"A good story flows like a river, revealing fresh territory, gathering tributary streams along the way. Lisa Dill's tale of a fortnight traveling along the muddy, moody Missouri is enlivened by a wealth of influences, including the wit of Mark Twain, the adventurous spirit of Lewis and Clark, the wisdom of Indigenous peoples, and the lore of scholars. Her own keen reflections flow through every page. Climb aboard the venerable boat she compares to 'a floating circus tent' and share the journey."

—SCOTT RUSSELL SANDERS, author of *The Way of Imagination* and *A Conservationist Manifesto*

"With *Around the Bend* Lisa Dill takes her place among other masterful contemporary writers—John McPhee, Elizabeth Kolbert, William Least Heat-Moon—captivated by the spirit and meaning of great American rivers. This book is delightful, witty, and deeply observed, fed by tributary streams of history, geography, and ecology. The Missouri has found its muse. Highly recommended."

—MCKAY JENKINS, author of *The Last Ridge: The Epic Story of America's First Mountain Soldiers and the Assault on Hitler's Europe*

"Lisa Dill writes exceedingly well about the story of her trip down the Missouri River, She shows us the living, breathing, silty life of the river as it wends its way across the continent. Her experiences and observations, made during her tortoise-like pace, provide a unique and fresh perspective and ultimately make a compelling case for why the river must be conserved by all seven states through which it lives and travels."

—CHARLENE PORSILD, author of *Gamblers and Dreamers: Women, Men, and Community in the Klondike*

BISON
BOOKS

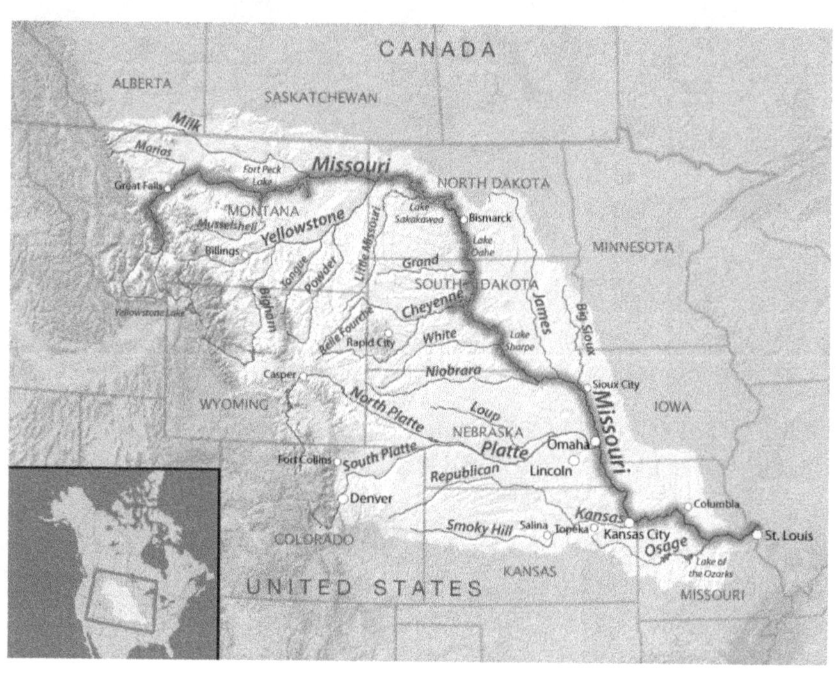
CANADA
ALBERTA
SASKATCHEWAN
Milk
Marias
Missouri
Fort Peck Lake
Great Falls
MONTANA
NORTH DAKOTA
Lake Sakakawea
Bismarck
Musselshell
Yellowstone
Billings
Little Missouri
Lake Oahe
MINNESOTA
Grand
Tongue
Powder
SOUTH DAKOTA
Bighorn
James
Big Sioux
Cheyenne
Yellowstone Lake
Belle Fourche
Rapid City
White
Lake Sharpe
Casper
Niobrara
Sioux City
WYOMING
North Platte
Loup
IOWA
NEBRASKA
Omaha
Platte
Fort Collins
South Platte
Lincoln
Republican
Denver
Columbia
Kansas
Smoky Hill
Salina
Topeka
Kansas City
St. Louis
COLORADO
Osage
Lake of the Ozarks
KANSAS
UNITED STATES
MISSOURI

AROUND THE BEND

Floating Down the Missouri River

Lisa G. Dill

University of Nebraska Press ✶ Lincoln

The University of Nebraska Press is part of a land-grant institution with campuses and programs on the past, present, and future homelands of the Pawnee, Ponca, Otoe-Missouria, Omaha, Dakota, Lakota, Kaw, Cheyenne, and Arapaho Peoples, as well as those of the relocated Ho-Chunk, Sac and Fox, and Iowa Peoples.

For customers in the EU with safety/GPSR concerns, contact:
gpsr@mare-nostrum.co.uk
Mare Nostrum Group BV
Mauritskade 21D
1091 GC Amsterdam
The Netherlands

Library of Congress Cataloging-in-Publication Data can be found at search.catalog.loc.gov:
ISBN 978-1-4962-3731-6 (paperback)

FRONTISPIECE. Missouri River map. Wikimedia Commons, Wikimedia Commons, https://en.m.wikipedia.org/wiki/File:Missouririvermap.jpg.

Set in Questa by A. Shahan.

For Mary, Dirk, Rod, and Lee, my co-conspirators.

And for Bryce and Jake, my future co-conspirators.

And for the river.

There are rivers of all lengths and sizes and of all degrees of wetness. There are rivers with all sorts of peculiarities and with widely varying claims to fame. But there is only one river with a personality, habits, dissipations, a sense of humor . . . a river that goes traveling sidewise, that interferes in politics, rearranges geography and dabbles in real estate; a river that plays hide and seek with you today and tomorrow follows you around like a pet dog with a dynamite cracker tied to its tail. That river is the Missouri.

—George Fitch, *American Magazine*, April 1907

Contents

Illustrations

Acknowledgments

This book would not have been possible without an army of people, and all errors are mine and mine alone. I would like to thank W. Clark Whitehorn, executive editor of Bison Books, for his support, guidance, and contributions to the manuscript. Rebecca Jefferson, Billie Smith-Haffener, Tish Fobben, Rosemary Sekora, Katrina Vassallo, and the team at Bison Books managed the book through the process, and it is greatly improved for all of their efforts. At the University of Delaware, both the book and I have been shepherded by John Ernest, McKay Jenkins, Gerald Kauffman, Cruce Stark, Meg Grotti, Jim Pizzuto, Michael Chajes, and the staff of the University of Delaware Library. I am a better writer and a better professor because of you. At Iowa Lakeside Laboratory, I thank my colleagues and friends Neil Bernstein, John Doershuk, Matt Fairchild, Rebecca Kauten, Katherine McCarville, and Paul Weihe, Lyndy Holdt and Friends of Lakeside Lab, and, at the University of Iowa Library, Dan Gall, whose willingness to answer scientific questions from a nonscientist enormously improved my writing. For their contributions to the research of this book and my understanding of the river, I thank David Swanson, Scott Mansker, Matt Hawley, Sam Stukel, George Edgermeyer, Robb Jacobson, Caroline Elliott, the Ioway Tribe of Kansas and Nebraska, Missouri River Relief, American Rivers, and Raygun (the Greatest Store in the Universe). I also thank the many marina, restaurant, and gas station workers, state and municipal park employees, and campground and hotel workers who took us in, despite what we must have looked and smelled like.

Writers cannot work alone. The book is immeasurably better because of my workshop members at Middlebury Bread Loaf and Orion, and my writing group: Mara Gorman, Jen Epler, Molly Giordano, Gitu Barua, Viet Dinh, and Dennis Lawson. It has also been strengthened by the friendship of Mark Nardone, Jane C. Miller, Beth Peyton, and Renata Golden. For their teaching, talent, expertise, and valued advice, I thank Scott Russell Sanders and Pam Houston.

Going down a river for several weeks and then writing a book about it requires the support of great friends, and in this I am immeasurably lucky. I owe a debt to Jillian Linster and her family and Kris Arthur Peterson and her family, who took me in before they'd ever met me. KC Van Dyke, Tiffany Wallace, Sandy Dente, and Nicki Paul cared for my animal family while I was gone, and for me when I returned. Jim Lee and Rachel Huerta supported my decisions and helped keep me going. Ciera Fisher, Dawn Apostolico, and Darrin Moore read draft after draft of the early chapters. Mary Skopec, Jim Kirby, Paulette Raughley, Ann and Dutch Miller, Bruce and David Venarde, Tom Mendenhall, Marvin Brown, Kathleen Olejnik, Toni Spille, Mike Hopkins, Lauren Hornberger, Allen Heggen, Susan Donley, Cheryl Rodriguez, Jennifer Follet, Michael McCamley, and Anne Hickey kept my eye on the ball and boosted my spirits the many times I needed them. Rosemary Wilson reminded me to celebrate. I thank Constantine Katsinis, for his faith in the absence of things not seen. And Mary Koechert and Richard Stobaugh made sure that I completed it, separately and as a team. You are each irreplaceable.

The Delaware Division of the Arts and Roxanne Stanulis helped fund my research, my writing, and my confidence, and I am deeply grateful for their support.

My students have been hearing about this book for years, and I thank each of them for their patience and support. Brandon Hunter and Liam Vita get a special nod, for talking me through the first big breakthrough, and Elizabeth Manning, Quinlan Kraft, Adaleigh Nare, Sherwood Molina, and Evan Borodin, for talking me through the end. I also thank Jordan Barry for his excellent photography.

Kimberly Richardson made sure the photos could be adapted for use in this book, and her friendship made sure I kept going forward. Prentiss Clark gave expanses of her time, expertise, and wisdom to see it down to the finish. Darlene Farabee first introduced me to the river, picked me up when I got off the boat, and supported me through ten years of writing. Thank you, my dear friends. This could not have happened without you.

My family, Glenn, Angie, Bryce, Jake, Sue, Atticus, Jem, D'Artagnan, and Ernie Dill, Meg Bohem, Glenore Jerrard, Lana Richards, Mary H. Gleysteen, and Mary Beekman supported me on the trip and through the years of work that followed it. And Mary, Dirk, Rod, and Lee Gleysteen, I thank you beyond measure.

Unfortunately, no book that takes a decade to write gets finished in time for everyone who contributed to it. To the memories of Janet and Glenn Dill, Charlie Brodigan, Dell Venarde, Sonia Sloan, Ron Gervason, Randall Burton, John Beekman, Judy Spille, and Lance Foster, you each and you all changed my life. I thank you, and I miss you.

AROUND THE BEND

Prologue

> Big rivers make me think of serpents, or dragons—always dangerous, never still.
>
> —Scott Russell Sanders

I walked down the boat ramp from the campground in the early light, tent under my arm, and whispered good morning to the river, as I did every morning. The river whispered in return, the center running fast over the stripped corpses of snagged trees, the edge lapping more quietly against the land, in conversation with itself. An older man, his plaid collared shirt straining against suspenders and the round of his belly, nodded to me as he loaded a bass boat onto an aluminum trailer with Missouri tags. The sun was swelling around the tips of the eastern trees downstream.

"Going fishing or coming fishing?" he asked, eyes in the shade of a trucker cap.

"Going to St. Louis, actually," I said, sloshing to our boat, anchored fore and aft in the river behind the safety of a small sandbar.

"From where?" he asked, pushing the brim of his cap up a little.

"Sioux City," I said, securing my tent in a storage box on the boat deck.

He stared at me, and then at the boat, his mouth hanging open a little. I turned to look up the river, pouring past us, about half a mile wide. The boat bobbed a little in the current. The August sky shifted invisibly from purple to blue.

"Well, I'll be damned," he said.

"You and me both, brother," I answered.

FIG. 1. The FloteBote, including canopy, braced in the Missouri. Photo by the author.

At the Christmas dinner table in 2012, my aunt announced that her first cousin Mary had decided to run the family's old pontoon boat down the Missouri River and then give it away. This was met by gasps, muffled laughter, and someone whispering, "They're all going to die." My uncle muttered dark prophecies about the boat sinking under the weight of the gas it'd need to carry. Cousins asked quite seriously if it would still float. No one thought this seemed like a reasonable idea.

I immediately asked if I could go along.

A few days later, my significant other, a man less engaged by the unknown than I am, went out to dinner with me, and he quite reasonably asked why I was going to go down a big river for no apparent reason.

"Well," I began, and petered out.

"What kind of boat is it?" Constantine asked.

"A pontoon boat. A lake boat. I've been on this boat all my life," I said.

I omitted a few pertinent details. There was a reason it had been around all my life. Mary and her brothers pooled their just-out-of-college resources in 1972 and bought a brand new twenty-four-foot Harris FloteBote. The family has a cottage on a lake in northwest Iowa, and by the early 1970s, their grandmother—my great-grandmother—needed a boat that would accommodate a proper seat. The FloteBote was, then, shiny and blue and quite the latest thing in lake travel. It flourished as queen of the family flotilla on Lake Okoboji for two generations, carrying children and great-grandparents and remote cousins and various dogs on gentle expeditions until the autumn of 2012, when it was deemed too "Beverly Hillbillies" for further use. The family bought a newer, bigger, shinier pontoon boat, and the FloteBote, a relic of a more glamorous age, languished in dry dock, its pontoons cracking and its canvas top rotting, waiting for someone to decide what to do with it.

Mary had decided.

"A pontoon boat," Constantine said. "From a lake."

"Well, yes," I said. "But how different can a river be?"

"How much do you know about rivers?" he asked.

I'd grown up in Wilmington, Delaware, less than two miles from the Delaware River. In the chronicles of American history, Washington crossed the Delaware in a rowboat to surprise the British in Trenton almost three decades before Lewis and Clark set off for the Pacific Ocean on the Missouri. I'd never gone properly "boating" on the Delaware, but I'd watched huge container ships full of bananas and crude oil and Toyotas and God knows what else head for the ports of Wilmington and Philadelphia and Camden. I'd ridden the state park ferry out to Fort Delaware, the island star fort constructed midriver just after the War of 1812. But I'd canoed and rafted and kayaked the smaller local tributaries since childhood. As long as we could avoid being hit by a container ship, I reasoned, we'd be fine. Constantine did not look convinced. He was Greek, the son of an ancient peninsular seagoing people who have an innate understanding of the capriciousness of water and wind.

There is a Greek expression: *matso halia*. It means, as I understand it, the rubble that is left after a chaotic event, like an earthquake, or a big storm. He muttered it under his breath, but he didn't try to change my mind.

What is a river? Scientifically, it's geography, geology, gravity, and water, moving from one point on a map to another. In another way, though, it's like us: the sum of its parts, comprised of every event, large and small, that affects it as it makes its way from headwaters to mouth. Every time I sloshed through the river from boat to land and back again, I was stepping into the history of the Missouri, and into the future of the Mississippi.

The ancient Greek philosopher Heraclitus said, "To those entering the same river, other and still other waters flow." He was speaking metaphysically, or so said Plato. But even if he was, Heraclitus was also touching on the truth of rivers. The water I stepped into the day I got on the FloteBote in the Big Sioux River would, some eight months later, move through the tidal currents of the Gulf of Mexico and eventually spin out into the Atlantic. From there, it probably crossed the ocean north of the equator to Africa, from which point it might have helped to drive one of the great storm systems that pound back across the Atlantic to batter my home on the East Coast. Heraclitus could have added a caveat: We may indeed step into new water every time we step into a river, but that water never really leaves us.

Seven months after that dinner with Constantine, I was sitting at the porch table at the lake house the night before we set sail with Mary and her brothers, Dirk, Rod, and Lee, and my mother's sister Meg. The screen door to the kitchen banged. From the porch on the other side of the house, the six of us turned from our card game to see who had arrived.

"Thought I should come have a last drink with you," our cousin Mary Helen said as she walked out to the porch. "Since you're all likely to drown, you know." And grinned at us.

"Not me," Meg said, shaking her head.

I'd arrived at the cottage on the lake that morning after a two-day drive and a fourteen-hour bus ride. Meg had picked me up from the bus station in Sioux City that morning. The original plan had been to take me straight from the bus to the boat, floating in a marina berth on the Big Sioux River southwest of town. Except that, the day before I arrived, the boat's motor wouldn't start.

"There are plenty of life jackets," Dirk said from the head of the table. His siblings and I laughed.

More than a hundred years ago, my great-great-grandfather and one of his nieces bought a piece of land high on a bluff overlooking West Okoboji, about sixty miles north of his hometown. They'd built the cottage, sharing every summer between the two halves of the family, and passed it down to their children and now, their children's children's children. Yet more cousins built their own cottage a few streets to the east of us. It's a lot of family, and a few of them I've never met.

Lee leaned toward me.

"You look pretty tired," he whispered.

I'd booked my bus ticket online before I left home, leaving my car with friends in eastern Iowa so I could get off the boat and shave half a day off my drive home, but I hadn't been able to figure out why it would take fourteen hours to get the three hundred miles from Iowa City to Sioux City. Turns out it's because first you have to go to Nebraska and spend about three hours—3:00 to 6:00 a.m.—in the Omaha bus depot. I sat awake the whole night, alternating between reading a book and watching the parade of shady characters who also spent their wee hours in the depot, while over our heads CNN chronicled the buildup to the arrival of the newest heir to the throne of Great Britain.

Once I finally got to the cottage, the four cousins hugged me and we got to work repacking the equipment and supplies. Rod had taken the dead motor to the marine store to get it repaired; he'd also pilfered an extra motor from the fishing boat.

I watched them all a little as we worked. As I had known the boat, they had known me my entire life. I am the oldest child of the oldest of their cousins, and the second child of my generation in the family. But to me they were literally relative strangers. I knew Lee best; he'd worked in eastern Pennsylvania for a while, so I'd spent a little time with him. The youngest, he had been a crew manager for Amtrak. All four of them lived in Seattle, and ten years earlier I'd stayed with Lee and his husband when I'd gone to Olympic National Park to interview a hiker.

Mary and I corresponded sporadically in the years before the trip. We were temperamentally well suited; despite a law degree, she'd spent her life working in an indie bookstore on Bainbridge Island in Washington and avidly working as a peace activist. But I'd seen her only three times in the last fifteen years. She sent me literary magazines and book suggestions; I sent her essays.

I hadn't seen Dirk or Rod since the late nineties. I'd been at the lake for a few days with Dirk, a retired teacher, and his sons when they were kids. I'd seen Rod at a family wedding around the same time, but both instances involved lots of events and other family, and I'd never spent any time with either of them by myself. All of them are enviably close to each other, probably the result of growing up on military bases around the world while their father, my great-uncle Rod, served as a career navy doctor.

Mary, the oldest, is almost twenty years older than I am.

Sitting around the porch table that night at the cottage, I wondered what the trip would be like for us as a family. I loved them, though largely in the abstract. And I wondered what a few weeks on a small, elderly boat would bring out in all of us. I was an outsider, albeit a pretty close one, to long history and all the shorthand, linguistic and emotional, that brings.

But I also wondered what the river was going to show me. As an undergrad I'd taken a writing class that required me to sit by a river for an hour once a week and then write about what I learned there. I learned a lot, but mostly I learned patience. That if I went to the river, it would always give me something: less than I hoped for, but more than I expected. That there is great beauty in the small things you start to see if you look long enough and closely enough. That bearing witness, even to the seemingly unimportant, almost always leads you to something important.

The Missouri isn't a river many of us are familiar with, but its reach, and its threat, impacts us all. In the early spring of 2019, the Missouri and some of its largest tributaries flooded badly, killing three people, damaging a million acres of farmland, and costing nearly $2.9 billion—$400 million alone in drowned beef cattle caught during calving season. In 2016 international press covered the standoff at the Standing Rock Sioux Reservation on the borders of North and South Dakota, where Native people and others protested—in vain—the construction of the Dakota Access Pipeline, which will tunnel natural gas under the Missouri. A pipeline breach, and thus a leak into the river, will taint bankside farmland all the way to St. Louis, and is more a question of when rather than if. In 2011 intense summer flooding came within a few feet of breaching a riverside nuclear power station in Nebraska, which would have sent a Fukushima-like plume of nuclear waste straight into the Mississippi, and from there, through the centers of Memphis and New Orleans. The Missouri is a river we should all pay attention to.

And it is a difficult river to get to know. At 2,300 miles long, its watershed covers 5 percent of the landmass of North America, but that land is sparsely populated until the river nears its mouth in St. Louis. It changes significantly as it moves from its headwaters in the Rocky Mountains to the great prairies of the upper Midwest. Our trip was only the final eight hundred miles, so I would get just a fraction of the river's full story.

In 2013 my interest in the Missouri was new. I'd admired it a few years earlier; I'd stood on its bank while visiting a friend in South Dakota, but it hadn't lurked in the back of my mind as an objective, the way climbers talk about the big technical mountains or rock faces that haunt their dreams. Even then it was threatening; during the floods of 2011, my friend called to tell me the South Dakota National Guard was sandbagging her town. But I wanted to see it, to learn whatever it had to teach me about itself, and about myself.

Around the table on the porch, just before I went to bed, Mary told us that this trip had been a lifelong, unfulfilled dream of their father's. She quoted from Bernard DeVoto, their father's favorite historian, who'd dedicated much of his career to Lewis and Clark and the Missouri: "One may lack words to express the impact of beauty but no one who has felt it remains untouched."

I went to sleep that night imagining the river, a hundred miles to the south, wondering what its impact would be on me.

1

The Missouri River

Too thick to drink, too thin to plow.

—Attributed to Mark Twain

Although many of us don't remember it, it is the Missouri River, and not the Mississippi, that is the longest in North America. The Missouri has played a crucial role in U.S. history; Lewis and Clark began their journey to the Pacific there, Samuel Clemens, before he became Mark Twain, learned to pilot a riverboat there, and it has supported human settlements since the Pleistocene. Until the completion of the Transcontinental Railroad, the Missouri served as one of the main thoroughfares for Manifest Destiny. And yet its reputation—ugly, foul-smelling, ruthless, and muddy—consigns it to the recesses of our collective memory, at least for most of us who live away from both its attractions and its menace. If the American consciousness has a river, it's the Mississippi, home of the paddleboat and Huckleberry Finn. The river of our subconscious, however, is the Missouri: opaque, ominous, and impossible to tame.

The Missouri rises in the northern Rockies and roars southeast through mountains and valleys and over waterfalls. It levels out as it crosses into the Dakotas and then cuts south, widening as it meanders through the farmland and cities of the northern plains. In the mid-nineteenth century, it stretched more than a mile across as it bisected the new state of Missouri. Steamboats carried settlers and supplies into the frontier as hunters and trappers shipped furs and meat to markets downstream. As we have throughout history, we tried to shape the river to do our bidding; we dammed, rerouted, channeled, and dredged it to maximize its utility and minimize both its power and its threats. The river's route has been changed so drastically that, in 1987, a group of Kansas City businessmen decided to find and excavate the wreck of a steamboat that sank in the river in 1856. The *Arabia* was found forty-five feet beneath a cornfield, nearly a mile from the river's present banks.

As the fur trade caved to silk and cotton, and as more efficient transportation became available, the Lower Missouri was slowly abandoned by nearly all but the U.S. Geological Survey, the Army Corps of Engineers, and those who live alongside it. Today, there is remarkably little river traffic, either industrial or recreational. Asian carp threaten native fish species. And the river itself, between its powerful current and the sheer tonnage of floating and submerged debris, makes both navigation and swimming a challenge. The Missouri runs to its confluence with the Mississippi nearly devoid of human traffic.

The coastline of South Dakota curved in toward the southeast ahead of us. Dirk, his father's old fishing hat drooping over his ears, stood at the helm, his eyes shaded but his jaw clenched tightly. The rest of us sat on the deck staring fixedly downstream, where we could just begin to see the long brown ribbon of water waiting for us at the confluence. The sun cracked through midsummer Midwestern clouds. As we got closer, I could track the strength of the coming current. Dirk muttered something I couldn't hear over the hum of the motor and nosed the pontoons to the west. South Dakota tapered away, and he sat down in the captain's chair, throttle at full, pushing the old, overloaded boat into the body of the Missouri River as close to straight across the current as he could manage.

In his memoir *Life on the Mississippi*, after first appropriating the whole of the Missouri as a tributary to make the Mississippi the longest river on the planet, Mark Twain describes the Missouri by citing the journals of Louis Joliet and Jacques Marquette, the first Europeans to navigate almost the full length of the Mississippi:

> A short distance below "a torrent of yellow mud rushed furiously athwart the calm blue current of the Mississippi, boiling and surging and sweeping in its course logs, branches, and uprooted trees." This was the mouth of the Missouri, "that savage river," which "descending from its mad career through a vast unknown

> of barbarism, poured its turbid floods into the bosom of its gentle sister."

The Missouri is still savage, still brimming with mud and secret menace. Kolks—surface whirlpools signifying something beneath the surface large enough to affect the current—churn across the river's surface, forcing boaters to focus more intently than drivers on snowy highways. When we first saw the Missouri, looming around the point of the Big Sioux confluence, the current looked like a mudslide. Dirk throttled forward, pushing the motor to jump into the fray, worried that the current would push us back, that we wouldn't make it into the river and would end up rudder-deep in the mud of the eastern bank, less than two miles into our journey.

"Ever gone swimming in a riptide?" Rod asked me. "I'd go with the backstroke. Just point your feet downstream. Someone will fish us out before Omaha."

I chose not to tell him that my physical training for this trip had been limited exclusively to swimming laps. Lots of them. My backstroke was just fine.

The banks of the Missouri looked a lot like the banks of the Big Sioux, the much smaller, much calmer tributary that we'd launched from. Scruffy, scrubby trees, weeds, a low western bank that showed glimpses of farmland through the tree breaks. A slightly higher eastern bank, with small stretches of sandy shoreline just wide enough for shorebirds, and a highway running south atop the berm.

The river was racing and muddy, but well within its banks. Sun broke through the clouds that stayed to the northwest behind us. Swallows tore back and forth across the river, chasing bugs. A family of Canada geese marched purposefully down the Iowa bank. I looked downstream, and then west, behind me, imagining the river rolling toward us from across most of the rest of the continent.

The Missouri River officially begins near Three Forks, in southern Montana, northwest of Yellowstone National Park. It crosses over five massive waterfalls and absorbs a succession of tributaries as it pounds its way east, where it flattens out into the Great Plains. Its first significant dam, near Fort Peck, Montana, provides more than a billion kilowatt-hours of hydroelectric power every year—roughly enough electricity to power every household in the United States for four or five days. Fort Peck is the largest hydroelectric fill dam in the United States, generating half as much power as the Hoover Dam, which lights up Las Vegas and much of Southern California. The Missouri and the dam together create Fort Peck Lake, which has a nearly 1,500-mile shoreline, longer than the coastline of the whole state of Florida.

From Fort Peck, the river flows into North Dakota, where it absorbs its ancient neighbor, the Yellowstone, roaring up from the southwest. The Yellowstone pours more volume into the Missouri than any of the other tributaries, mostly the result of snowmelt from the Absaroka and Gallatin mountains in Wyoming and Montana. The Yellowstone, at the confluence, is larger than the Missouri. Below the confluence, the river flows into Lake Sakakawea, a reservoir created by the construction of the Garrison Dam in central North Dakota.

The lake is named, of course, for the Lemhi Shoshone woman most of us learned about in elementary school and called Sacagawea, which means "Bird Woman" in the Hidatsa language. Lake Sakakawea—Native linguists deem this to be the correct pronunciation of her name—is the third largest manmade lake in the United States. It's 180 feet deep at the dam, and provides hydroelectric power, flood control, and recreation to the area, fifty miles outside Bismarck. It's full of fish: Chinook salmon, Walleye, Brown, Rainbow, and Lake trout, and huge Northern pike, which are routinely up to six feet long and can weigh more than fifty pounds. It's also considered to be the southwestern demarcation of the great glaciers of the Pleistocene era.

About two and a half million years ago, what are now the Upper Missouri, Yellowstone, and Musselshell Rivers flowed north into a single lake in central Canada, which probably drained into Hudson Bay. Some eighty-five thousand years ago, during the Pleistocene era, what scientists refer to as the Wisconsin Glaciation covered all of Canada, the upper Midwest, the upper Rockies, and as far east as New England with a massive ice sheet. Geological signs of the Wisconsin Glaciation can still be seen all over the northern United States and Canada, including in New York City's Central Park. The ice carved and shaped the northern half of the continent, pushing up hills and scattering boulders in its wake, and so altering the Bering Straits that a land bridge formed between Asia and North America.

FIG. 2. Manitou Bluffs, made of limestone, in Boone County, Missouri. Photo by the author.

Sometime between seventeen thousand and thirteen thousand years ago, the Laurentide ice sheet, one of the largest of the Wisconsin's glacial sections, blocked the Yellowstone, Missouri, and Musselshell Rivers' access to Hudson Bay, forcing them southeast. The three rivers rerouted themselves around the glacial mass, carving a new drainage.

Geologists believe that in the last two million years, multiple glacial events happened in what is now the Missouri River Valley, and with every advance, all the rivers along the way were relocated. Below Glasgow, Missouri, 230 miles west of the Missouri's confluence with the Mississippi, the river valley is visibly narrower, in part because it's younger, geologically speaking, than the upstream areas, but also because the rock in that area erodes at a different pace than the bedrock upstream. The trouble with accurate reconstruction of the preglacial river is simple: As the glaciers retreated to the Arctic, they obliterated most of the evidence of what had been beneath them.

What is now the Lower Missouri originally rose somewhere near Yankton, South Dakota, and the rerouted western rivers sought it out. The shape and path of the Missouri in North Dakota and through South Dakota to Yankton—deep and narrow—is the result of that push. Today, the Upper Missouri River Valley, more or less, follows along the southern border of the colossal expanse of ice that finally retreated from the Great Plains at just about the same time that the first humans crossed the Bering land bridge and began settling the Western Hemisphere.

Humans are close to the river here, just west of Sioux City, Iowa. Cars go past on the highway above us, and I wonder if the people riding in them can see us, and if they're wondering just what the hell we're doing out here. They won't be alone.

Sioux City is the first big town below the last of the dams. The part of the river we would sail, the Lower Missouri, picks up speed and strength as it moves unimpaired toward its terminus in St. Louis. It also absorbs the last of its big tributaries—the Platte in Nebraska and the Osage in Missouri—adding their strength and might, and the impact of whatever weather events are occurring upstream.

The Missouri moves through some of the most dramatic changes in weather patterns in North America. Early in the twentieth century, the definition of a humid climate was considered to be twenty inches (or more) of annual rainfall. By the middle of the century, climate was redefined as "available moisture"—the moisture available from rain and air content—and the mountains of the American West were redesignated from an "arid" to a "steppe" climate.

The United States' climate shifts from the east's humid zone to the central's steppe zone beginning in western Minnesota, in a narrow band that runs almost straight south through the country to east Texas. A slightly wider swath, encompassing most of the state of North Dakota, thinning as it goes south to cover only a slice of the Texas panhandle and on down to the Gulf of Mexico, is considered "dry sub-humid." This is what early explorers referred to as the "desert"—the dry, sandy, treeless expanse of the southern plains. West of that, all the way to the rainforests of Oregon and Washington, is a patchy, swirly mass of semiarid and arid climate that makes up the great ranges of the intermountain west.

This means that the more western tributaries of the Missouri—like the Moreau River in western South Dakota—may absorb fifteen or more inches of rain a year in their watersheds, but only a half inch of that may reach the Missouri. On the other side of the climate line, a tiny river like the Little Sioux, draining from Spirit Lake in northwest Iowa, inside the sub-humid zone, can send more than three inches into the Missouri.

This change in climate helps to explain the power and fury of the Lower Missouri, and part of its difference from the Mississippi. The Mississippi River runs its whole route in humid or sub-humid zones, and its tributaries are—except during flood and drought years—relatively consistent. The Missouri, on the other hand, still reflects the identities of its two ancient forbears: the narrow, relatively peaceful river of the mountains and steppes and the wide, wandering river it becomes in the plains. Ninety-five major tributaries and any number of smaller rivers feed into the Missouri from Montana to St. Louis, and, below the confluence during flood years, up to 70 percent of the Mississippi's water comes from the Missouri. This despite the dams that try to control water flow levels in the upper river, and the physical and geological differences between the Upper and Lower Missouri. When the cousins agreed to my joining them on the trip, I began tracking snowfall and snowmelt and then rainfall in the Midwest and the Rocky Mountains in a slightly compulsive fashion, visions of the South Dakota National Guard's sandbags stacking up in my mind.

And I got lucky. The year 2013 produced a very mild winter and the beginnings of a drought in the Midwest and upper Rockies. While this wasn't great news for the farmers and ranchers of the Wheat Belt, it meant that our trip would be safe.

Ish.

At the least, it meant that we wouldn't be ordered off the river by the various governmental agencies that control the Missouri. A half hour into the first day of our trip, I started to relax. The river was fast, but once we'd safely crossed into it, it wasn't threatening. There were no container ships; the Missouri is too shallow and too striated with sandbars. There also were no visible threats to the boat, no trees sailing downstream toward us at alarming speed, or snagged in sand bars midstream. The banks were not cliffs, not heavily forested, and certainly not removed from civilization, at least so far.

Dirk relaxed his death grip on the wheel a fraction.

"I'm not optimistic, but so far things are going better than I expected," he said.

We rounded our first bend and spotted a small green marker on the eastern bank. Mile marker 793: the distance from here to the Mississippi confluence. Plenty of time, space, and water for Dirk's optimism to wane and confirm the extended family's open belief that the five of us were utterly insane.

Periodically over the next few weeks, we would come to agree with them. And the people and officials who met us on our trip, while more polite than our loved ones, all shared an expression that conveyed something between shock and pity. Particularly the officials.

The various agencies responsible for the river work hard to contain its threats. There are four major dams along the Missouri as it moves through South Dakota and close to the point where, during the Pleistocene, the ancient upper river merged with its lower counterpart. And, as it moves toward its final dam, just northwest of Yankton, South Dakota, the last vestiges of the "wild" Missouri flow, if not into submission, at least into some version of a feral state.

After the floods of '93 finally receded, the Corps of Engineers and state agencies up and down the Missouri developed plans, protocols, and new strategies to prevent it from happening again. The most visible of these changes were the levees, huge land walls built atop the bluffs to keep the river out of the towns.

The river is officially managed by the U.S. Army Corps of Engineers, with additional regulation by state and federal agencies, especially the U.S. Fish and Wildlife Service, which administers the Endangered Species Act, and the U.S. Environmental Protection Agency, which handles the Clean Water Act. Law enforcement and conservation agencies from the states along the Missouri's banks deal with the humans and animals who work, live, and play on it. In between those agencies is the U.S. Geological Survey, a purely scientific organization, working on behalf of the states, tribal governments, and various federal trust resources that the river impacts.

The USGS Midwestern Region includes most of the Missouri, the Upper Mississippi, the Ohio and the Platte Rivers and the whole of the Illinois River. They study ecosystems, water, climate, hazards, energy and minerals, and environmental health. Their scientists are working on everything from energy production and dam discharge to the science needed to protect the Missouri's most threatened species, the Interior Least tern, the Piping plover, and the Pallid sturgeon. And one of its primary points of interest on the Missouri River is the question, or problem, of restoration.

Restoration as a principle is fairly simple: to return an ecosystem to its, or at least *a*, more natural state. Pull the dams and the wing dikes, ban dredging and channel maintenance, forbid development along the riverbanks, empty the floodplains of human structures and farmland, and let the river be itself—let it be a river. As a fact, however, restoration is an extraordinarily complicated and controversial idea. With a river as strong and as full of sediment as the Missouri, a river that, along with several of its largest tributaries, rises in the Rockies to disperse the snowmelt, restoration would not simply result in a "natural" river. It would allow the Missouri to begin moving around the landscape again, changing its channel as it chooses, with no regard for human—or socioeconomic—interests.

The river, at mile marker 793, is roughly two hundred yards wide. While the Corps of Engineers' river charts indicated that it is less than fifteen feet deep, the sediment levels rendered the bottom invisible. It might have been two feet, or it might have been one hundred. To the west, breaks in the bank trees revealed tidy Nebraskan crops of corn and soybeans. To the east, the banks rise to thirty- or forty-foot bluffs, crested with roads and occasional houses.

According to Robert Jacobson, retired chief of the USGS River Studies Branch in Columbia, Missouri, the restoration of any river or ecosystem—particularly large, multipurpose rivers like the Missouri—to a precontact, predisturbance version is impossible. Even if the many governmental, private, and corporate interests could agree to such a plan, it would be difficult for anyone to clarify exactly what that restoration would look like. And what do we mean by "precontact"? In the case of the Missouri, does it mean before Lewis and Clark? Before Columbus? Before humans arrived in North America?

Practically speaking, restoration at this point means recovering it to a more natural, but not pristine, condition. There is no realistic way to undo the impact, intentional and unintentional, that human contact has made on any ecosystem. Instead, those working toward restoration and recovery on the Missouri are making small but significant changes in flow releases from the reservoirs to return the river's flow to a more natural level. They're also acquiring small areas of the floodplain along parts of the river and reengineering the navigation channel to provide more habitat diversity for the river's fish. All this, Jacobson says, while still maintaining the human requirements of the river: flood control, floodplain agriculture, navigation, water supply, power generation, and recreation.

It is a big, muddy, nondescript river without much scenic value or recreational opportunity. It doesn't smell; it does sustain millions of the descendants of the mosquitoes that plagued the Corps of Discovery in 1804. Its boat traffic is mainly limited to fishers, law enforcement, and a small number of sand dredging operations. The history of flooding means that there is very little of anything manmade on its banks, save massive power plants and a couple of airports.

And yet, as I watch a string of wild turkeys pick their way along the shoreline, and flinch when the first of many Asian carp leaps three feet in the air beside the boat, I begin to see what is beautiful about the Lower Missouri. It's not the scenery; the Missouri will never compete aesthetically with high-mountain rivers like its tributary the Yellowstone, or the upper Hudson, or even the Susquehanna as it carves its huge cleft through eastern Maryland.

What makes the Missouri beautiful is something in its refusal to play by our rules. After more than a century of humans redirecting, channeling, and dredging, it still jumps its banks and goes where it chooses. Its power is unspeakably dangerous; more than fifty people died in its floodwaters from 1993 to 2019. The floods ravaged farmlands and swamped the few cities close to its banks. It is a complex, difficult, threatening river. And its lack of traditional beauty, from its mud-brown water to its scruffy banks, limits its appeal for tourism. The Mississippi has Huck Finn, Memphis, and New Orleans. The Lower Missouri has virtually nothing.

And that nothingness protects it. The Missouri is a forgotten river, all but abandoned by both commercial and recreational interests. Apart from maintaining what must be maintained to sustain the dredging industry and protect against the next inevitable flood, the river is left largely to its own devices. Those people who remain have installed floating docks and built their homes as high atop the levees as they can. The river, below its central dams, is no longer wild. It has been chiseled and narrowed to serve our purposes and protect our interests. It has been colonized by a foreign species that has no predators and no clear means of suppression. The river bottom is being sucked up and sold for concrete and industrial use. Neither Lewis nor Clark would recognize the Lower Missouri today.

But it steadfastly maintains itself: still muddy, still riddled with sandbars and submerged trees and logs racing invisibly downstream just below the surface. Despite all the human efforts to force it into submission, despite its manifest alterations, it continues to refuse to live within its constraints. It runs downstream to the Mississippi—a river that has been even more aggressively contained—as a vivid reminder that our capacity for control is limited. And the Missouri River allows us to see, if we're willing to look closely, that there is great beauty in its refusal to be either drunk or plowed.

2

Lewis and Clark and the Corps of Discovery

> We are to ascend the Missouri River with a boat as far as it is navigable. We expect to be gone eighteen months or two years. If we make great discoveries as we expect, the United States has promised to make us great rewards, more than we are promised.
>
> —Sergeant John Ordway, Corps of Discovery

Sometime in the summer of 1802, President Thomas Jefferson picked up a new copy of Alexander Mackenzie's book *Voyages from Montreal.* In 1793 the Scottish Mackenzie, nine companions, and a dog became the first Europeans to cross the North American continent north of Mexico by completing an overland passage across Canada. The book also sketched out an ambitious imperial plan for Great Britain: to seize control of the Columbia River, which runs from southwestern Canada through what is now Washington State and empties into the Pacific in what is now Oregon. This would almost certainly assure British domination of Asian markets for furs and agricultural goods. Jefferson, long aware that the young United States was under threat from European powers intent on maintaining a colonial presence in North America, began planning an expedition through the soon-to-be purchased Louisiana Territory, to settle forever the question of the American West.

By the spring of 1803, as Jefferson's plans were beginning to take shape, he received letters from Secretary of the Treasury Albert Gallatin and French naturalist Bernard Germain de Lacépède, both urging (from their own perspectives) the necessity of a U.S. claim to the area surrounding the Missouri. "The future destinies of the Missouri country are of vast importance to the United States," wrote Gallatin. Lacépède envisioned a strung-together system of rivers, canals, and portages that could link New York City directly to the mouth of the Columbia, allowing easy transport of goods—not just furs, but crops, because farmers wouldn't settle the West without a means to get those crops to markets—from west to east and back, and then on to Europe and Asia.

Jefferson agreed, and instructed his presidential secretary, twenty-nine-year-old U.S. Army Captain Meriwether Lewis, to design a plan to navigate, survey, and explore the Missouri River, long considered the best route by which to achieve those goals. Lewis began to sketch out a proposal for an expedition requiring fifteen men and expected to last up to two years. Though no historical record exists to confirm it, the initial plan must have seemed, to at least some people, complete folly.

The four cousins and I entered the Missouri from the Big Sioux River, on the border between Iowa and South Dakota, in late July 2013. Our trip did not originate in presidential orders, or with congressional approval or funding. We had no pretensions to geopolitical discovery or international imperialism. But I did do some planning, well beyond ensuring that I could get to shore if and when the forty-year-old boat sank.

The Great Recession had been hard on me. As co-owner of a two-woman professional writing company almost exclusively reliant on a single corporate client, when that client cut off all its contractors, I had little luck finding work for two years and had drained my retirement account. By the fall of 2011, I'd begun working as an adjunct instructor of writing and literature at any local college that would have me. Paying my bills often meant commuting to three different colleges in two states, teaching as many as six courses each semester, and tutoring and doing manual labor at a local horse farm in the summers, when teaching positions were harder to come by.

When I heard Mary's crazy idea that Christmas Day, I'd signed on imagining a long weekend, maybe four or five days, for a couple of magazine articles. The whole journey—estimated at close to a month—seemed irrational both practically and financially. Mary, Dirk, and

Lee were retired. Rod could work remotely, even on a boat. I had no such options.

One night in early February, I walked into the living room. We'd finished dinner, and Constantine had gone in to watch television while I cleaned up the kitchen. I glanced at the screen, stopped, and looked again.

"What the hell is Whoopi Goldberg doing on *Star Trek*?" I asked.

What I meant was, Why was Whoopi Goldberg, actress, comedian, and winner of an Academy Award, on a nineties *Star Trek* spinoff? What I got back was something more like a character study.

"She's a time-traveler they found in the 1890s, in San Francisco, where she was with Mark Twain, and she helped them figure out how to fix the . . ." Constantine kept talking about what she helped fix, and how she fit into the *Star Trek* universe, and how Mark Twain dealt with *Star Trek*. Eventually I sat down next to him and opened a book.

About five hours later I woke up. Constantine slept on beside me. I stared at the green light of the smoke detector on the ceiling, thinking about summer and the lack of work, panicking as quietly as I could.

And suddenly the phrase "The Innocents Aboard" scrolled across my eyes in large red letters, like an EMERGENCY EXIT sign. Mark Twain's best-selling book in his lifetime was *The Innocents Abroad*, about American tourists in Europe and the Holy Land. I'd written a paper about it in grad school. Provoked by Whoopi Goldberg, Constantine, and *Star Trek*, it had morphed and returned to me. I reached over to the bedside table for a notepad and pencil, and started scribbling in the dark.

"What are you doing?" he mumbled, rolling over.

"I'm going down the river," I said. I had five months to plan, and almost nothing to lose.

Lewis and Clark took more than a year to make their plans, but they had everything to lose.

On the Fourth of July 1803, Jefferson appointed Lewis to command the expedition. The president dispatched the young captain to Philadelphia to study with the doctors and scholars of the American Philosophical Society. Founded by Benjamin Franklin, the Philosophical Society housed much of the best nineteenth-century knowledge in science, medicine, and geopolitics.

The first thing Lewis did, however, was commission his old friend from the army, thirty-two-year-old Lieutenant William Clark, to colead the expedition and start selecting men. Clark, youngest brother of Revolutionary War hero General George Clark, had extensive wilderness experience and a more logistical mind than Lewis. William Clark had resigned from the army for health reasons in 1796 and returned to his family's plantation outside Louisville, Kentucky. He received Lewis's commission in mid-July and began recruiting candidates from around the new nation. They wanted excellent hunters, healthy, strong men with proven survival skills who were brave and, ideally, unmarried. Almost one-third of the "permanent" corps members came from the Kentucky frontier, near Louisville and Clarksville, and were known as "the nine young men from Kentucky."

I, a youngish woman from Delaware, had a simpler need: money. The trip itself would not be overly expensive, apart from fuel; the challenge for me would be paying the bills at home while sitting on a boat in the Midwest.

The solution came unexpectedly. A much-loved friend of the family died, and her sons gave me her car. When I emailed the elder son to tell him that their gift would make my trip possible, he wrote back to tell me how pleased he was that his mother would be part of my expedition, and how pleased she would have been as well. I sold my aging Jeep, paid my August bills in advance, hired a house sitter to care for the dog and the cat, and took a month's leave of absence from tutoring. Finally, in late July, I drove to Iowa City, left the car with a friend, and made my way to the lake. Lewis, on the other hand, put in a requisition to Congress for $2,500—exactly half what I got for the Jeep 210 years later—that was immediately approved.

Lewis used most of his budget on equipment and supplies, including rifles, medical supplies, cartography equipment, gifts for the Native tribes, whiskey, and more than seven hundred pounds of salt. His most expensive purchase was a chronometer, a crucial tool in mapmaking and distance calculations. While in Pittsburgh, Lewis made one final purchase: For twenty dollars, he bought an adult Newfoundland dog he named Seaman.

My packing list was less substantial. A tent, sleeping pad, and bag. A small propane camping stove, with four canisters of gas. A sizable first-aid kit, including Ace bandages, Vetrap, and a snakebite kit. Extra-strength mosquito repellant and waterproof sunscreen. Shorts and tank tops that I was willing to sacrifice to the river. A couple of long-sleeved shirts and a hat. A battered pair of Teva sandals. Rain gear. A camera, basic toiletries, my cell phone. Out of nostalgia, my brass compass. A small journal a friend had given me for Christmas. Finally, my Kindle, which contained, among other things, the complete journals of Lewis and Clark.

After completing his scientific and medical studies in Philadelphia, Lewis traveled to Pittsburgh, where he commissioned a keelboat he designed himself: fifty-five feet long, eight feet wide, with a thirty-two-foot forward mast. The captains had sleeping quarters in the cabin above decks. The men slept in the hold, which was also capable of storing twelve tons of cargo, though Lewis also bought two pirogues, flat-bottomed dugout canoes shaped from whole tree trunks, in case they'd need more room. The keelboat was designed so that it could be rowed, poled, sailed, or cordelled: pulled upstream by heavy ropes.

The FloteBote, on the other hand, was a forty-one-year-old pontoon boat, twenty-four feet long and seven feet wide. In its youth, it had an aluminum frame that carried a canvas canopy; when we set sail, the frame (and the canopy) had long since rotted away. The last time I'd been on it, ten of us had taken it out for a family swimming party and nearly swamped it. Four of us dove off and swam to shore to get the pontoons back above water. On that adventure, all we'd had with us were towels.

In advance of our trip, Dirk and Lee had bought six large plastic storage tubs, four for our belongings, one for tools, equipment, and charts, and one for camping gear. We also had a six-foot ice chest of food, a box portajohn, two anchors, and six five-gallon plastic gas cans. Dirk had packed five or six bottles of Crown Royal, to thank or bribe marina managers who might give us a berth overnight. I'd thrown in a pricy four-pack of Belgian beer. He also firmly established that, with the exception of the launch, no more than four of us could be on the boat at the same time, to keep it afloat.

In August of 1803, Lewis, Seaman, and a handful of men Lewis had recruited left Pittsburgh and sailed the keelboat down the Ohio to meet up with Clark and his recruits in Kentucky. Once they reached the

Mississippi, they turned the boat upstream, and in struggling against the current it became clear that their original plan of fifteen men would never get them up the Missouri. They hired twenty-four more men from military outposts in Illinois, plus another twelve French Canadian rivermen, called *engagés*. These men would accompany the corps as far as the Mandan Native villages, more than 1,600 miles upstream, the furthest point any European had reached on the Missouri River. At the time the corps set off, the only things the Western world knew surely enough to put on a map west of the Mississippi were four tiny dots: St. Louis, St. Charles (the last European settlement in what would become Missouri), the Mandan tribal villages in what is now North Dakota, and the mouth of the Columbia River, on the Pacific Ocean, another 1,500 miles away. In May of 1804, the corps prepared to set sail.

A few days before I got to the lake house, Dirk and Rod had gone to the public library and printed off more than two hundred pages of river charts. Produced by the Army Corps of Engineers, our charts mapped the Missouri from the confluence of the Big Sioux River to the confluence with the Mississippi. The cousins paid extra to print the charts in color; every significant bend, sandbar, boat ramp, daybeacon, and marina for more than eight hundred miles was clearly indicated. Every directional change for boat traffic was specified, in case the daybeacons had come down or been obscured by bank growth.

Today, rivers navigable by motorized boat traffic are organized similarly to interstates. Daybeacons, large green or red triangular signs, are placed along the banks at seemingly random intervals, both upstream and downstream (they are called "daybeacons," presumably, because when they were initially installed on the Lower Missouri in the early 1920s, they were kerosene lamps, hung from posts along the navigation channel). Green means you continue straight along the boat channel, a trough about fourteen feet deep that runs some twenty yards off the bank. Red means you must cross the river and move into the channel off the opposite bank. Every few miles, all boat traffic swaps sides of the river. Sometimes, these moves make obvious sense; there is a large sandbar, or a boat ramp, or some natural or manmade obstacle in the river. Most of the time, however, the shift has no visible purpose. The whole process is more unnerving if there is oncoming boat traffic.

There are also dayboards, diamond-shaped signs that correlate to specific locations on the charts, so you can know exactly where you are. This would be comforting, if there weren't also caveats announcing that the river has moved a good bit since the dayboards were installed, so you can only be somewhat sure of exactly where you are.

The charts provided all of this information, along with mile markers, boat ramps and docks, and surrounding towns. Dirk stowed them in a series of gallon Ziploc bags, along with a GPS, to counter the inaccuracies of the dayboards. It turned out that Ziploc bags were among the most essential of our gear. The Corps of Discovery had no such luxuries.

They did, however, have a partial map. In 1795 James Mackay and John Evans set off from St. Louis to explore the Missouri River as far to the northwest as the Mandan villages where, eight years later, the corps would spend their first winter. Mackay was a Scottish trapper looking for new trade opportunities. Evans was a Welshman searching for proof of the Welsh prince Madoc, who legend claimed had fled Wales in a boat in the twelfth century, arrived in North America, and married into a Native tribe, and whose descendants had blue eyes and spoke a version of Welsh. Of the two, Mackay was the more successful. Lewis and Clark had Mackay and Evans's map of the river up to what is now Washburn, North Dakota, and had consulted with Mackay in St. Louis about the first leg of the trip.

"I wish we had the journals of Lewis and Clark with us," Mary said, as the boat settled into the relative calm of the center of the river. I pulled my Kindle from its Ziploc bag and read aloud from their entry for our launch date, July 28, in 1804.

> Saturday July 28th 1804. cloudy morning. we Set out eairly proceded on past a high Bottom prarie on N. S. Some Timber on the Ridge back of those praries above the Bottom prarie the hills make in close to the River verry high & Steep. we passd. the mouth of a Small Creek on N. S. named *Round Knob Creek*. the wind Blew hard from N. E. *G. Drewyer* joined us at 11 oC with one Deer. we Came to a hi clift or Buut one hun[dred] feet the Barge Struck a

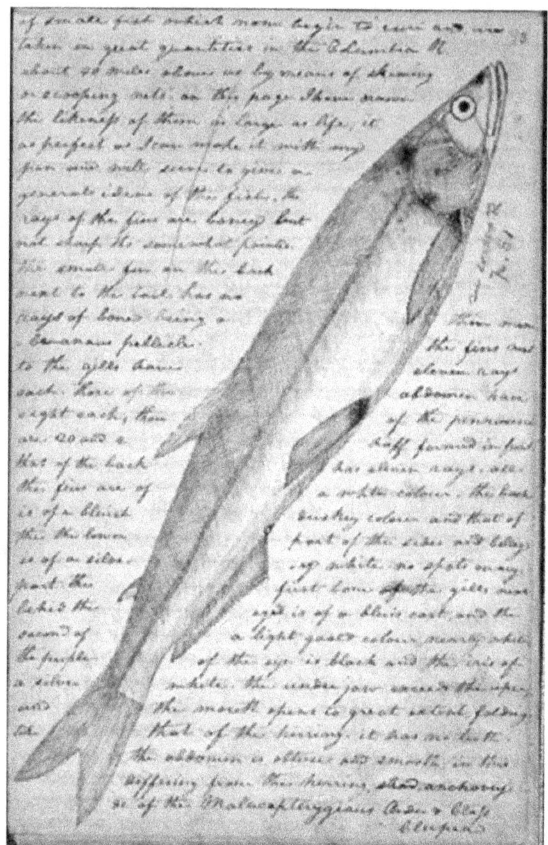

FIG. 3. Fish illustration from the journal of William Clark. From Meriwether Lewis and William Clark, *The Definitive Journals of Lewis and Clark*, vol. 6, *Down the Columbia to Fort Clatsop* (Bison Books, 2002).

> Sand Bare on *the Side of the River on the Star Bord S. in Campe on the north Side of the [river]* at the foot of a iLand CaLd the Bluf iLand we Rowed 10 Miles that day. the hunterers Comin and Brought one indian with [them]. ~ Joseph Whitehouse

At his writing, Whitehouse and the corps were nearly a month of travel downstream from our location.

Joseph Whitehouse was born in Virginia in 1775. His family moved to Kentucky in 1784; sometime after that, he enlisted in the army and was stationed at Fort Kaskaskia, in southern Illinois, on the Mississippi River. He met traders and Native people, learned about life beside a big river, and it was there that he volunteered, in January 1804, to join the Corps of Discovery.

We have lists and receipts for the things Lewis bought and requisitioned for the men, but none of the surviving journals discuss the day-to-day experience of life on their boat. Clark's journals contain ongoing records of weather, hunting and fishing successes, and the issues of managing a group of up to fifty-four people. He wasted neither time nor paper on personal experiences or descriptions of the river. Once he began writing, Lewis was the more eloquent, illustrating his journals with drawings of animals, plants, and fish, but his entries were sporadic until the corps was some six months into their trip. Historians are fairly confident that Lewis and Clark's journals were edited before they were turned over to the White House.

My journal, like the men of the corps, was bound in leather. Unlike them, however, I did most of my writing on the boat, not on land by the campfire every evening. Even on dry land, my penmanship doesn't come close to that of an eighteenth century Virginia schoolboy. On the boat, it vacillated between marginally legible and gibberish. On nearly every page, sentences are boxed and surrounded by stars or question marks, things for me to look up once I got home to the internet.

Placed side by side, however, my entries don't differ that much from Whitehouse's:

> 7/28/2013: Sun and clouds. Significant clouds to the northwest for first hour. Dirk says Decatur, NE by 8 p.m. Three Great Blue heron. Trailer park on IA side at Wood City boat dock, NE side wooded. Homemade Slip-and-slide down bank made of old billboard fabric—unreadable but bold. Bass boat passed us at Sioux City RR bridge. Very few people fishing. 2 geese walking down Iowa bank—3rd charged out to meet them, neck low, at speed. Then recognized them and relaxed. Burned pilings on the NE side—how?

But the one thing I did do that none of the corps journalists did was jot down, from time to time, the conversations of my companions.

"I'm glad we didn't get the pontoons water-tested before we put the boat in," Dirk said from the helm, eyeing the river suspiciously as it unwound before us.

"Excellent call," Rod said.

I peered over the side at the edge of pontoon I could see. No visible cracks, anyway. At least on the top of that starboard pontoon. Mary moved to the foredeck and lay down, head-first, to watch the river pass beneath us. Rod, Lee, and I simply looked around.

Eight hundred miles upstream from St. Louis, the Missouri is a muddy brown color, like peanut butter, or coffee with too much cream. It's impossible to see through, though periodically Asian carp would hurl themselves into the air to remind us that there was life below us as well. There is a small, sandy beach along the left bank; Nebraska rises more bluntly on the right, the cutbank above the river lined with scrub trees. We came around a bend and spotted a little girl with a dog on the Iowa bank. Seeing us, she ran and hid behind a bush, peering at us. I looked past her at the trees, imagining what it might have looked like when the corps passed this way, and how terrifying it would have been if they spotted a human hiding on the shore, watching them.

The untested pontoons were sitting pretty low in the water. Rod had agreed to come on board for the first few miles but was getting off near a bridge downstream from Sioux City to follow us in his van while getting some work done by phone. We'd agreed that we'd take turns in the van so that everyone had equal time on the river. When we spotted the bridge, Dirk steered us carefully up to a fallen tree that hung out over the river and dropped the motor into idle. Mary, Lee, and I held the boat by the tree branches while Rod clambered on the trunk and picked his way to dry land. We waved to him as we let go and floated off downstream.

"The good news is," Lee said, watching Rod make his way up to the bridge, "we can't really get lost."

"Speaking of which," Dirk said, steering us back toward the center of the river, "can you hand me the GPS? I think it's in with the charts."

"Here's a conversation Lewis and Clark never had," said Lee, snapping the lid off one of the boxes.

In August 1804 Clark sent eighteen-year-old Private George Shannon to retrieve two pack horses that had gotten loose. A Pennsylvanian and the youngest member of the corps, Shannon promptly got lost. He wandered around what is now northeastern Nebraska for sixteen days, subsisting on wild grapes and the few rabbits he could shoot. The corps finally caught up with him, nearly starving, somewhere across the river from present-day Yankton, South Dakota. In 2001, in anticipation of the bicentennial of the expedition, Nebraska towns all along the river vied to register themselves as part of the official Shannon Trail. Those of us who live in the original colonies have learned to be skeptical about "George Washington Slept Here" markers; in small Nebraska towns up and down the river, similar markers read "George Shannon May Have Been Lost Here."

Shannon's problem was that he vastly underestimated how slowly the main party was moving. Once he located the river, he raced upstream, moving farther and farther ahead of them each day. Though sails, poles, and oars were often at work, the primary engine moving the corps west was the men themselves, wading waist-deep in the river or along the shore while hauling the boat, thirty tons of supplies, and the small cannon mounted on the bow over their shoulders by rope. They averaged about ten river miles a day on the upstream journey.

In contrast, going downstream with a motor, we were shooting for almost forty-five river miles on our first day, heading for a marina in Decatur, Nebraska. The mile markers—assuming they were where they were supposed to be—suggested that we were making about eight miles an hour.

The clouds stayed behind us to the northwest. Sunlight sparkled across the muddy surface of the river. Insects, nearly invisible, danced and swarmed just above the water. Bank swallows, their short, dark silhouettes like Stealth bombers, dove from Nebraska to Iowa and back after the bugs, skimming across the surface of the river. The first time we passed one of their nesting colonies, a stretch of riverbank riddled with one- to two-inch round holes, I thought it was a snake colony and looked about nervously for a floating snarl of water moccasins. At one point, we sailed through the bank-to-bank path of a Red Admiral butterfly. Unfazed by our arrival into its commute, it alit on the lid of a storage box next to me, rested there for a few seconds, and, presumably having caught its breath, resumed its flight to Iowa.

What we didn't encounter, perhaps because of our speed, were mosquitoes.

In the early nineteenth century, the only successful mosquito repellent was smoke. Native tribes often added herbs that proved very effective in driving away mosquitoes. The Blackfoot tribe laid fringed sagewort on their campfire coals; the ensuing smoke was such a deterrent to mosquitoes that bands of wild horses would come into camp and huddle around the fires, helping the Blackfoot to become one of the dominant mounted powers of the northern Rockies.

As the expedition couldn't build fires on the boats, the men coated themselves in a gooey mixture of tallow and hog lard. Since many of them were in the river for most of the day, this didn't work, and their suffering is much remarked upon in the journals. Spelling was not yet regularized in the United States; though they all spelled "mosquito" differently, they all mentioned them repeatedly. Clark alone brought them up so often that the word is spelled nineteen ways in his journals. Lewis recounted that Seaman the dog was so tormented that he kept the men up all night, whining and scratching.

On our boat, we were all aware that in 1804 no one yet knew that mosquitoes were responsible for much more than torment. Malaria was rampant in the nation's new capitol in those days, built on the sediment and marshes of the Potomac, though no one knew why. Today, we also know they also carry dengue, West Nile virus, and a number of forms of encephalitis. I had two bottles of deet in my storage box; Mary had bought a Racket Zapper, a battery-operated Ping-Pong-racket-sized flyswatter that claimed to electrocute pests with every swing. For the record, it didn't. But the mosquitoes left us alone, at least until we stopped moving.

Whenever Lewis and Clark stopped moving, they had trouble with their men. Young, healthy, mostly unmarried men come with their own issues. And while their boat was much bigger, they faced an uncertain timeline with no possible exit strategies, no assurance that they'd make it home alive, and plenty of unexpected, often unimaginable problems. The men fought; they broke into the whiskey; there was dereliction of duty and three cases of desertion. And those are just the problems Lewis and Clark felt compelled to record for posterity.

But for all the problems, there were also remarkable moments of courage. In October of 1804, as the river began to ice up around them, they reached the Mandan tribal villages in what is now North Dakota. There, Lewis and Clark signed on a French trapper and translator who had been living with the Mandans. They also recruited his wife, a thirteen- or fourteen-year-old Shoshone girl named Sakakawea. The trapper, Toussaint Charbonneau, had either bought her or won her at cards from the Hidatsa, who had kidnapped her as a child. She, when her husband agreed that they would join the corps together, about a thousand miles into what would be a nearly five-thousand-mile journey, was about five months pregnant with her first child. Clark nicknamed her "Janey." By the end of the trip, he and Lewis considered her one of the most critical elements of their success. Clark would, after her death, bring her children to be raised in his own household.

The corps hunkered down through a vicious winter on the northern plains from November until April 1805. On February 11 Sakakawea gave birth to a son, whom she named Jean-Baptiste. Two months later, when the corps moved west and off their map, she strapped the baby onto her back and moved with them.

Like all American children, I'd learned about Sakakawea in elementary school. Never before, however, had I imagined what her experience must have been like. A stranger, surrounded by strangers, moving into familiar but forgotten lands. And utterly dependent on those strangers for her survival.

My survival was only slightly less of a concern.

Not far upstream from our launch site, the corps saw their first grizzly bear. They had their first meeting with the Teton Sioux, the first of the many western tribes whose power and threat the nineteenth-century U.S. government took seriously. The journals record that even in Missouri, wolves stood openly on the riverbanks watching them move upstream. The men killed their first bison. Saw their first pronghorn antelope.

Lewis had promised Jefferson more than just journals and a trade passage to Asia. Renaissance men, they had agreed that Lewis would, where practicable, send home samples of both flora and fauna that the corps found. They didn't send home a live pronghorn or a bison. They did, however, somewhere east of our launch site, trap a Prairie dog and ship it back, alive, to Jefferson in Washington. It took the men—some forty-five of them born and trained wilderness experts—an entire day.

What's interesting about the Prairie dog isn't that they shipped it home. What's interesting is that they caught it—after a day of frustrations, by finally flooding an underground den and rescuing the half-drowned occupant—in September of 1804. They couldn't ship it back to Washington until April 1805. Which meant that they kept it alive—built it a cage, fed it from their own stores, melted snow to give it water, cared for it—for more than six months, and then shipped it with instructions for its care downstream to St. Louis, and then overland to Washington. It traveled to St. Louis, presumably with adequate food supplied by the corps, with the three men who'd been dismissed from the corps for desertion, and then down the Mississippi to the Gulf of Mexico and around Florida to the harbor in Baltimore, doubtless the most well-traveled Prairie dog of its time. Regardless, along with one captured and caged magpie, it made it safely back to the White House, living examples of the biodiversity of the west. The Prairie dog was simply the first of many animals no European American had ever encountered.

We know that Jefferson kept the Prairie dog, at least, for several weeks before shipping it to the Peale Museum in Baltimore; what became of the magpie is unclear. Did they roam freely in the new White House, the Prairie dog chewing on the baseboards, the magpie alighting on the banisters?

What's also not clear is what Jefferson hoped for from the men's journals; presumably, he wanted a thorough and multidimensional record of the expedition. We don't know how many or which of the men were literate enough to record their experiences; we have no idea if other journals were lost, destroyed on the trip, or if, like Whitehouse's, they might turn up one day from the corner of an old trunk, where they have been moldering in an attic for more than two centuries. There is some evidence that at least one other man kept a journal; reports concur that Robert Frazer kept papers in his saddlebags. However, they have never been found.

But I've got to imagine that if the journal I kept of my trip was destined, not for my own use and perusal but for the president of the United States and, potentially, the Cabinet, the Congress, and the American people, I would have written it very differently. For sure, I'd have been more detailed in my notes.

The corps' journals leave us with six versions of the experience. They are each devoid of self-awareness, of self-doubt, of the kinds of thoughts and emotions that any diarist might include in a text that no one—or at least, no one beyond immediate family—might read. But as someone who followed vaguely in at least some of their footsteps, I can identify with them a bit, especially with Whitehouse. A private. A latecomer to the expedition. I can imagine at least the edges of what he must have been thinking.

Fear. Most of the men were in their twenties, an age at which most of us believe ourselves immortal. But even in your twenties, the idea of venturing into unmapped, uncharted territory full of unimaginable animals and legendarily hostile Native tribes must have caused at least a little trepidation. Whitehouse was twenty-nine when they set off.

I wasn't worried about animals or violent altercations with other humans. I was absolutely certain that the boat would sink, probably on day 3 or 4. Either the pontoons would crack under the weight of our equipment or we'd hit a submerged tree or a sandbank, but the chances of the boat staying above water for eight hundred miles seemed low. If it did go down, I had a plastic pouch on a string around my neck to make sure my cell phone and my driver's license survived, and so they could ID my body, in case the Missouri lived up to its reputation and I couldn't swim to shore.

My mother, who had given me the plastic pouch, was afraid a container ship wouldn't see us and would run us down. While there aren't container ships on the Missouri, every time we were passed by a massive dredging barge, I half-expected their wake to swamp us. Once or twice they nearly did.

I was also a little concerned about everyone's health. We had full cell service most of the time on the river (apparently radio waves are strengthened on big rivers, where there is nothing blocking the signal), but I didn't know the cousins' medical history, and they didn't know mine. Presumably they knew each other's, which was at least something. And I hadn't been certified in CPR since I was a lifeguard in college.

"I'm allergic to penicillin and morphine," I said tentatively, apropos of nothing.

Lee looked at me and raised an eyebrow.

"And black walnuts," I said. He laughed then.

But like me, what Whitehouse and the rest of the corps must have felt was excitement. Even in the early nineteenth century, rumors about the western frontier were alluring. The landscape, the animals, the Native tribes. The gold. After months of training and preparation, the men of the corps must have been incredibly excited to see whatever was out there. They didn't write it down, but especially at the outset, they must have been eager to be moving west at last.

And it was Whitehouse who, albeit after the journey was complete, finally inserted a little of himself into his writing. In December 1806, four months after the journey was complete, Whitehouse wrote a preface to his journal, in anticipation of publication:

> Though the events, which compose my Journal, may have little in itself to strike the imagination of those who love to be astonished; nevertheless, when it is consider'd, that we explored those Waters, which had never before borne any other Vessell . . . traversed those Forests and plains, where no American Citizen, or European had ever before presented themselves . . . I cannot in justice to myself omit saying, that the manly, and soldier-like behaviour; and enterprizing abilities; of both Captain Lewis, and Captain Clark, claim my utmost gratitude: and the humanity shown at all times by them, to those under their command, on this perilous and important Voyage of discovery.

It is the sole insight into the minds of the men, though no doubt colored by his survival. I may not have confronted grizzly bears or, as Whitehouse did, fallen overboard several times, but I do know that it's easier to be sanguine about an experience after it's been proven not to have killed you. But I did, unlike Whitehouse, jot down fragments of what I was seeing and feeling, and the occasional metaphysical observation.

> Lay in the prow, throb of engine on my ribs. Watch water slip past the pontoons, feel spray on shoulders. My head probably level with the Corps when they were in the pirogues. No boats or people, but cottonwood fluff floating everywhere. Remembering so many trips on this boat sitting where I'm lying now, my then smaller toes pointed to reach the water, water sluicing around them, wondering what fish were below me, looking up at us as we passed over them, wondering if the muskies of Lake Okoboji would come to check if my toes were actually food. This boat, and the people on it, were huge parts of my childhood.

Dirk had said, earlier, that riverboating provided a very pointed view because you can't see the countryside. I wrote:

> Going down a river is like tunnel vision, or life. You can see to, but not through, the next bend.

And then:

> Don't get too flowery.

I can't clearly articulate, even to myself, even now, why I went on the trip, beyond the middle-of-the-night red-letter vision and the general appeal of doing something so interesting. "Who wouldn't go on this trip?" is still my standard answer when the question is posed.

The men of the corps must have felt this as well. Lewis and particularly Clark vetted their men carefully, so there must have been some level of pride in being selected. And likewise, there must have been some glamour in imagining the life of an explorer, especially upon a victorious return. Columbus had landed in the New World only 312 years earlier. James Cook had died only five years before the corps set out. The idea of being the first American citizens to see the western half of the continent must have carried with it some level of cachet.

In their aftermath, millions of European Americans settled, lived, procreated, and died on the river's banks. But I was getting to see it, to some extent, as the corps had. At the least, I was getting to see it in a steady block. See all the things—birds, fish, animals, bugs, humans, terrain—that existed in, with, and alongside it, a little more than two hundred years after they did.

And I was getting to see all this with members of my own family that I both knew and didn't know, that I shared blood and history and all the joy and damage that family brings, that geographical and generational distance both enhance and impair. And perhaps, once it was over, assuming we all survived, those distances would be reduced for the five of us.

Chaos theory tells us that if we look closely enough at seemingly random events, patterns begin to emerge: 209 years and two months, almost to the day, after the Corps of Discovery set off from St. Charles,

Missouri, on their grand adventure, my four cousins and I sailed into the center of the Missouri to begin our own. We launched close to the site of the corps' first important meeting with the Yankton Sioux, nearly four months into their trip. Lewis and Clark could not have dreamed of the tools we brought to our expedition. Apart from the motor and the backup motor, we had GPS satellite data and river charts, an expectation of safe and friendly harbors, MedEvac helicopters, and reasonably accurate weather prediction. By the time the corps reached our starting point, all of their horses had been stolen. We had road support in the form of a 2002 Volkswagen Vanagon. Most ominously, a few miles downstream from our launch site, Lewis and Clark had already buried the first of their men.

Charles Floyd was a Kentucky native and a neighbor of William Clark, handpicked for the expedition two weeks after Clark received the orders from Lewis and President Jefferson. Despite Floyd's youth and relative inexperience, the men elected him to serve as sergeant once the Corps of Discovery began assembling across the Mississippi from St. Louis. Little is known of Floyd's childhood on the frontier; born in the final years of the American Revolution, he grew up near present-day St. Matthews, Kentucky, just outside Louisville. By 1802 he was a local constable and mail carrier between Louisville and Vincennes, in southern Indiana, which at the time meant distributing mail across a hundred-mile route teeming with hazards. In the spring of 1803, General George Clark and his youngest brother, William, moved in across the Ohio River and presumably got to know the young Floyd as he delivered the mail. Sometime around July 18, William Clark began assembling the Corps of Discovery. Charles Floyd's enlistment papers show that he joined on August 1.

For the next ten months, he and the other men worked and trained to prepare for their journey. Finally, the corps headed upstream and into the unknown. Floyd kept a journal; his entries, like Clark's, reflect a pragmatist's approach to exploration, a daily account of miles traveled and weather faced and problems developing or solved. On the day of the expedition's departure from St. Charles, he wrote:

> Monday [May] 21st, 1804. Left St. Charles 4:00 p.m. Showery. Encamped on the north side of the river.

His journal doesn't convey a sense of the man holding the pen. But it says something about Charles Floyd that it is Clark, and not Floyd himself, who first recorded, on July 30, that Floyd was "very unwell, with a bad cold." Three weeks later, on August 20, Charles Floyd died. He was, we think, twenty-four years old.

The Corps of Discovery gave Floyd a full military funeral on the eastern bank of the Missouri. His grave, though it has been moved three times by the U.S. Park Service as the bluff it rests in has eroded, is marked by a one-hundred-foot sandstone obelisk, erected in 1900. It was the first site in the country to be established on the National Register of Historic Places.

When Sergeant Floyd died, Lewis and Clark must have wondered, in their own minds if not to each other, how many more of the corps would lose their lives, if, indeed, if any of them would survive the trip. As we floated past his monument, visible from the river, less than an hour into our expedition, I looked surreptitiously at my four cousins, all a generation older than me.

"Do you still have your appendix?" Rod asked me.

"Yes," I said.

"Most people going on this trip have theirs prophylactically removed," he said. I laughed, nervously, and poked a little at my lower right quadrant.

This does make one wonder how many people go on this trip.

Historians believe that Charles Floyd died of a ruptured appendix, today cured by one of the simplest surgical procedures known to medicine. But at the turn of the nineteenth century, it was a death sentence. Floyd would have died even if he'd been safely at home in his bed in Kentucky.

But he wasn't. He remains on the western coastline of the state of Iowa to this day, proudly cared for by the people of the city that has grown up around his grave, the only member of the corps to die on the expedition. Floyd's monument isn't his only tribute, however.

On our drive to the boat, earlier that morning, we'd stopped at a park in the small town of Alton, Iowa, to use their restrooms. Mary had pointed out that it might be quite some time before we saw a bathroom that had a roof again. I walked down a small slope, past picnic tables and a playground, to a narrow stream overhung with cottonwoods.

I plucked a small, heart-shaped leaf off a branch over my head and dropped it in, watching it glide downstream toward the Missouri. My grandfather and his brother, the father of these cousins, were born in Alton just over a hundred years ago, and a hundred years after Lewis and Clark embarked on their great adventure. All my life, the one salient story I knew of my grandfather's childhood was that every winter, as soon as this small river froze solid, he and his brother would strap on their ice skates, like Hans Brinker, and skate three miles upstream to the relative metropolis of Orange City to play with their cousins, then skate back down and home again before dark.

It is the Floyd River, named by Lewis and Clark themselves to honor their dead sergeant. It is the first tributary to enter the Missouri downstream from his grave.

If we look closely enough at seemingly random events, patterns begin to emerge. My grandfather died when I was seven, and his brother, these cousins' father, became my de facto grandfather. Now his children and I, separated most of my life by a continent and all my life by a generation, had come together on the banks of Charles Floyd's river, and the centuries came together as well, loosely, like the entwined branches of close-growing trees.

3

Endangered Species of the Missouri

No human being, however great or
powerful, was ever so free as a fish.

—John Ruskin

Early the next morning, returning from breakfast after our first night on the river, Lee and I were crossing a pedestrian bridge in Decatur, Nebraska, when we spotted a small white and tan bird walking on the riverbank, pausing as she picked her way through the sand on delicate, knobby legs to wait for the tiny white puff of a chick that trailed her. We stopped to watch for a few minutes, parent and child nearly the same color as the bank.

"It might be a Piping plover," Lee said. And I wished I'd brought binoculars.

I'm not what my birding friends would call a "birder." I can identify most of the birds local to my home: Cardinals, Robins, Blue jays, Catbirds, the omnipresent Starlings, Red-tailed hawks. Somewhere in the woods around my house is at least one Great Horned owl; I've only seen it once, but after sunset I can hear it hooting from the trees, and I've found owl pellets, the undigested remnants of fur and bone, lodged in the grass in my backyard. The waterfowl are also familiar, Canada and Snow geese, Mallards, Snowy egrets, Mute swans, Bald eagles, and my favorite, the Great Blue heron, huge and prehistoric. Once, very early on a summer morning in Pennsylvania, I was driving down a country lane when I saw the lights of an oncoming car stopped in the road, and the silhouette of something slender. When I got closer, I realized it was a Great Blue, standing stock-still on the yellow lane divider, as tall as my car. The other driver and I idled on either side of it, transfixed, for almost ten minutes until it suddenly unfolded itself, like origami in reverse, and lifted from the pavement.

I knew that the Piping plover was one of two endangered species of birds on the Missouri. I'd searched in vain for an Audubon *Guide to the Midwest* on arriving in Iowa City; if one exists, I've never been able to locate it. My own *Guide to the Mid-Atlantic* is well-thumbed and annotated, but it was no use to me on the Missouri.

The Lower Missouri is home to countless species of birds. We saw predictable Canada geese, followed by an unexpected American White pelican, paddling upstream alone, a month earlier than her migration schedules forecast. Great Blue herons stalked the shadows beneath overhanging trees, and swallows darted from bank to bank chasing insects. As we moved downstream, Bald eagles began to appear in startling numbers; I kept a running tab in my journal until I could no longer keep up with them. Some days later, in western Missouri, a guy from St. Joseph would tell me that, despite going out on his boat several times a week for years, he'd never seen a Bald eagle on the river. I told him I'd seen thirty or forty just that day, about twenty miles upstream from his dock.

The Piping plover breeds on the sandbars and beaches of the river, and its status is endangered almost entirely because of the loss of those habitats. As sand dredging operations suck up sand from the river bottom and farming, recreation, and development reach for the riverbanks, safe locations for plover nests become harder to find.

They are sturdy little birds, with narrow black bands around the backs of their short necks and long yellow legs; at adulthood they measure six to seven inches tall, and are decidedly plump. They make quick piping calls, often many over a few seconds, when alerting each other to danger. In breeding season, the males scratch out five or six different potential nests in grassy sand above the waterline, clearing the larger stones and debris with their feet. A breeding pair will then take up to ten days to select the best of these sites and then get down to the business of laying and incubating eggs. Plovers are monogamous during breeding seasons, and take turns caring for the eggs, with one partner sliding into the nest as the other slides out, keeping the eggs protected almost constantly.

Lee and I leaned against the bridge and watched the little family peck their way down the shore and out of sight.

We'd arrived at Pop-n-Doc's Marina in Decatur the evening before in dramatic fashion. The marina is carved in behind a twenty- or thirty-foot levee, with a narrow entrance on the southwestern bank of the river that's hard to spot if you don't know where to look. As we didn't, we overshot it. Dirk shouted out to Lee, who was driving, as we sailed past. Near the entrance there were a number of boats fishing or cruising, so Lee abandoned the idea of a marine U-turn, pushed the engine into reverse, and backed the FloteBote upstream, through the entrance, and straight into a slip in the U-shaped marina.

We did attract some significant attention from the people enjoying a drink on the restaurant deck overlooking the boatyard.

"Well, we just took that Beverly Hillbillies thing to a whole new level," I said to Mary as we fished our wallets out of the plastic tubs and walked up the long wooden staircase to the restaurant at the top of the levee. Apart from our entrance ass-end first, our boat was smaller, dingier, and much, much older than the sleek speedboats and luxurious pontoon boats berthed in the marina. Up on the deck, some of the patrons started taking pictures of it.

"Maybe we'll make the local paper," she whispered.

Once we'd paid the overnight slip fee, Mary went off to find a bathroom, and I went back to the boat to help Dirk and Lee assemble the wooden canopy they'd designed to replace the broken aluminum frame. It was essentially an A-frame, constructed of two-by-eights and bolts, and draped with mosquito netting and silver tarps affixed by bungee cords and large metal hand clamps. It looked, in a word, ridiculous. And it didn't reduce the attention we were still getting from the restaurant.

While we were finishing the frame, Rod appeared, having caught up to us in the van, and walked down to the slip with Mary. We had a brief conversation about sleeping arrangements; Mary and I would sleep on the boat, Rod would pop the camper roof and sleep in the marina's parking lot, and Dirk and Lee reserved a cabin in an off-season hunter's camp. With a shower. Then we climbed back up the wooden staircase to the restaurant, and Dirk bought us each a beer.

Most of the other patrons were local recreational boaters and fishers. The most prominent food fish this far upstream is the Walleye, the largest of the perch family. Walleyes can weigh up to thirty pounds, but what makes them special is their eyes. Like many predators, walleyes have tapetum lucidum in their eyes, a layer of reflective tissue behind their retinas, which gives them excellent night vision but also causes their eyes to shine when lit in the dark, even in the silty water of the Missouri. Which makes them somewhat easier to catch, at least at dusk and dawn.

A waitress came by and plunked plates of the fried Walleye dinner special in front of us, and we dove into our food as if we'd been living on the boat for weeks and hadn't had a homecooked breakfast in the cottage twelve hours earlier. When I looked up, the bar crowd was staring at us, if possible, even more closely.

There are nearly a hundred species of native fish in the Lower Missouri from the Gavins Point Dam in South Dakota, some sixty river miles upstream from our launch, to St. Louis. They range from the tiny Pygmy sunfish, about an inch and a half long, to the Alligator gar, which can be ten feet long, weigh up to 350 pounds, and, as the name suggests, has a long, narrow mouth lined with needle-like fangs. There's the American Paddlefish, a huge spoon-billed fish that dates back 125 million years, weighs nearly 140 pounds, and though not endangered, is thought to be the last survivor of its species left on earth. Two species of catfish live in the Missouri: the Flathead (100 pounds) and the Blue; according to a mid-twentieth-century steamboat captain, a 315-pound Blue catfish was caught east of Jefferson City in 1866. And finally, there's the Pallid sturgeon, smallest of the river's monster fish, nearly six feet long, topping out at about 70 pounds, and arguably the ugliest of them all.

The only fish I would actually see in the river on the whole trip was the Asian carp, the invasive fish that has infiltrated Midwestern lakes and rivers, recognizable because they leap dramatically from the water when boats pass near them, and those I would see only in flashes. The Missouri is too murky to spot fish even in the shallows near the banks, which, in my case, is a blessing. If I'd seen an Alligator gar or a Paddlefish, I'd have been afraid to set foot in the river, which would have made getting on and off the boat a challenge. But the Pallid sturgeon, long, pale, and every bit as prehistoric-looking as the Horseshoe crab, engenders affection if you look at it long enough, like the Ugliest Dog in America that they show on morning news shows.

The Pallid evolved, more or less in its present form, some seventy million years ago, in the Cretaceous period. In 1928 a Decatur farmer dug a sixty-five pound bone out of his fields; it was part of the hind leg of a still-unidentified dinosaur from the same period. At the end of the Cretaceous, the asteroid-induced mass extinction wiped out the dinosaurs, but the Pallid, safe in the depths of the Missouri, survived, and remains virtually unchanged to this day.

They are not, like most modern fish, scaled. They are covered in what are called "scutes," large hexagonal plates of cartilage that form a coat of bone-like armor. As they mature, the upper scutes harden into sharp points along the top of their backs, protecting them from predators. They don't have bones; their skeletons are also built from cartilage. Like their name suggests, they are a silvery, muddy tan, with long, flat, arrowhead-shaped heads, triangular bodies, and tails that rise to an angled point like the rear fender of a 1950s Cadillac. And, though they sit at the top of the Missouri's aquatic food chain, Pallids are toothless, swallowing whole the small invertebrates, fish, and mollusks that comprise their diets. They sense their prey through the tips of four barbels, arranged in a box around their mouths and dangling like fleshy whiskers off the flat bottoms of their heads. The only way to distinguish the Pallid sturgeon from the Shovelnose sturgeon, also living (and flourishing) in the Missouri, is that the Pallid's upper two barbels are shorter than its lower two.

In videos, Pallids materialize into frame from the murky water of the Missouri like ghostly, armored sharks, hovering above the river bottom, probing for food. Apart from visiting captive-bred Pallids at the National Fish Hatchery in Yankton, South Dakota, I will probably never see one. Like the river itself, they are outside our memory, forgotten through their invisibility except to those who are working to save them.

It's hard to know how many Pallids there are today in the Lower Missouri, though the number is certainly small. The dredging industry and efforts to maintain the boat channel have altered the gravel beds and natural channels that sturgeon need for spawning. Female Pallids don't reach sexual maturity until they're about fifteen years old, and both sexes can live to be over fifty, sometimes up to one hundred. A lot like humans. Female Pallids produce eggs only every two or three years, and if nesting conditions are not to their liking, they can reabsorb the unspawned eggs and avoid reproduction indefinitely. Each spawning female lays thousands of eggs, and once they've hatched, the "fingerlings"—most the size of a human fingernail—drift back downstream across the hundreds of miles their parents migrated to fertilize them. The period of drift leaves the larvae vulnerable to any number of threats, and even in ideal conditions only a handful of them live to adulthood.

This has an ecological purpose, of course. The Missouri can't support tens of thousands of seventy-pound carnivorous fish. But as spawning sites disappear from the Missouri and its tributaries, fewer and fewer of those handfuls survive.

The U.S. Fish and Wildlife Service staff at the Gavins Point Fish Hatchery, just below the last downstream dam on the river in Yankton, South Dakota, have been breeding Pallids since the 1990s. They extract both eggs and sperm from live, wild-caught adults, fertilize them by hand with turkey feathers, and then wait two weeks for the eggs to hatch, at which point the fingerlings are deposited in family-unit tanks to maximize genetic diversity and minimize the chance of inbreeding in the wild. The parents are returned to the places on the river where they were caught, and the babies are carefully raised and tended to all day, every day, until they are more than a year old, which makes them more likely to survive to adulthood in the wild. The hatchery has released tens of thousands of young Pallids into the river from Montana to Missouri, in hopes of bringing the population back to stability, but these great relics of the distant past remain gravely endangered, and particularly below the dams, their numbers are consistently low.

A few years after the trip, I took a group of undergraduates and graduate students to the hatchery. Our guide, Sam Stukel of the Fish and Wildlife Service, reached into a tank with a net, pulled out a six-week old Pallid sturgeon, and held it in front of us. It opened and closed its little round mouth, but it didn't struggle. I gasped a little and asked if I could touch it. He said yes, and I gently ran the point of one finger down its soft, firm side. It felt like soft steel, and a little bit like a miracle. Later, one of the grad students told me that she thought for a second that I might burst into tears.

"I thought I would burst into flames," I said.

FIG. 4. The author meets an adult Pallid sturgeon at Gavins Point National Fish Hatchery. Courtesy Jordan Barry.

Captive-born Pallids are each microchipped and sometimes equipped with tiny radio transmitters as scientists up and down the Missouri study them and strategize ways to keep the species viable. River fishers would almost certainly report any Pallids they caught and released. Anecdotally, anyway, this doesn't appear to happen often. It hasn't been legal to keep a Pallid since 1990, even if you could catch one and get it to shore. However, before they were placed on the endangered species list, they were prized for their size, and both their meat and roe were apparently delicious. The river's fishers hope that the Pallids will recover and become, once again, a trophy catch.

The Delaware River, back by my house, had such a thriving Atlantic sturgeon population until the mid-twentieth century that an entire riverside town in New Jersey grew up around a caviar canning plant. By the 1950s pollution had caused the oxygen level in the Delaware to plummet, forcing the sturgeon to seek spawning sites elsewhere, and the industry (and the town) collapsed. The Missouri has never supported a commercial fishing industry. The current is so strong, the river channel so dangerous, and the water so muddy that fishing on it is, and always has been, recreational. One of the people we met at Pop-n-Doc's during our Walleye dinner was a fisherman who told us that the best approach to Walleye fishing on the river was to use a weight and bump the hook along the bottom. Which also seems like a reasonable means of hooking a Pallid. That there are virtually no reports of fishers catching Pallids speaks to their rarity.

Over the 750 miles of our trip, we must have encountered a few, if invisibly. They must have been able to hear the vibrations of our little outboard motor as we spluttered down the river, rarely more than fourteen feet above the river bottom (most fish can hear; they are earless but have a form of hearing organs inside their heads). An old sturgeon today would have living memory, if they have memory, of the Missouri before the prevalence of small motorboats, when traffic on the river was propelled by oars, sails, or poles, excepting the occasional steamboat moving people and supplies upstream and down.

But it's what's outside even the oldest Pallid's living memory that catches my imagination. There are only a handful of animals left on the planet whose ancestors were here with the dinosaurs, whose essential appearances are unchanged from that distant, almost fantastical period, and almost all of them live in water. At the Museum of the Rockies in Bozeman, Montana, there is a nearly complete Pallid fossil, thirty-one inches long and seventy million years old. It looks, even to the untrained eye, exactly like a modern Pallid.

The Museum of the Rockies also held, for almost twenty years, one of the most complete *Tyrannosaurus rex* skeletons ever found. Montana's *T. rex*, who died sixty-six million years ago, stands twelve feet high and is thirty-eight feet long, and paleontologists estimate it weighed nearly six tons when it was alive. In 2019 it was moved to the Smithsonian's National Museum of Natural History in Washington DC and renamed the Wankel *T. rex*, after Kathy Wankel, who originally found it near the Fort Peck Dam on the Upper Missouri River. And so the Pallid fossil in the museum, who died roughly 100,000 sturgeon generations earlier than the *T. rex*, and the Pallids gliding through the mud and silt of the Missouri River bottom right now, are one of a very few living connections between the *T. rex*'s world and our own.

Back at Pop-n-Doc's, we finished our Walleye and fries (for the record, the Walleye was delicious), and the waitress appeared with a second round of beers, sent to us by a couple sitting near us on the deck. We thanked them and invited them to join us at our table. The Wambergs came from North Bend, in eastern Nebraska, and had flown their private plane up to Decatur for the evening. Having witnessed our notable entry into the marina and the subsequent transformation of the boat into a farcical version of the *African Queen*, they asked where we were heading. Dirk told them.

"Life's too short not to do stuff like this," Mr. Wamberg said, almost longingly, staring over the deck railing at our moored flotsam.

"And may get shorter quickly," Dirk replied.

The sun sank toward the Nebraska horizon and disappeared, and the Wambergs suggested that they might join us for dinner the next night in Omaha. Eventually, Mary and I climbed down to the boat, unrolled our sleeping bags overtop the pontoons, brushed our teeth over the railings, sprayed on some deet, and went to bed. We were awakened at 1:30 a.m., when "God Bless America" and "America the Beautiful" blasted out from the deck speakers, presumably the last-call alert at Pop-n-Doc's. A clearly drunk couple had a loud argument in the parking lot for a few minutes. Mary got back to sleep but I lay awake for a while, listening to a pair of bullfrogs throbbing to each other while crickets and cicadas thrummed, and staring through the mosquito net at what I think was the Little Dipper. I wondered, before I finally fell back to sleep, if Lewis and Clark and the guys had heard and seen the same when they'd been around here, and what they'd been thinking about if they had.

The next morning, as I brushed my teeth over the railing of the boat, birds were already darting around the marina, making an early start on their breakfasts. I could hear, somewhere nearby, the distinctive rattling call of a Kingfisher, and looked up, hoping to spot him diving for a fish.

The final endangered animal on the Missouri is the Interior Least tern, smallest of the terns—though they were removed from the endangered species list in 2019, their numbers remain low. Like Kingfishers, they are divers, plunging into the current for fish and small invertebrates, which is most of the reason I'm pretty sure I never saw one. Lewis and Clark recorded the first sighting of a Least tern near what's now Omaha, a long day's modern boat ride downstream from Decatur. They are crow-sized, white-and-gray birds, hard to spot unless you are actively looking for them, or unless they are diving. Like the Piping plover, they breed on bare sand and sandbars, and so are losing nest habitat to bank traffic and dredging. They are most often seen flying alone. It's possible I saw one flying about, or standing on a sandbar or shoreline, and simply didn't register it. It's more likely, however, that any whose habitat we did pass through chose to hide from us.

The common denominator between all three of the endangered animals of the Lower Missouri is habitat loss, and the most visible threat to their habitat is dredging operations. Dredging is a standard practice on modern rivers, deepening the river channel by removing the buildup of sand and gravel—the silt—from the river bottom. This, in a shallow, fast, dammed river like the Missouri, makes navigation safer for midsized boat traffic and gives the river itself greater volume capacity, presumably reducing flooding. The dredged material is sold for construction projects, like highways, and the waste material, the stuff not suitable for construction, is often used to strengthen, repair, or build levees.

Silt is created when bedrock and boulders upstream erode into a river. As this erosion rolls downstream, it bounces off the other debris in the riverbed, reducing in size from boulders to large rocks to cobbles to gravel to sand. This travels the length of the river, building up wetlands, creating islands and sandbars, and distributing new landmasses into the river channel. Silt is how rivers are able to shift themselves around the landscape, building up at a bend, for example, and moving the river into a different direction or across a new angle.

In the winter of 1880–81, the combination of extreme cold and heavy snow in what is now central and southeastern South Dakota caused ice dams and flooding so severe that the residents of Vermillion, built along the northern bank of the Missouri very close to the Iowa state line, abandoned what was left of their town and moved atop a bluff about a mile to the northwest, safe from the river's edge. More than 130 buildings washed completely away, and eyewitnesses reported that the river was more than two miles wide at the height of the floods. By the time the town was rebuilt, however, the river also had moved itself about a mile to the southeast, in part due to the silt buildup that developed during the flooding.

Silt is an essential part of a river's contribution to its watershed. It creates wetlands, distributes sand and gravel—material through which water can easily drain—and creates habitat for the animals that live in and on the water. In a "natural" river, channel buildup is spread across the shallows, banks, oxbows, and sandbars during flood season, and this is where Pallids, Piping plovers, and Least terns lay their eggs. On a dammed river, humans need to get involved. Silt sediment builds up behind the dams and prevents the natural development of new landmass below them. Dredging, done to keep the channel's depth stable and enable safe boat traffic, removes tons of sediment every year from the Lower Missouri, keeping the river in its bed, but removing existing fish habitat and preventing the development of new sandbars and banks for the birds. Ironically, deepening the channel increases the river's flow rate and, therefore, creates a higher flooding risk, so using the removed sediment to stabilize the levees creates a cycle of flooding and required flood maintenance.

And, for Least terns, Piping plovers, and Pallid sturgeon, it dramatically limits the development of new nesting grounds. In drought years, massive sand bars and sandy islands rise from the river, and terns and plovers are easy to spot in protected spots on the river with the naked eye, but in normal years, they are nearly invisible, even if you know where to look.

It's likely that what Lee and I were looking at that morning from the footbridge was actually a Killdeer and her chick. Killdeer are cousins of the Piping plover, birds that have so well adapted to coexisting with humans by nesting in sand and gravel wherever they can find it that they can be seen routinely in parking lots and playgrounds. It's equally likely that none of the unidentified birds I watched wheeling above the river was a Least tern. I've seen both species on the river since the trip, and they prefer the wilder, quieter sections of the river in which to raise their young. The U.S. Fish and Wildlife Service post signs barring humans from known breeding sites, especially in dry years, when the river is low and sandbars are plentiful.

Dredging is necessary if we are to utilize dams as sources of hydroelectric power and limit our dependence on fossil-fuel-powered electricity generation. It's necessary, as well, to allow even small private boats to use the river. I benefited from the efforts of the dredge industry in many ways, from a relatively safe and navigable river channel, to the stability of the banks where we anchored the boat, to the construction of the highways and bridges that got me halfway across the continent to the river to begin with. It's a complicated problem without quick or easy solutions, and even those of us who care about endangered animals are complicit in the problems that endanger them to begin with. Would the world notice if we existed without the Least tern or the Pallid sturgeon? If there are Killdeer to be seen, do we need the Piping plover along the Missouri?

The answer is that we do. Not just because these three animals are special and, in their own ways, nice to look at if we are lucky enough to see one, but because, as conservation researchers suggested in the 1980s, plant and animal species are to ecosystems what rivets are to the wings of an airplane. You may be able to land safely if one is lost, but every additional loss increases the likelihood of disaster for everyone involved. In 2018, five years after I went down the Missouri, the United Nations reported that one million species around the world were at risk of extinction. It's a lot of rivets to try to land without. We can no longer claim ignorance to the effects of our impact on the planet. We must work to find solutions to those impacts, for ourselves as much as for the species we threaten.

Once the mother and chick—Killdeers? Piping plovers?—disappeared, Lee and I walked back to the marina and down the wooden staircase to the boat. Waving goodbye to the restaurant workers, we pulled out of the berth and slipped, prow-first this time, back into the Missouri. I saw a small plane rise above the trees along the western bank and head toward the river; I assumed it was a crop duster off to spray the fields of Iowa, but it banked south and stayed with the river. Pretty quickly it caught up to us and circled over our heads twice. It was, we realized, the Wambergs, the couple who'd bought us the round of beers the night before. They waggled their wings at us, circled one last time, and turned northwest for home. We continued southeast, letting the river show us what it was, and maybe what we were as well.

4

Engineering the River

> Reports will be presented here . . . which will demonstrate the feasibility and practicability of improving the Missouri so that it will become one of the great highways of trade.
>
> —John M. Thayer, governor of Nebraska, 1891

Our second morning on the river was clear and sunny, with high puffy clouds dimly reflected in the murky, shifting surface of the water. In some parts of the country, before Europeans arrived and began building along the riverbanks, rivers ran clear from head to mouth, but the Missouri has always been muddy. Until the dams were built in the twentieth century, the two muddiest rivers in the world—the rivers with the highest silt content—were the Colorado and the Missouri. The Nile was a distant third.

Dirk took the first turn at the helm for the sixty-five miles from Decatur to Omaha. Lee was in the van, so Mary, Rod, and I sat on the deck under the tarp tent (the ends rolled up and clamped to the frame, providing good sun protection but also the constant threat of head trauma). It was warm but not hot; I stretched my bare calves into the sun from the storage box I was sitting on and looked around. Both banks were wooded, with no signs of human life. Swallows turned and wheeled over the shallows, so the bugs must have been lingering closer to shore. Out in the center of the river, it smelled vaguely of mud, and something sharp and tangy, a little like vinegar or hot bark mulch. On both sides, near the banks, big gravel "islands" began to appear. Rod sat on one of the supply boxes across the deck from me on the Iowa side of the boat. I asked him what the rock piles were.

"Probably wing dikes that were overrun during the 2011 floods," he said, pointing to one of them. Wing dikes are just one example of the tools river engineers have developed to try to manage the river. Made of tons of what's called riprap, piles of fist-sized gravel, wing dikes jut into the center of the river to force the fastest currents into the middle, allowing the water to push any submerged obstacles in the navigation channel downstream.

A little farther down, we floated past a long string of what are called revetments, wooden pilings that are wired together in sets of three and driven into the river, looking like nothing quite so much as three- or four-foot-high clothespins lining the river. The revetments we passed had probably been in place in the river since sometime in the mid-twentieth century.

The Missouri is designated as a national recreational river for the hundred-mile stretch between the Fort Randall Dam near Pickstown, South Dakota, to Ponca State Park in Nebraska, about twenty-five miles upstream from our launch site in Sioux City. This is not the same as a national wild and scenic river designation. A 149-mile stretch of the Upper Missouri in Montana, upstream of the first of the dams, holds that, but the national recreational river area marks the final stretch of the "wild" Missouri, at least as far as a dammed river can be considered wild. From Sioux City to St. Louis, almost eight hundred miles, the river has been engineered, albeit in fits and starts, with mixed and sometimes disastrous results, since the end of the nineteenth century.

The river upstream from Sioux City looks very different from itself below the city. Where the Missouri has not been engineered, it sprawls through the land, wide and wild, with sand bars scattered across its breadth and very little human development along its high natural banks. From Sioux City downstream, sand bars are few and far between, the banks are carefully managed with riprap and other stabilizing materials, and the buildings, much closer to the water, are mostly atop and amid levees, designed to keep the river where it belongs.

The river technologies we were passing, wing dikes and revetments, are only the most visible tools. Within fifteen years of the Corps of Discovery's safe return from the Pacific, Congress began discussing the ways the Missouri could be tamed and used as a shipping lane. Construction had begun on the Erie Canal in 1817, connecting the Great

Lakes to the Atlantic across the whole of New York, and the Rivers and Harbors Act of 1824 provided federal funds to make the Ohio and Mississippi Rivers safely navigable. There was even talk of digging a canal across the top of the Florida panhandle to speed up shipping from the Gulf of Mexico to Atlantic ports. The Constitution and an 1824 Supreme Court decision gave the federal government authority over interstate commerce and, since until the advent of the railroad rivers could help move goods and services (like furs and crops, or the mail), over multistate rivers as well.

In 1819 and 1820 Congress authorized a survey of the Missouri to assess its potential. Over the next sixty years, as steamboat travel on the Missouri flourished, money arrived periodically from Washington to help clear snagged trees and shipwrecks. By 1881 all the territories along the Lower Missouri had become states, and the Dakotas and Montana would follow in 1889. For South Dakota, Iowa, Nebraska, Kansas and the northwest corner of Missouri, politicians and cartographers used the river to delineate state borders, just as the Mississippi separates eastern states from western ones. What the politicians and cartographers didn't realize, however, was that the Missouri River has never been as well behaved as the Mississippi.

All natural rivers have recognizable floodplains, expanses of land level with the riverbanks, where snowmelt- and rain-induced floodwaters reach. But because of a number of geological and geographical factors—the soft, alluvial soil of the Great Plains, which erodes much more easily than clay or bedrock; the velocity of the Missouri as it absorbs its great Midwestern tributaries, the Platte, the Kansas, and the Osage; and the heavy silt load that the Missouri carries down from the Rockies—the Missouri didn't just flood before the twentieth century. It moved itself around the landscape, changing its channel as silt built up and got distributed, finding simpler gravitational geography during flood years, and demonstrating no concern whatsoever about its impact on human lives or laws.

The most dramatic example of these shifts happened to what's now Carter Lake, Iowa, a suburb of the small city of Council Bluffs. Council Bluffs sits in the southwest corner of Iowa, directly across the Missouri from Omaha. In 1877 a flood prompted the river to move a little more than a mile to the east of its bed, and stranded a small slice of

Council Bluffs on the new western shore of the Missouri, which had been, up to that point, in Nebraska. During the flood, an oxbow in the river—a horseshoe-shaped bend in a meandering river that forms as the river floods and contracts—silted up at both ends, forming an oxbow lake. The new lake wrapped around the northeast edge of the detached section of Council Bluffs, and the area was named Carter Lake. It remains an Iowa city to this day, its residents Iowa citizens, paying Iowa property taxes and holding Iowa driver's licenses, fully encircled by Nebraska.

As we made our way toward Omaha, I watched a Turkey vulture wheel through the thermals high over the river, its bald head extended below its wings as it hunted for carrion. On the Iowa bank, a few small weekend houses and trailers showed signs of summer life; by one of them, someone had shored up their bank and retaining wall with old tires, and made a Slip 'N Slide into the river out of an old bedsheet. Along the Nebraska coast, several trees lay crown-down in the water, all facing southeast. Even in the shallowest water along the shore, the Missouri's current is so strong that if a tree falls in the river in any direction, it will end up pointing downstream.

This was the other big navigational problem with the Lower Missouri; even in the center, even during high-water years, the river was extremely shallow. When Lewis and Clark and the men headed upstream, they were pulling the keelboat by ropes over their shoulders against the powerful current, but for most of that journey they were walking in the river, not on the banks. Much of the river was at most four feet deep; by comparison, the Mississippi River at St. Louis is reliably twenty feet deep, without human intervention to keep it at that depth, and nearly two hundred feet deep in places as it approaches the Gulf of Mexico. The Corp's keelboat was fifty-five feet long and was hauling a few thousand pounds of supplies at the start of the journey, and getting it upstream through the shallows, in summer in the southern plains, must have been incredibly hard work.

We, on the other hand, puttered cheerfully downstream with an outboard motor. The draw—the water depth required to keep a boat afloat—for a pontoon boat ranges from ten inches to two feet. At our eight miles an hour, our motor speed augmented considerably by the current, we'd have a nine-hour day getting to Omaha. About an hour in, Dirk called me to the helm and told me to take over. He'd explained about the daybeacons the day before, so I understood the rules of the river. But when I stepped in and took the helm for the first time, the river made sure I knew that we were traveling only as easily as it would let us.

A pontoon boat, even on a lake, is not the most agile of watercraft. On the river, it pulled hard toward the center, a little like a car that's out of alignment and just wants to veer in one direction or the other. The wheel was vibrating so hard that I clung to it just to make sure it didn't fly off the boat. The whole thing felt a bit like what I imagine steering a bathtub might be like, if someone decided to sail a bathtub down the longest river on the continent. Mary called out something from the prow, pointing at a red and white diamond-shaped sign poking up from the weeds on the western bank. A daybeacon: I needed to cross the river to the channel on the other side. I turned the wheel, feeling the pontoons push against the current, and began a slow diagonal pass to the eastern side, just as a huge barge, piled two stories high with cranes and equipment and looking like a floating construction site, came upstream around the bend straight toward me, a few hundred yards away. I took a deep breath and waited for it to turn and cross the river as well.

In 1881, after the historic late winter flood that swamped Vermillion, South Dakota, and other towns along the Lower Missouri, Major Charles Suter of the Army Corps of Engineers announced a strategy to "turn the river on itself" to contain the river's natural channel and deepen the riverbed. Dikes would force the current into a single channel, rather than letting it spread across two or three (or more) channels in the wide, meandering, untamed river. The current would become narrower and considerably stronger; he reasoned that the river's new current would naturally scour the bottom, clearing silt buildup and debris, a simple, self-sustaining management system. He asked Congress for $8 million to engineer the river from St. Louis to Sioux City. Suter's plan of attack began with addressing the silt load. He estimated that eleven billion cubic feet of silt might move through the river in a single year. As a reference, eleven billion cubic feet is enough to bury a square mile of flat ground in silt two hundred feet deep.

The strategy started with reshaping the course of the river. By installing revetment structures called clump dikes along outside bends, the river channel would be forced into the center of the river. The revetments were driven twenty to thirty feet into the river bottom and reached up to two hundred feet toward the center of the river. To manage the silt, handwoven willow mats that measured nearly two acres apiece were laid from the riverbank's rise into the water, past the ends of the dikes, and then were covered with riprap to submerge the mats. Water could flow through the willow, but the silt would build up against the wood and rocks. Over time, the silt would form new banks and the river would become narrower and faster. By constructing these clump dikes strategically, the channel would narrow, the river would deepen, and, Suter reasoned, the Missouri could become a navigable river, at least between St. Louis and the South Dakota border.

Farmers, businessmen, and local politicians were all on board. The Transcontinental Railroad had been completed in 1869, and train tracks ran on high ground all along the Missouri. This meant that farmers and ranchers could get their crops and livestock to the big city markets, but the railroads had no real competition, and the price of shipping by rail varied enormously by region. According to the Missouri River Convention of 1891, the railroads charged 0.79 cents per ton of freight per mile in the North Central District (Ohio, Michigan, Indiana, Illinois, and Wisconsin). This went up to 1.06 cents for Iowa, Nebraska, Minnesota, the Dakotas, Wyoming, and Montana, and 1.35 cents for Missouri, Texas, Kansas, Arkansas, Colorado, New Mexico, and Indian Territory, now Oklahoma. The railroads claimed that the North Central states were older and the rail lines more established, which was certainly true, but politicians at the convention pointed out that those states also had free access to the Great Lakes, the easily navigable Ohio and Mississippi Rivers, and the Erie Canal. Wrangling the Missouri River under control would force competition with the railroads and drive down expenses for the farmers, hunters, and trappers of the northern plains.

Delegates from Iowa, Nebraska, Kansas, and Missouri pressured Congress to support Suter's plan, and in 1882 Congress approved it, not with the $8 million Suter had requested, however, but with $850,000. Suter began work, focusing on the river between Lexington, Missouri, about forty miles east of Kansas City, and Charleston, Kansas. Congressional support continued through the 1880s, creating the

FIG. 5. Corps of Engineers workers topping willow mats with riprap, 1930s. Photo by U.S. Army Corps of Engineers.

Missouri River Commission. However, ongoing funding was spread across not only the Corps of Engineers' plans but local organizations along the riverbanks as well. Rapid growth in cities and industries along the river competed with the commission's plans and federal funding. By 1902, twenty-one years after Suter's initial proposal, the Corps of Engineers had managed only forty-five miles of a consistent six-foot channel upstream from Jefferson City, Missouri. Out of a total request for $7,150,000 in allocations over those years, the corps had received $3,280,201.

Theodore Roosevelt supported river development, and for a brief period the Missouri became a focal point for improvements. Steamboats and specially designed barges began traveling through the lower river, moving passengers, equipment, and freight up and down the river. This led to the creation of port terminal facilities in Kansas City. In 1911 barges hauled a little more than a thousand tons of freight through the city. By 1914 that number had risen to nearly fourteen thousand tons. In 1915 political and private interests turned against the Corps of Engineers, but it was global conflict that brought Missouri River management to a standstill.

I steered the FloteBote across the channel Suter had imagined, the helm vibrating even more strongly in my hands, and watched the barge that was still heading toward us. It was massive. They could certainly see us; the bridge on a twenty-first-century barge in the Missouri is about twelve feet off the deck, which is not that much higher than the deck of the FloteBote. I got to where the chart said the channel was on the eastern side of the river, about fifteen feet from the bank, and turned us straight toward the barge. It wasn't until the barge turned its nose toward the western bank that I realized I'd stopped breathing completely.

Mary and Rod waved to the pilot as he passed us. I swore at him in a whisper. I kept the pontoons straight as we crossed into their wake, the FloteBote bucking like a scared horse. The rudder fought against me, but the water stayed in the river and off the boat. By the time we got to the green daybeacon on the Iowa bank, we'd made it through the wake and were back in calm water. The use of daybeacons on the Missouri began in the 1920s with kerosene lanterns suspended from ten-foot posts. If a well-shaped tree happened to be growing in just the right spot, the lanterns were hung from the lower branches. Lantern tenders could earn nine dollars a month to keep the lamps clean, fueled, and lit.

As the United States entered World War I, the federal government abandoned all work on the Missouri and shifted all its workboats to the Mississippi as war resources, the Mississippi being a deeper, calmer, and better-behaved river. When the Corps of Engineers came home from Europe, the river had taken back much of the forty-five mile section that had been improved. The district engineer felt that this proved the river's recalcitrance and suggested abandoning the improvement project altogether in 1921, and limiting the corps' involvement to only what maintenance was absolutely necessary.

Local government and private interest disagreed, and in 1925 future president Herbert Hoover, then secretary of commerce, gave a speech before the Missouri River Navigation Association in which he imagined a nine-foot-deep navigation channel that reached from St. Louis to Sioux City. The corps, then led by Major Cleveland Gee, countered with a six-foot-deep channel that ended in Omaha. Congress authorized $12 million in appropriations in early 1929 to see the grand plans of Hoover, by then the president, to fruition.

Thousands of young men were hired to work on the river. Quarter boats lined the banks, barges with two-story dormitories and dining halls built atop them for the workers to eat and sleep in. As the Great Depression began, crews of workers graded the banks to install dikes with steam-powered pile drivers. By 1930 eroded river edges had been smoothed, banked, and piled with riprap. Revetments stabilized the banks and contained the channel, and where the river had once meandered, forked, and oxbowed, it now curved sinuously through the farmland toward the Mississippi. The silt better contained in rocks and mats, the current rolled down a centralized channel, keeping itself (mostly) clear of sandbars and debris. And by 1932 the Corps of Engineers estimated that a six-foot channel to Sioux City was more than 90 percent finished.

My steering confidence boosted by having not gotten us all killed by the barge, I got accustomed to the vibration of the wheel and took one hand off to fish my ringing cell phone out of my pocket. Cell signal is strangely strong on open stretches of the river, even as the land we were passing through looked more and more remote. It was Constantine.

"You have cell service?" he asked, surprised. "I expected to get voice mail."

I cheerfully told him about the close call with the barge. He managed to conceal his concerns. We talked for a few moments, him asking where we were, me explaining how we only sort of knew for sure. I could almost hear him shaking his head. I steered us across the river again and as we straightened out by the Nebraska bank I looked around the next bend and saw a pair of speedboats tearing toward us, crossing on the command of the daybeacons, but not slowing down.

"Boats," I said into the phone. "I have to go."

"Ok," he said, a little nervously. "Call me—"

"Oh, shit," I said, and dropped the phone.

The wake from the speedboats, much smaller than the barge but moving much faster in single file, was heading toward us like a wave. I turned the boat into the wake, instinctively, like you turn a car into a spin on icy roads.

"No!" Dirk yelled, but it was too late. The waves broke over the left pontoon and sent a cascade of water over the prow, soaking the carpet. I swore again, methodically, under my breath.

Once we got past the wake, Dirk assured me that the speedboats should have slowed down while passing us, and that it wasn't my fault, but I was pretty sure he was just being kind.

With the success of the Lower Missouri's management, the states along the upper river lobbied for similar management from Sioux City to the edge of the Rocky Mountains. Legislative responses to the Depression included the National Industrial Recovery Act, which funded construction of the Fort Peck Dam on the Upper Missouri in Montana. Construction on the dam, which would one day be 20,000 feet long and 250 feet high, began in 1933. The same year, the Corps of Engineers removed the Missouri River from the Upper Mississippi Valley Division and created the new Missouri River Division.

As Major Suter's navigation channel became a reality, more than fifty years after he envisioned it, commercial interests began moving freight on the river. In 1937 Federal Barge Lines, a government entity, moved sixty thousand tons of grain from Kansas to St. Louis. In 1938 they doubled that. Private companies soon followed, though the Corps of Engineers often sailed with heavy loads to ensure that the channel depth could handle the boats.

The engineering created some problems for itself, however. In some places, the river could no longer move its own sediment, causing silt to build up in the channel. At some of the bigger confluences, so much silt came into the river from tributaries that the Missouri couldn't distribute it. The only solution for these issues was to start dredging.

Modern dredgers are used all over the world, to clear silt from rivers, ports, and lake- and oceanfronts. This serves two purposes on rivers: It keeps navigation channels deep enough for boats, and in the event of environmental contamination, it removes silt holding pollutants and toxins. Modern dredgers use giant suction tubes to clear silt. In shallow water, like in ports (or the Missouri), they have what looks a little like one of those bars of revolving rags that cleans the top of your car in a car wash. For dredging, the bar is equipped with a cutting tool that loosens the silt and debris on the river bottom. The suction tube sucks the silt up and shoots it onto a pair of barges lashed together, which can be moved up- or downstream by tow boat. We saw plenty of dredgers along the river. The removed silt is hauled off and sold, mainly as industrial sand and gravel.

Mary took the helm from me after about an hour, and we were, once again, the only boat on the river. We came around a bend to a huge industrial complex, wrapped in razor wire and studded with closed-circuit cameras.

"What is that?" I asked.

"Nuclear power plant," Mary answered, watching it as we went by. A little way downstream, a huge drainpipe poured mud-colored water into the river, foam circling around the mouth.

The Fort Calhoun Nuclear Generating Station is owned by the Omaha Public Power district and, when it was operating, provided 25 percent of the company's power outlay. In 2011 flooding surrounded the plant, the water reaching to within two feet of the intake valves and causing a fire. Although providentially the reactor had been shut down and defueled in April of that year for routine maintenance, the fire shut down electricity to the plant for more than ninety minutes, disabling the cooling pools for spent fuel rods, and creating a "Red Event" emergency, the most serious threat level the plant, and anything and anyone downstream, had ever experienced. After the crisis was handled, the plant was shut down for three years, and in 2016 it was closed for good.

We crossed through the DeSoto Bend and into the DeSoto National Wildlife Refuge, more than eight thousand acres split between Iowa and Nebraska. The banks didn't look all that different, but there was a lot of cottonwood fluff drifting across the river. I looked at the river carefully. In 1968, Rod told us, two treasure hunters used historical maps to locate the wreck of the steamboat *Bertrand*, which had struck a log in the Missouri in the spring of 1865 and sunk. The wreck was carefully excavated, but because it was found on federal land, the contents belonged to the American people. More than five hundred thousand artifacts were removed from the wreck, including clothing, preserved food, and building supplies destined for the frontier. Much of the collection is on display in a museum at the wildlife refuge visitor center near Missouri Valley, Iowa.

We were beginning to see increasing boat traffic, and after a few more miles, it became clear why. Fifteen miles north of Omaha, the

N. P. Dodge Park Marina was, we hoped, where the FloteBote would be spending the night. Called Dodge Park by the people of Omaha, the park, a campsite of Lewis and Clark, is more than forty-four acres of recreational area that was given to the city in the 1930s. It was developed as a park in the 1960s, and we knew it had a marine fueling station and more than three hundred boat slips in the marina.

What we didn't know was whether or not they would let us in. Lee, who was driving the Vanagon, had gotten to the marina an hour or so earlier, but we had a stretch of poor cell service on the river and had no idea what was going on. Dirk took over the helm and steered us into the marina, cut in off the river the way Pop-n-Doc's had been, with tall stone levees on both sides of the marina entrance.

Once we got in, Rod got through to Lee, who said that the park rangers were not feeling inclined to let us spend the night, because berths are supposed to be reserved twenty-four hours in advance. We pulled up to the end of a dock and tied up loosely, and Dirk got off and walked up to the ranger station. Mary and I went off in search of a restroom, and by the time we returned, Dirk was back, smiling broadly.

"They aren't very happy about it," he said, "but we talked them into it."

He got back on the boat and we moved slowly through the docks, most of the slips filled with glossy speedboats and new, or at least much newer, pontoon boats. People milled around the docks, watching us, but at least not laughing or pointing. That I could see, anyway. We found our slip number and pulled in. Next door, a father and a couple of teenagers were washing a shiny red speedboat.

To their credit, they didn't even turn around. But the two-by-four tent frame and the silver tarp, on our tiny boat sitting low in the slip, was bound to attract some attention.

Dirk and Lee had managed to talk their way into a place for the boat overnight, but there was no chance we could spend the night on the boat. Apparently the marina gates were padlocked at some relatively early hour, so Rod wouldn't even be able to park the van there overnight. We gathered our bags, such as they were, and walked back to the van.

In the van, Lee began calling hotels in Omaha. To our rising anxiety, they were all either full or didn't have two rooms. Ultimately, we got lucky with a Microtel across the river in Council Bluffs. Despite our attire and appearances, we stopped at a nice steak place, and despite our attire and appearances, they let us in. We ordered a bottle of wine; the boys had steaks, Mary had vegetarian pasta, and I had salmon, in direct violation of my father's credo to never eat seafood in a landlocked state. After dinner, we crossed the river, loaded all our slightly dirty bags from the boat boxes onto one of those brass luggage trolleys, and walked into the lobby to check in.

We probably could have made the trip without all the engineering that has been done by the Corps of Engineers, though it would have required a whole different level of planning. Our time frame would have worked, if the year was the perfect balance of not too much rain and not too much drought, so the river was neither too high or too low. The draw on the FloteBote would have worked in the shallows, though we would have had to keep watch for sandbars and shoals, and be careful to keep the motor out of the mud. We'd also have had to keep a close eye on floating and submerged trees; like the *Bertrand*, most of the hundreds of steamboats that sank on the Missouri sank because they ran into submerged logs or floating trees. It would have been more difficult, and it would have required plenty of skill and quite a bit more luck.

But when you look at a heavily engineered river, the Hudson uptown in New York City, for example, or the Schuylkill in Philadelphia, once you start to understand what you're seeing, it's a little heartbreaking. Certainly, if humans are going to live by rivers, and we have to, we also have to make sure that we can do so safely. But we are learning, the hard way, of course, as we always tend to, that our control over nature is not a guarantee of safety, and that more technology is not always a solution. The Corps of Engineers, along with Fish and Wildlife and the Geological Survey, are beginning to restore some of the wetlands along the Missouri, in places where it works for both the river and the people who work and live along it. This restoration will allow a number of positive things to happen. Moderate floods will have somewhere to go. Species who need shallow water or stable banks to breed will find them. And the river itself will be able to breathe.

5

Drought

The waters from the sea will dry up,
And the river will be parched and dry.

—Isaiah 19:5

Waking the next morning in a bed was disorienting, even after only two nights on the boat. On the upside, though, there was a shower, and as much coffee as I could drink. We drove back to the marina, where, as promised the night before, we had to wait for the park rangers to sign us in to get back to the boat. They still weren't pleased. Happily, the boat deck was dry, but it had been cold enough overnight that the ice was still solid in the water cooler. Mary opted to drive the van, so the rest of us got the FloteBote out of the slip and made our way out of the marina. Just at the break in the levee that opened into the river, we pulled up to the bankside fuel station, and a young man clambered down to help us.

"My turn," I said, pulling my credit card out faster than the others, who were busy lining up our red plastic gas cans on the foredeck. To his credit, the kid tried not to look amazed. I ended up buying almost twenty-three gallons of fuel. There were two six-gallon tanks for the outboard, and we carried three five-gallon tanks on the boat. We switched the fuel tanks on the outboard every four hours or so; the second the motor sputtered, whoever was closest to the back dove for a gas can. As Rod and Lee lined the full cans up along the stern, Dirk slid us back into the river channel. It was Sunday, and the river was already busy with boaters. I turned to look back at the gas dock, and saw the kid pointing us out to one of his colleagues.

When we got a half mile or so from the marina, the traffic thinned out. We passed a family on a pontoon boat, anchored in the river, having a picnic, a couple of kids staring openly at us over their fishing rods.

"Just think," I said to Lee, waving around at the FloteBote, "in thirty or forty years, they can have all this."

We floated past the end of a runway, edged with high chain-link fencing and razor wire, at Omaha International Airport, and I was quietly grateful that no planes were landing or taking off. The runways at my local airport, Philadelphia, are right up against the Delaware River, and almost all planes coming in for a landing approach low over the river. I'd never thought, looking out a plane window as the traffic on I-95 grew from small blobs into distinct cars, how alarming that must be for small boat traffic. Past the airport, the landscape became increasingly industrial: rusty railroad bridges, high-voltage wires, abandoned bridge pilings, and several highway bridges. If the rural first few days of the trip had me remembering the canoe scenes in *The Fellowship of the Ring*, this urban riverscape was more evocative of Cormac McCarthy, or the post-pandemic setting of *Station Eleven*. The bases of the bridges showed lots of variations in dark water stains up and down the concrete, and I tried to imagine what the river looked like at its highest, when the river's surface was many yards above the water levels we were floating down. The drought that had begun the winter before, while safeguarding my trip, was already making itself visible.

According to the National Academy of Sciences, the Missouri River Basin was drier in the first decade of the twenty-first century than at any point in the last 1,300 years. In the next decade, 2012, 2013, and 2017 were considered "flash drought" years. The National Oceanographic and Atmospheric Administration identifies a flash drought as a perfect combination of low precipitation, abnormally high temperatures, elevated winds, and increased solar radiation. They are called "flash" droughts because, if they are not anticipated and planned for quickly enough, they can have profound and dire economic impacts on agriculture and irrigation, hydropower, and tourism, all while increasing the threats to the plants and animals that depend on river systems even more than we do.

Drought at this level is familiar in the deserts of the American Southwest, and to the extent that most Americans are aware of severe river drought in this country, their knowledge stems from the Colorado

River Basin. The Colorado rises in Rocky Mountain National Park in north central Colorado. The Missouri rises about 350 miles northwest of that. While the Missouri runs through a semiarid climate for most of its length (until it gets close to its mouth in St. Louis), the Colorado moves between semiarid and arid over its entire run. However, drought in the Missouri River stems from exactly the same source as it does in the Colorado: a vast reduction of the Rocky Mountain snowpack, coinciding with the rise in temperature brought on by climate change. Add in elevated temperatures across the planet, and particularly a string of the hottest summers and years ever recorded, and you get a perfect mix of reduced runoff followed by lack of rain and increased evaporation.

Hot droughts aren't new to American desert climates, but the twenty-first-century state of the Missouri's basin has surprised scientists around the country. Dendrochronologists, the scientists who study and date trees by variations in their rings, can also identify periods of flooding and drought stress on the trees they study. Apart from a period of extended drought in the 1200s, the last time the Missouri River Basin was this dry was sometime in the eighth century.

Back in the twenty-first century, we stopped in a marina at the southern end of Omaha because, Dirk said, we could walk to the National Park Service's headquarters for the Lewis and Clark National Historic Trail. The park service staff showed us a small exhibit, including a taxidermized Prairie dog, though presumably not the one the corps had sent to Washington. It was nice to get off the boat for a few minutes and move around a little, though. When we got back to the marina and were getting ready to cast off, a guy pulled up near us on a bass boat equipped with a special prow for bowfishing. I'd never seen a bowfishing boat before. To be honest, I'd never even heard of bowfishing. Bowfishing boats have an elevated little platform above the prow with railings for the archer to lean against, presumably to stabilize what would have to be a very complicated aiming process. All in all, while it seemed like a much more sporting option, particularly for the fish, I couldn't imagine how anyone could fish by sight in the muddy water of the Missouri, through which nothing—not a plant, not a rock, and certainly not a fish—was visible.

"Where you headed?" the guy asked, while I imagined trying to shoot a fish with an arrow.

"St. Louis," I said.

"Wow," he answered, looking at the FloteBote.

"If the motor holds out," Dirk said.

"If the pontoons hold out," Lee said.

"If the food holds out," Rod said. We all laughed, but they guy stared at us for a minute, clearly wondering how much of that was true.

I had confidence in the food, anyway. What was the most surprising to me was that he was the first person in a day and a half who'd asked.

We pulled out of the marina and back into the river. As we sailed through the last of the vaguely apocalyptic landscape below Omaha, a Red-tailed hawk crossed the river ahead of us, hassled by a flurry of small birds, and I noticed that the land around us was getting hillier and more wooded. Rod opened the big cooler and he and I assembled salami, cheese, and tomato sandwiches on rusk buns for everyone. Lee passed around cups of the last of the raspberry lemonade, and we ate quietly as the motor chugged us downstream. We also had the dwindling contents of a big bag of homemade oatmeal raisin cookies, and while we rationed them carefully, they always gave me a little boost of energy and good spirits. It's not that the days were particularly rigorous, sitting on a motorboat, puttering downstream. It's more that spending hours sitting in the sun, with very little physical activity, tends to make me sluggish and a little cranky, and I didn't want the cousins to have to put up with that. They were, at least in front of me, continually cheerful, and I intended to be likewise.

About twenty miles south of Omaha, the Platte River pours into the Missouri from the west, one of the largest river confluences we would encounter. The Platte rises in western Nebraska, formed by the merging of the North Platte and the South Platte, both of which roll down from the eastern slope of the Rocky Mountains. We knew where it would come in thanks to the Corps of Engineers charts, but we'd heard from the dinner gang at Pop-n-Doc's that the confluence of the Platte and the Missouri was treacherous. We were all watching the western bank get narrower, and I thought of our entry into the Missouri from the Big Sioux, the churning, muddy water thundering toward us as we accelerated toward it.

The Platte drains much of Nebraska and (via the North and South Plattes) a good bit of southeast Wyoming and northeast Colorado; it is the furthest downstream of the Missouri's tributaries to drain the Rocky Mountains. It has always been, like the Missouri, a shallow, braided, sandy river, challenging to navigate and largely ignored by industrial transportation. Throughout the twentieth century, however, the Platte has diminished substantially. Agricultural irrigation in Nebraska depends heavily on the Platte, and both the North and South Plattes are becoming ever more essential to the western water supply as the Colorado and Wyoming groundwater level runs low. Add to that the same diminishing Rocky Mountain snowpack and rising ground temperatures, and one of the Missouri's largest tributaries is sending considerably less water to the Missouri than it was even fifty years ago.

During the fall and winter of 2022–23, there were regular opinion pieces in some news outlets of the Rockies and West Coast arguing for the construction of a pipeline to carry water from the Missouri to the Colorado River Basin. While the stories I read never specified where on the Missouri they envisioned this pipeline's placement, I can see any number of problems with the idea. I'm assuming that they're talking about the Missouri once it starts to widen and strengthen in the great flatlands of eastern Montana and the Dakotas, not the small river it is at its headwaters. But pipelines are complicated in the Midwest; they can't run aboveground in tornado country, but they can't get belowground in the mountains once they get west of the plains, and presumably they would freeze and burst if carrying water in any of these places in winter. Beyond that, the Missouri, while perhaps not as drastically and perpetually low as the Colorado, is also suffering through drought conditions, and from exactly the same causes. Perhaps most importantly, though, the ranchers, farmers, and residents of the northern plains also need that water, for irrigation, for electricity, and for drinking. Fortunately, the heavy unexpected snowfall of the winters and springs of 2023 and 2024, in the Rocky and Sierra Nevada in particular, eased conditions in the far West, but it is nearly certain that in coming years, severe drought will return to the Colorado River Basin, just as it will to the Missouri's.

And the Colorado River Basin is not the only place in need. From the northern Nebraska border, west into Wyoming, and then narrowing all the way down below the Texas panhandle, between one hundred and four hundred feet below the ground, lies the Ogallala

Aquifer, the largest underground water resource in the country. It's shaped something like an outboard motor, or maybe a jellyfish, a fat east–west oblong with a long south-reaching tail. It underlies nearly 175,000 square miles of the central plains, is estimated to have begun forming between two and six million years ago, and, until the middle of the twentieth century, almost no one lived atop it. After World War II, however, diesel pumps made mass crop irrigation feasible and transformed the region into a global agricultural powerhouse. But for the last twenty years or so, it has become increasingly apparent that the aquifer is running low, and unlike rivers and lakes, aquifers are not refillable. At least not quickly. Which means that the row crop farmers and cattle ranchers of all these states—Wyoming, Colorado, Nebraska, Kansas, Oklahoma, and northern Texas—are going to need to find millions of gallons of water elsewhere.

Presumably it was both of these factors, the pipeline discussions and the state of the aquifer, that prompted Missouri lawmakers, in early 2024, to begin work on bills aiming to limit or prevent other states from accessing Missouri's water. It's an understandable impulse for elected officials, wanting to ensure protections for their own voters. However, it's also a recipe for disaster. If Americans begin fighting each other over water, we will all lose.

We began to see clear signs of the confluence with the Platte just north of river mile 595. Buoys guided us in toward the center of the Missouri, as far as possible from the spot where the rivers came together. As the land tapered off, a stone dike almost a hundred yards long kept the rivers apart, slowing the rush of either one into the other. It would not take anything like the flood levels we'd seen on the bridge bases in Omaha to submerge the dike and turn that confluence into a churning whitewater.

It was remarkably calm, given all the buildup. In aerial photos, the Platte looks muddier than the Missouri at the confluence, probably the result of the shallower, sandier course it takes through Nebraska. When we got safely below the confluence, I looked upstream at the Platte. It was wider than the Missouri, but side by side they looked nearly identical: scrubby trees on their banks, sandy beaches in their flats, row crop fields peeking through the trees to east and west, like a photographic image that's been split and then copied back onto itself.

A wide sandbar nuzzled up from the Missouri some thirty yards in from the Nebraska bank. Sandbars, even here in the managed section of the river, are often enormous. This one stretched downstream for nearly fifty yards, maybe ten feet wide at its center, looking like the East Coast's Atlantic barrier islands in miniature. They are, of course, essential nesting habitat for birds like the Least tern and Piping plover. I couldn't make out any tiny puffs pecking around, though.

We passed the sandbar and the river stretched in front of us, with scrubby trees ranging down both sides.

"Infinite variety it certainly isn't," Dirk said, looking around.

It's hard to tell, from the middle of the river, what species the trees along the banks are. I'd spotted silver maples and swamp oaks, a huge American sycamore, and cottonwoods and willows when we pulled over to a lonely stretch of Nebraska shoreline for a leg-stretching bathroom break, but from the boat I couldn't clearly identify any but the willows. What was apparent here, though, was that most of the trees close to the river were dead. Whether this was the result of weather, fungus, or an insect infestation was unclear.

A greenish dragonfly flew up over the rail and landed on Lee's hand, and I leaned over to take a look. At that, it took off again and landed on the lid of the boat box nearest the steering console. I grabbed my camera to take a photo; later, I identified it as a green eastern pondhawk. It sat for a few minutes on the lid, presumably resting.

"You better have gas money," Rod told it, and it flew off.

South of the Platte, the Missouri grows wider, no doubt a consequence of the addition of all the water flowing in from Colorado, five hundred miles to the west. Of course, that means that drought conditions in the Rocky Mountains impact the Platte, which impacts the Missouri, which in turn impacts the Mississippi, seemingly safe in the westernmost reaches of the continent's humid zone. Seven months before we set sail, however, the Mississippi, in the throes of its own drought, ran so shallow that the U.S. Coast Guard patrolled the section of the river between St. Louis and Cairo, Illinois, nearly two hundred miles downstream, trying to divert large boats. The Mississippi was so low that for eight hours a day, boat traffic was slowed to one way, alternating upstream or down every hour. For the other sixteen hours, the river was closed. The Mississippi is a very different river from the

Missouri; thousands of barges move mountains of goods up and down the Mississippi every month. The Corps of Engineers dredged the river channel and removed tons of rock to make the shallow water safer to navigate. This limited boat access on the Mississippi, traffic that in January is almost exclusively commercial. In a typical January in the early twenty-first century, barge traffic on the Mississippi moved more than $2 billion in agricultural goods alone, and more than $3 billion more in chemicals, petroleum, crude oil, and coal. The Mississippi's falling water levels meant those products had to be shipped by other means and made a significant and grim impact on a river shipping industry just emerging from the Great Recession.

In short, significant droughts affect far more than irrigation. At my house on the East Coast, the first visible signs of drought to people whose livelihoods aren't intertwined with rivers come in the form of household limitations: no watering lawns, for example, or washing cars. I'd heard neighbors complain as their yards turned tan; I tended to be happy that I didn't have to mow my grass, and that I could justify my filthy car without embarrassment. But significant and prolonged drought in the basins of these three massive rivers, the Colorado, the Missouri, and the Mississippi, would be, and in the minds of some scientists, will be, catastrophic. It won't just be shipping and agricultural irrigation that will be impacted. And in terms of household use, it won't just be lawns and car washes. Drinking water, particularly in desert areas, could become gravely low.

We all learned in elementary school that the planet is something like 80 percent water. What we may not know is that, according to the National Geographic Society, only 3 percent of that is fresh; beyond that, only 1.2 percent is available for drinking and irrigation. While that is still a vast quantity of water, the amount of fresh water we use every day is also vast. The U.S. Geological Survey estimates that the average American uses between 80 and 100 gallons a day, from drinking to cooking to bathing to cleaning. The EPA reports that the United States used 9 billion gallons per day for landscape irrigation in 2017 alone. A USDA report from 2018 says that American farms and ranches used 83.4 million acre-feet of water for irrigation that year. An acre-foot means the quantity of water needed to cover an acre of land in one foot of water; that's 325,851 gallons. In total, American farms and ranches use 27.176 trillion gallons of water a year for irrigation. Lake Tahoe, for comparison, contains about 37 trillion gallons of water.

The United Nations estimates that as of 2025, two-thirds of the humans on the planet live in water-stressed locations. Since the turn of the twenty-first century, there have already been 543 violent conflicts either over or weaponizing water, or both, according to the Pacific Institute, a global think tank working on worldwide water resiliency. There's a reason the Wall Street robber barons, who made fortunes betting on the U.S. mortgage bubble that caused the Great Recession and ruined countless Americans' lives, have now turned their attention—and their investment capital—to water.

It's almost impossible to consider, the idea of serious drought while floating down a big river like the Missouri, even during a drought year. But indicators are there. The 2013 charts from the Corps of Engineers, for example, show the Missouri River channel depth near the mouth of the Platte as nine feet, down from the relative depth of fourteen feet upstream. In the late winter of 2024, the marina from which we launched the FloteBote announced that it would be closed for the 2024 season, the result of low water and high silt buildup. The watermarks on pilings and bridge bases are stark reminders of floods; you focus on the highest ones, imagining how much water it took to stain cement that far above your head. It's easy to forget to wonder how low those marks might go below the surface. And it's hard to picture this landscape without all this water moving through it.

Rod laid down on the prow and fell asleep. I pulled the river charts out of their Ziploc bag and had a look. The charts identify the counties around the river, some of the larger towns and cities, and provide GPS coordinates in various places. They also identify every daybeacon and bend by name. Many of the daybeacons are named for either the nearest bend or the county they're in, but some of them don't seem to have any correlation to anything in particular. We were coming up to the Lillian Daybeacon, on the Iowa side; nearly a mile downstream from that, in Nebraska, is the Weeping Water Daybeacon.

The charts also show the wing dikes jutting into the navigation channel, giving you a rough idea of how far from the shoreline you need to keep the boat, and where there is space to pull over to the shore in case a passenger needs a bathroom break behind a bush. The charts we had said they had last been revised in 2011; they didn't say if that revision was before or after that summer's floods.

We made our way around the Lower Copeland Bend, which made me smile; my brother and I had both had Copeland friends in our elementary school classes, and a boat ramp with a long, low floating dock appeared on the Nebraska side. It had an aluminum gangway leading up the side of a boat ramp, with what appeared to be a parking lot at the top. We pulled up against the dock, and Mary came down to us.

"How was the day?" she asked, as Lee pitched an anchor off the back of the FloteBote and Rod jumped down from the prow and splashed to the shore, holding us by hand.

"Pretty good," I said. Dirk went up to the parking lot to talk with whoever was in charge. We'd arrived at Nebraska City's Riverside Park. They have a campground, but overnighting a boat is not a common event. Dirk returned after a bit and said we had permission to leave the boat in the river overnight, but the park wasn't responsible if the lines broke and it drifted away downstream to Kansas. Or if someone stole it.

We all turned and looked at the FloteBote, its silver tarp rolled damply to the midpoint on our timber A-frame, the grubby pontoons a hair higher in the water now that no one was aboard.

"I mean, sure . . ." I trailed off.

Rod and Dirk discussed the best way to anchor the boat into the rocks and rubble on the bank, so it would be tied fore and aft on the downstream side of the floating dock. They pronounced it secure, and I scrambled back on board to grab my purse. We all climbed up the boat ramp and piled into the Vanagon to find some early supper.

Dirk and Lee got rooms at Lied Lodge, the headquarters of the Arbor Day Society. Rod would sleep in the van in the boat ramp parking lot, and Mary and I would once again sleep on the boat. We found a restaurant that didn't seem to mind our appearances, and just after sunset, Mary and I made our way back down the boat ramp and sloshed back to the boat.

"I'll be right up here, so call if you need me," Rod shouted down to us, and went to park the Vanagon.

Mary and I pulled the mosquito netting and the tarps from the frame and secured them down around the boat with clamps as well as we could. We sprayed on some bug repellant, brushed our teeth once again over the side of the boat, unrolled our sleeping bags, and crawled into bed. I made a few notes in my journal and pulled out my book and was asleep in an hour.

When I woke, it was pitch dark out the canopy of netting on the prow, but I could hear something. I lifted my head a little toward the rear of the FloteBote and realized it was men's voices, speaking low, the sound underlaid by a small boat motor, and getting louder. The boat puttered somewhere nearby, not downstream of us so much as to the port side. I lifted my head further and felt around me for some kind of weapon. My hand first touched my Kindle, and then the corner of the portajohn. All the giant wrenches and things were safely inside their box, somewhere in the darkness.

There was a crash, what sounded like metal scraping across rocks, somewhere ahead of me to my right side. Mary and I both rose simultaneously into what a generous yoga instructor would call the cobra pose and froze. The voices raised to yells, though I couldn't understand what they were saying. There was a loud scrabbling in the rocky bank, and the sound of men—one? three?—fumbling up the boat ramp.

I grabbed my phone and checked the time. It was 10:30 p.m.

Mary and I remained silent. After what seemed like an hour, but was probably fifteen minutes, I lowered myself back to the boat deck. The FloteBote has a solid frame surrounding the main part of the deck, so I couldn't see anything, but I lay there, straining to hear and hearing only the hum of insects and the thrum of frogs, and the gentle splashing of the river against the pontoons, for a long time before I fell back to sleep. Before dawn, I came through the netting onto the foredeck, toothbrush in hand, to find an aluminum bass boat with two seats and a forward steering column tied to the branches of a downed tree about ten yards downstream from the FloteBote. Maybe they'd been aiming for our parking spot in the dark and only realized at the last minute that it was already taken by what must have looked like a floating circus tent. Despite all the crashing, the bass boat was afloat and appeared undamaged. And quite empty, apart from a low pile of boxes between the seats.

I turned my back on the bass boat and looked out at the river. The light was just beginning to rise over Iowa, and low clouds hung behind the tree line. The eastern horizon loomed red and angry, a dark omen.

6

Flooding

> The signal corps at Yankton, D. T., reports the river risen fifteen feet in the past twenty-four hours. The water in the lower town is four feet deep. There is a gorge above and below. The water is still rising.
>
> —*Omaha Daily Bee*, April 5, 1881

At daybreak, the Missouri looks its wildest. Even on a clear morning, the semidarkness conceals the signs of human impact on the river and the landscape. South of Omaha, the river moves back into more or less wild country. It's heavily wooded along the banks, hilly on the Nebraska side. To the east, Iowa rises more slowly, but a few miles from the river the Loess Hills, a formation of sharp hills, rise up to two hundred feet high, the accumulation of soil blown across the valleys of the retreating glaciers and that both settled and eroded as plants began to take hold in the Holocene warmth that followed the Ice Age. Today they reach from eastern South Dakota down the western edge of Iowa and taper off into northwestern Missouri. The eastern floodplain of the Missouri, the flatlands that stretch between the river and the hills, is low and flat and primarily farmland, but in a number of spots, farmers have given land back to the states and let patches return to the wetlands, which probably comprised the whole area before Europeans arrived.

To the west, on this rainy morning, the lights of Nebraska City overrode the misty, dark magic trick of early morning on the river. Mary and I packed up our sleeping bags and called Rod, and by the time we stepped off the boat to splash our way to land, the Vanagon was idling at the top of the boat ramp. We drove to the lodge and picked up Lee and Dirk, who were quite a bit cleaner than the rest of us, stopped for a hot breakfast at Mary's Cafe, and returned to the boat ramp at about nine. Lee decided to drive, and the rest of us dug around in the boat boxes for our raingear. We'd checked the forecast on a weather app: a high of sixty-eight degrees, with twenty-mile-per-hour winds and moderate to heavy rain. We had to cover almost sixty-five miles to the next stopping point, a small boat ramp in Rulo, Nebraska, on the Kansas border. In accordance with the rules of tempting fate, it was the highest-mileage day of the whole trip.

It was raining lightly as we tried to get the FloteBote ready for the day. Rod used a pole to square the silver tarp over the A-frame, and I moved around underneath it, rolling the ends and clamping them to the crossbeams. Over and over, I forgot the beams were above me and banged my head as I straightened up. Once we were finished, the boat was covered from stern to bow by a plastic silver pup tent that rose to about six feet at the peak. It covered everything except about a foot of the deck on each side, but we had to leave the sides rolled up for visibility. The rain knocked softly on the lids of the boat boxes and the cooler, and raindrops bounced back toward the clouds from the surface of the river.

As we got ready to pull the two anchors, two men in dark uniforms backed a small aluminum patrol boat marked "U.S. Geological Survey" down the ramp and into the river. They nodded to us and looked at the bass boat, but didn't ask any questions. One of them drove the truck and trailer back up to the parking lot as the other moved around the boat. As the first walked back down to the dock, an older pickup truck pulled up in front of the ramp. Two men peered out the open window, staring at the guys in uniforms. I tapped Rod on the shoulder and nodded at them.

"Think those are the night visitors?" I asked quietly.

As if in answer, the truck sped away, quite a bit faster than seemed appropriate for a public parking lot. I wondered, again, what the late-night crash landing had been about. There wasn't a boat ramp across the river, and there weren't any visible structures or roads or means of getting a boat on the river over there. I glanced over at the bass boat as the Geological Survey boat pulled away, and wondered what was in the boxes, now getting rained on in the open hull. Was it drugs? Stolen property? It seemed unlikely that anyone would leave that alone, on a river, loosely tied to a fallen tree.

As we got everything squared away on the deck, a man and his young son walked down the dock. The boy was staring at us, fascinated.

"What kind of boat is that, Dad?"

His father made a reply, too quietly for us to hear, and tried to pull the boy along beside him.

"I never saw a boat like that, Dad," the kid said.

Me neither, I thought, and grinned at him. He just stared back at me, frowning, presumably trying to work out what we were up to.

Rod walked the front anchor up to the prow and handed it to Mary so he could climb on board, and Dirk pulled up the rear anchor. Rod turned the motor on and we reversed into the rainy river, pointed the prow downstream, and got back under way. I waved goodbye to the boy and his father, by then at the end of the floating dock. Only the dad waved back. Dirk, Mary, and I pulled up our hoods and huddled as much as we could under the tarp as the wind and rain picked up, and we set off downstream.

If the Missouri River appears in the national news in this country, it is almost always because it is flooding. There are two main causes of severe river flooding: ice jams in cold weather, or extreme rains in warm. Ice jams happen when there is a sudden thaw after a cold winter, most often in late winter, or an early spring rain. The meltwater or rain swells the river, which breaks up the heavy surface ice, and the ice chunks move downstream until they snag on things, and then on each other, until they block the entire river, as if someone dropped an impervious dam into the river channel overnight. With nowhere to go, the water pours out of the river channel and over the banks. Jams form where rivers are braided or shallow, or when they run up against manmade structures like bridge abutments. Which pretty much describes the whole of the Lower Missouri. The trouble is that the locations where ice jams might form are very hard to predict accurately, and when they happen, riverside communities sometimes have very little advance warning.

At the beginning of March 2019, after a long winter of temperatures steadily below freezing, a massive snowstorm passed through the Rockies and the northern plains, leaving up to three feet of snow on the ground. And on the frozen river. Suddenly, between March 9 and 11, the temperature rose to sixty degrees, accompanied by more than an inch of rain in some places. The result was a massive series of ice dams, and the effects along the Missouri River were catastrophic. In Iowa more than thirty levees collapsed or were breached. In Hamburg, Iowa, they had been unable to raise enough money to construct a permanent high-water levee, and the one that had saved them in previous floods failed them. The river breached it, and water stood roof-high in the town and surrounding fields in parts of the city for more than a month. In Nebraska the city of Fremont was completely surrounded by flood water, with the National Guard setting up convoys to get food and drinking water to residents who couldn't or didn't evacuate. In western Missouri, at one point, I-29 stood under fifteen feet of flood water. The standing water in fields delayed planting and devastated the cattle industry, as beef cattle in Nebraska and Kansas were calving at the time. All told, between January and June of 2019, nearly fourteen million people were affected as the flooding moved south with the Mississippi and Arkansas Rivers. The governor of Iowa declared $1.6 billion in damages. Nebraska reported $440 million in crop losses and $400 million in cattle losses. A year later, as the COVID-19 pandemic lockdown took hold, the reason steak prices were so high wasn't only because of supply chain impacts and shipping problems: The beef industry had lost a significant portion of its 2020 stock to the river.

In the fall of 2019, four *New York Times* reporters developed a map of the flooding that draws together the full impact of that catastrophic winter and spring. It shows not only the flood events in the Midwest but the full slow-moving catastrophe that made its way down the Missouri to the Mississippi, and then out into the Gulf of Mexico. Even in the gulf, the destruction continued; agricultural fertilizers, pesticide, and herbicide runoff in the floodwaters created a dead zone in the gulf roughly the size of the state of New Hampshire.

Back on the FloteBote, Rod drove as the rain and wind became steady. He sang some travel songs and quoted from *Mary Poppins* and cajoled Dirk into breaking into our small and precious supply of brownies to boost morale. Once the sugar kicked in, I moved to the wheel and sat down to drive. I stared hard at the river ahead of me, my shoulders hunched a little, concentrating the same way you do when you're driving in a snowstorm at night, with snowflakes highlighted in the headlights and streaming at the windshield like comets, trying to hypnotize you. Except, of course, there isn't a windshield.

My wet-weather gear was designed more for a short backpacking trip, and not, for example, deep-sea fishing in a spring gale. By the time I took the wheel, my pants were soaked through. After a half hour, I couldn't unclasp my fingers from the wheel. Dirk peered at me.

"We need to check her for signs of hypothermia. First sign: poor judgment."

"She's on a boat in the pouring rain, in the middle of the Missouri River," Rod said.

"Right. So hypothermia it is," I said, trying not to let my teeth chatter.

It was, more simply put, deeply unpleasant.

Lee called us to say that he had found a place where we could pull over and meet him for a hot lunch. He told us to come ashore at Riverside Park, in Brownsville, Nebraska.

"How will we know if we're in the right place?" I asked, still hunched and freezing behind the wheel.

"He says we just look for the *Meriweather Lewis*," Rod answered. Who, last I checked, had been dead for more than a century.

Dirk pulled out the charts and found Brownsville, almost exactly at the midpoint between Nebraska City and Rulo. At the last mile marker before Brownsville, Dirk moved up next to me, I slowly unpeeled my white, wet fingers from the wheel, and he took over steering. I'd gotten perfectly adept at steering in the river but bringing it in for a landing made me nervous, even when I knew what that landing zone looked like.

Sure enough, through the easing rain we spotted what looked like a huge white building just on the bank of the river on the Nebraska side. As we got closer, it began to take shape, a massive, slightly tattered side-wheel dredge boat. The *Meriwether Lewis* was launched in 1931, only about half built at the time, to help the Corps of Engineers wrestle the river into shape for navigation. At almost 269 feet long, once they finished building it, the ship could house up to fifty-eight people and dig twenty feet down into the river channel. In the mid-seventies, it was given to the Nebraska State Historical Society, who moved it to a dry berth in Brownsville, right on the bank of the river. It serves as a museum now. Below it, I could see the Vanagon, and Lee standing in front of it, looking a little like a Red Cross worker, waving to us.

We pulled ashore and hopped onto the ground, and I realized that it had stopped raining. Mary looked at me closely and asked if I was really okay.

"I'm pretty cold," I said, my hands still half-balled into loose fists.

"Come warm up," she said, and walked me to the van.

Lee had brought us bacon, lettuce, and tomato sandwiches and sweet potato fries, and had two thermoses of coffee. We stood in the mud around the van, leaning on the frame to keep the interior dry. Rod handed me a packet of french fries; my hands, still stiff, couldn't hold them, and they scattered across the ground, a tasty, if damp, snack for the birds and rodents.

Taking a sip of coffee, Rod looked at his siblings.

"This is the day the spouses predicted," he said. I laughed. The others just nodded, solemnly.

Once we'd eaten, I unzipped my raincoat and stuffed my hands under my sweatshirt, my fingers icy and damp against my skin. Lee checked the weather report, and said it looked like the rain had passed us.

"Good," Mary said, "because Lee bought me a present."

He opened the back of the van and presented a flat, brown, wooden object. After he fiddled with it for a moment, it unfolded itself into a slat-backed wooden rocker. He reached into a pocket and produced a corncob pipe.

"Here you go, Mrs. Clampett," he said, as the rest of us laughed. My fingers moved against new warm skin, still cold but starting to tingle. Mary stuffed the pipe into her mouth and plopped down in the rocker, and we laughed again.

We took a look around, the break in the weather holding. The *Meriwether Lewis* was not open, so I walked along it, trying to imagine what it must have looked like, and sounded like, in its heyday. Down by the bank, I reached up and plucked a leaf almost the size of my hand from an overhanging branch. Here was a tree I knew well. It was a big eastern sycamore, very near the westernmost reach of its native territory.

The sycamore is one of my favorite species of trees. These can be massive, often growing next to or close to water. They are very long-lived; a friend in Maryland has one on her property, right on the bank of a creek, that is estimated to be more than four hundred years old. They have a flat, greenish-gray bark that peels off in uneven chunks, more solid than paper birch bark, revealing a stunning white layer. Another friend once told me that people sometimes call them "ghost trees" because they glow in the moonlight. This one was not as big as my friend's tree, and presumably nowhere near as old. But it pleased me to recognize it, here on its western boundary. I carried the leaf carefully back to the boat and folded it to fit into my journal.

Mary allowed us to convince her to finish the day in the van with Lee, even though the rain seemed to have stopped, and Rod, Dirk, and I waved to them as we turned the FloteBote, complete with the rocker, back into the current and set off downstream again, warmer and happier, our stomachs full from the warm meal.

Two years before our trip, there was some bad flooding throughout the Lower Missouri caused by neither ice jams nor extreme rain. The winter and early spring of 2010–11 was much wetter than anticipated in the Upper Missouri valley. Long-term weather forecasting predicted a dry summer, but once again, the reservoirs behind the major dams on the river were overflowing, and to prevent the dams from bursting, the Corps of Engineers released much higher than normal levels of water from the dams in North and South Dakota. Unfortunately, the summer weather models were wrong, and even moderate rain, combined with the water released from the reservoirs, touched off several months of severe flooding. While most of the major cities on the Missouri had strengthened their flood defenses, in many small communities, levee funding had been limited and the protections were in precarious shape. In Hamburg, Iowa, the Corps of Engineers came into the town at the last minute and created a makeshift levee addition that added eight or nine feet to the barrier, and in that case, saved the town; it was the same levee that would fail eight years later in the 2019 flood. The 2011 floods swamped more than ten bridges across the river, and made river crossing impossible in two hundred-mile stretches in Iowa, Nebraska, and Missouri. Almost everywhere we stopped, if there weren't signs of the floodwater, people told us their stories.

The flood that everyone in the Midwest uses as a benchmark, however, happened twenty years before we set sail: The Great Flood of 1993. One of the most costly flood events in the history of the United

States, flooding began in April and lasted until October. It killed more than fifty people, the deadliest natural disaster in the country until Hurricane Katrina. About 30,000 square miles were flooded, roughly an area the size of South Carolina. Of that, more than a million acres of farmland were under water.

From a scientific perspective, the Great Flood actually started in the summer 1991, when Mount Pinatubo, a volcano in The Philippines, erupted. The second-largest volcanic eruption of the twentieth century, the eruption sent a plume of ash almost twelve miles into the atmosphere. Big sulfuric eruptions allow drops of sulfuric acid to block the sun, which creates what scientists call "volcanic winter." This, in turn, may result in natural "cloud seeding," where particles in clouds increase the clouds' capacity to produce rain. These events meant that the river was primed to flood, and the winter of 1992 pushed it further with heavy snowfall in the Rockies, creating above-average soil moisture and reservoir levels on the Upper Missouri. This meant there was very little capacity for either soil or bodies of water to absorb or hold on to what would be extraordinary amounts of rain. The spring of 1993 continued the pattern. In May Sioux Falls, South Dakota, got more than seven inches of rain in one three-hour period. Much of the region's soil was saturated by the first of June, meaning all rainfall after that, whether it fell on earth or pavement, would run off into streams and rivers. And rain it did; in some places, precipitation was more than 700 percent above normal.

The water began to recede in June, but in July the rain returned. Kansas City saw more than seven inches above normal for the month. The surrounding states' National Guard units sandbagged as fast as they could, not just along the Missouri and Mississippi, but around all their tributaries as well. By July all boat traffic on the Missouri, private and commercial, was banned. All told, during that year almost all seven hundred of the levees along the Lower Missouri were breached. On August 1, 1993, at the Missouri-Mississippi confluence in St. Louis, over a million cubic feet of water—roughly 748 million gallons, almost 100 million gallons more than an eight-lane, fifty-meter Olympic swimming pool holds—poured into the Mississippi every second. In normal weather, the flow rate at the confluence is 14,000 gallons a second.

President Bill Clinton flew in to tour the damage and asked Congress for $2.5 billion in federal disaster relief, almost $5.5 billion in 2024 dollars. This, it turned out, would be inadequate. Estimates of the damage totaled somewhere between $12 and $16 billion, plus of course, the loss of lives. It would be December before the crisis was declared over.

Altogether, some areas along the Missouri were in flood stage for almost a hundred days in 1993. Even after the water receded, tons of sand from the river bottom covered crop fields, livestock pastures, and houses. Acres of planted row crops drowned, suffocated, or were washed away. Houses and buildings were lost completely. There was some good news from Kansas City, however.

The most catastrophic flood to hit Kansas City happened in 1951. It was a larger flood than the 1993 event, but the levees around Kansas City at the time were not remotely large enough to contain it. Both the Kansas City Stockyard and the Kansas City Airport were destroyed. However, in the aftermath, the Corps of Engineers and others significantly strengthened and enlarged the levee system around Kansas City, and forty-two years later, the levees held.

Back on the river, mist rose in soft, swirling puffs from the surface of the water and drifted into the trees. Above us, more eagles than I'd ever seen in one place peered imperiously at us as we floated below them, apparently displeased that we were noisily cutting through their territory. Five female wild turkeys strutted along the shore, seemingly unfazed by the predators overhead.

Unsurprisingly, there was no other traffic on the river. The wind had settled a lot, and the river smelled tangy and cool, like mud. Still cold in my wet pants, I wrapped a towel around my waist and looked out over the water.

Rod was driving and suddenly he pointed ahead of us. A big, rounded, tan object bobbed on the surface. He steered us a little closer to the Iowa side, and as we came alongside it, we realized it was a dead fish. It was enormous, its white belly turned to the sky, at least three feet long.

"Carp," Dirk said, watching it slide behind us as we puttered downstream.

"I thought it was Bambi," Rod said.

I shuddered a little. Death is, as always, close by on the river, but it would be upsetting to see a fawn. Or any other large mammal. However, even dead mammals have a part to play in sustaining a healthy river, and perhaps even more so in a river that has been altered by human interests in ways that make flooding more of a challenge.

Flood control is one of the Corps of Engineers' highest priorities. The problem is that, once a river has been engineered as much as the Missouri has, the options for control reduce to a very few, and most of them come with diminishing returns. A "wild" river would flood, shift its channel, change its flow, and the land alongside the river would change as well. Silt and sand buildup, along with all the dead biomass the water carries—plants, animals, and microorganisms—mix into the land surrounding the river, keeping it fertile. The nutrients feed the soil, and the sand sinks in, keeping the soil porous so that it drains more easily. Where the water can recede to wetlands along a river's banks, the more inland soil gets the benefits of occasional severe floods with a space for the land to drain. These are the floodplains, the marshy mix of standing water, mud, and water-tolerant plants that surround natural bodies of water. While floodplains might not be able to absorb extreme flooding, they are nature's response to the threats of wild rivers.

The Missouri is no longer wild, though. As we have developed the land as close to the river as possible, making the most of that rich, fertile earth, we have drained the wetlands, leaving floodwaters nowhere to go.

Wetland restoration has been happening alongside large bodies of water for decades now, all around the world. My home state, Delaware, makes up about half of the landmass of the Delmarva Peninsula, a point of land bounded by the Delaware and the Chesapeake Bays and edged by the Atlantic. Strategically recreating and placing wetlands allows our fragile environment to absorb what it can from these enormous waterways.

Restoring wetlands, at least along the Missouri, is fairly easy. If you don't drain land in the floodplain, don't plow it, don't build on it or pave it, if you just let it be, it will begin to return itself to a wetland on its own. Fairly quickly, rainwater will pool and then pond into large, shallow marshes. Dry-soil plants will die off, and their decomposition will build up the base of the ponds and provide nutrition for plant and animal life. As soon as this water deepens to an inch or so, insects arrive, and soon after that, birds and reptiles follow. It's the birds that provide the most complex and interesting additions to the mix, though.

Anyone who's ever plucked the feathers from a wild waterbird knows how much material those feathers carry. Today, of course, that knowledge is mainly limited to wildfowl hunters. A few years ago, scientists joined some Midwestern hunters in order to see what wild ducks and geese were carrying with them from one body of water to the next. They found seeds and spores from flowering plants, fungi, and algae but also the eggs of macro- and micro-invertebrates, including water insects and small shellfish. They also found fish eggs. All these tiny life forms, floating around in a lake somewhere, stick to the skin and feathers of wildfowl as the birds paddle around feeding. When the birds take off and land in another body of water, say, a one-inch-deep marshy pond, a mile or so inland from the Missouri River, the seeds and eggs fall off, settle into whichever environment suits them, and, if conditions are right, sprout or hatch.

Obviously, an inch or two of water couldn't support some, or even most, of the fish living in even a small pond. Once a Small-mouth bass, for example, outgrew the water levels, it would die, and sink to the bottom, feeding the rest of the small ecosystem, strengthening it and making it possible for further life to begin.

In several places between the Loess Hills and the river in Iowa, this process is already taking place. Iowa farmers have donated some of their acreage to the state Department of Natural Resources, and department officials have let those lands go fallow. According to the department's website, before Europeans settled in Iowa, about 11 percent of the state—between four and six million acres—were wetlands. Today, 95 percent of those have been drained and made into farmland.

It doesn't take long for the land to recover, despite probably a century or more of use for row crops. After only a few years of restoration, there are large areas of standing water. If you walk out to one of these wetlands, the life that surrounds you makes you wonder how this bit of land could ever have been anything else. Under the water, submerged plants like coontail flourish. Across the surface, floating plants like duckweed, American lotus, and lily pads move slowly with breeze, or bird splashdown, or human footsteps. Around the edges of the ponds, smartweed or pinkweed blooms, surrounded by sedges, bullrushes, and cattails. Frogs sit motionless in the shadows, carefully watching dragonflies and gnats. In daylight, that might be all you see. If you backed away, birds would appear: not just ducks and geese, splashing in to deposit new prospective life, but Great Blue and Green herons, Red-winged blackbirds, and Bitterns would settle down to hunt in the cattails and reeds. Maybe, if the area got big enough, some of Iowa's restored population of Trumpeter swans, the largest American waterfowl, might turn up to build a nest and raise a clutch of cygnets. Small mammals would move in, attracted by the fresh water and available prey, and those would in turn lure out the avian predators, the Bald eagles and Harriers. Turtles would come, and snakes. At night, the wetlands come even further to life. Bats flit above the ponds, diving for mosquitoes. Muskrats emerge from their dens, and owls hunt anything they can hear moving through the tall plants and mucky earth around the water.

As ever, nature is in conflict with human economic interest. Every one of those donated acres lessens the yield from the farmers who need those crops to survive in a world in which farming is an essential, but deeply challenging, profession. Every one of those farmers pays taxes on both crop sales and land, taxes that support schools, public safety, and infrastructure. But as weather grows increasingly severe, as drought years are followed by very wet years, and as rising temperatures strengthen storms, the strategies we deploy to protect ourselves from flooding will need to adapt. We will have to find ways to balance environmental need with economic need. Simple floodplain and wetland management will not prevent the kinds of floods that overran the Missouri's valley in the bad years, but they could help. They are already helping life to return to those spaces, even after a century of agriculture.

Dirk drove for a while, and then I took over again for the last leg. Rod, looking at the charts, said that the boat ramp in Rulo was at mile marker 503.

"We just passed 513," I said, as the rain began again.

He looked down at the chart again.

"Whoops," he said. "I think it's 498."

I swore very quietly, and began the slow turn across the river at the Corning Landing daybeacon. In rain and cold, five more miles is demoralizing.

Finally the boat ramp appeared, a dark, wet dock in front of a dark, wet park. It was after 5 p.m., and the only car in the park was the Vanagon. We got everything secured on the boat and Mary and Lee walked out to greet us.

"I've reserved two cabins at the White Cloud Casino," Lee said. "Any takers?"

I looked around the wet boat. Mary and Dirk both announced that they would sleep on deck. Rod, as usual, would sleep in the pop-up camper in the van. I plucked limply at the wet plastic on my wet legs.

"I'm in," I said. I dug my backpack out of the box I shared with Lee and passed his duffel bag to him. We all climbed in the Vanagon and Rod drove us through a darkening evening. The rain, mercifully, had stopped.

"Welcome to Kansas," Dirk said from the front passenger seat, and I looked around in surprise. I'd been to Kansas before, at least to Kansas City, Kansas, and it had lived up to the broad assumptions non-Midwesterners have about the Midwest generally and Kansas specifically: It was flat. Now the Vanagon climbed up a long slope, both sides of the road heavily forested. We came out of the woods and wound around farmland and past some typical Midwestern farmhouses, lights glowing warmly from the windows. A light blue water tower loomed over us.

"Iowa Tribe KS & NE" was painted on it in large black letters. Our trip had just become multinational.

7

The Ioway Tribe of Kansas and Nebraska

> To the Ioway, the river is not a barrier. It is a road.
> It is a street in a neighborhood, connecting us.
>
> —Lance Foster, director, Ioway Tribe National Park, and tribal historical officer

In October of 1837, a group of Ioway tribal leaders traveled to Washington to argue that an earlier treaty signed by their former chief White Cloud was not valid, and to try to negotiate a new treaty. They were led by No Heart, White Cloud's younger brother, who had been a great warrior in his youth. Now in middle age, he presented the United States with a hand-drawn map. The map looks a bit like a riverbank tree, tipping sideways to reach the sun, with a long trunk running the length of the page, and branches reaching in all directions around it. Running along and between the branches are small dots and circles, almost like the tree has been strung with small lights. No Heart told U.S. officials that the map "is the land of my forefathers. We have always owned this land. It bears our name."

The "trunk," the long line, is the Mississippi River. The "branch" that comes down into the page at the top left is Nyisoje, the Missouri. All the other branches are rivers as well. And the dots and circles are Ioway villages, hunting camps, and pathways around the landscape of what would, a few years later, become the state of Iowa. It bears their name. But it no longer belongs to them.

In northeast Iowa, along the Mississippi River and near the Wisconsin border, Effigy Mounds National Monument preserves some two

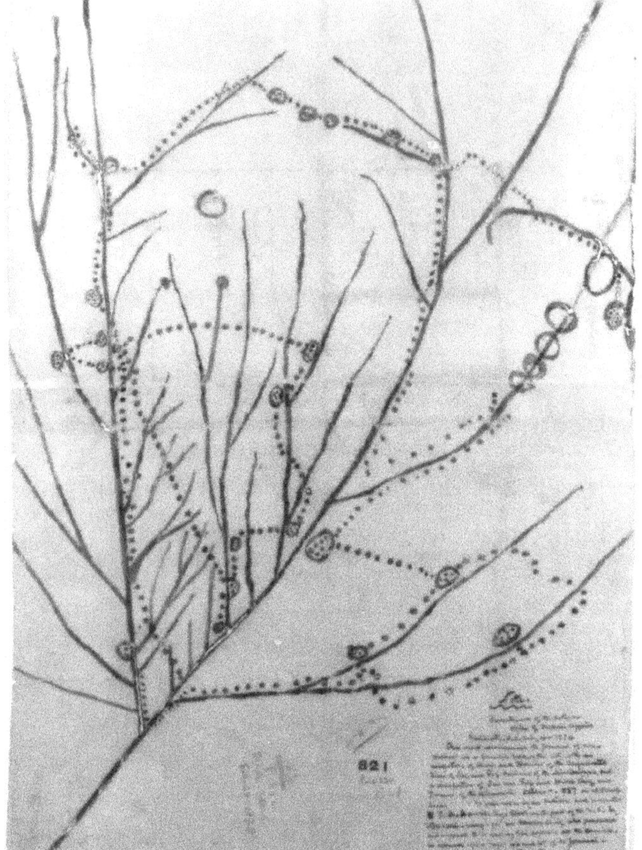

FIG. 6. Map of Ioway lands in relation to the Missouri River, 1837. Library of Congress.

hundred precontact earth mounds. Archaeologists estimate that the Oneota people constructed the mounds between 900 and 1250 CE, but there is evidence of large-scale settlement throughout the area for at least eight thousand years. The mounds on this site served a number of purposes; while some of them are burial mounds, the bulk of them are ceremonial, built in the shape of animals, in particular bears and birds.

Over time, the Oneota people separated, possibly to search out better land for hunting and farming and spread across the eastern reaches of the Midwest. The Ho-Chunk moved north, into what are now Wisconsin and Minnesota. The Missouria went south, to what would become Missouri. The Otoe settled along the west banks of the Missouri River. And the Ioway, who call themselves and their language Báxoje, People of the Gray Snow, spread across the wetlands, lakes, and prairies between the Mississippi and the Missouri.

Before Europeans came to North America, the Ioway were farmers and hunters, growing corn, beans, and squash and hunting bison, deer, elk, and beaver. The Ioway also moved into southern Minnesota, near what is now Pipestone, named for the deposit of the mineral that northern plains tribes used for ceremonial pipes. Guardians of the pipestone, the Ioway quarried stone and crafted pipes, but they also allowed other tribes, even tribes they fought with, to come peacefully and take their own supply. Pipestone, known scientifically as catlinite, a relatively soft, dark red stone, is easy to work, and easy to decorate. Pipestone pipes were an essential part of Plains culture, and pipes have been found that date back more than three thousand years.

The first recorded contact between the Ioway and Europeans came in 1676, when a French Jesuit priest mentions in his journal that he'd met some Ioway. But in less than two centuries, the Ioway people would be entirely gone from the land they had lived on for millennia. Today, the Ioway live on two sovereign reservations, the split the result of an intratribal conflict in the mid-nineteenth century. One is in Oklahoma, near the town of Fallis. The other is a small patchwork of about twelve thousand acres of hills, woodlands, prairies, and arable land that straddles the northeast corner of the Kansas–Nebraska border, and it was into this that the Vanagon drove, still a little damp, in search of dinner and a place to spend the night.

As you crest the hill by the water tower, you can see the bright lights and collection of buildings that make up the tribal center. There's a government building, a health center, a fish and wildlife conservation office, a collection of big metal sheds, a gas station, and a casino. There are a set of animal pens and a rodeo arena. Tucked in behind those on the downslope, near a small stand of burr oaks, is a large stone building that looks a little like a church. On the other side of the trees are four small A-frame cedar shake cabins, each something like a studio apartment, which serve as the casino's hotel rooms.

We pulled up to the casino's doors and Rod stopped under the portico to let us out. By the time I got out the sliding side door, the young Ioway man in a security uniform who was posted at the door, was laughing out loud. I told Rod I'd wait for him and introduced myself. His name was Kyle, he told me, still laughing. He was an artist, a painter. And he was considering moving to Oklahoma, where there is a better market for Indian art. I asked him what kinds of things he painted.

"Giant Snickers bars, that kind of thing," he said.

Rod materialized from the growing darkness and we chatted for a few minutes. Kyle, like everybody else, looked both amused and bemused by the idea of our trip. Mary waved to us from inside, and Kyle held the door for us as we walked into the casino.

Casino White Cloud is, in comparison to Atlantic City or Vegas, a small operation. However, it's considerably bigger than the sole hotel casino I had passed through in my one night in Reno. They offer slot machines, table games, and bingo. Even at 8 p.m. on a Monday night in late July, there were a good number of people playing slots. We crossed the big room, the lights and noise startling after days of nothing but sun and trees and outboard and wind. They'd closed their buffet down earlier, not expecting a flood of cold, hungry boaters, but they let us go into their restaurant and have some sandwiches for supper.

After we ate, Rod, Dirk, and Mary drove Lee and me down the hill to the cabins. I unlocked the door, dropped my pack on the leather sofa, and went and took a shower. Once I was warm, I called home and then crawled into bed.

Before the nineteenth century, the Ioway lived in wooden lodges, framed with willow and clad in elm and cottonwood bark. The women of the tribe built and owned the houses, which would last about ten years. The women also handled the bulk of the farming and processed deer and bison hides. The men made tools, hunted and fished, and protected the tribe. It takes three to five acres of farmland to support a family, and the reaping and storing of seeds in fall was a critical part of their year, so that they would be able to replant the next spring.

The Ioway designate themselves into clans: the Sky Clans, Buffalo, Pigeon, and Owl, and the Earth Clans, Black Bear, Wolf, Eagle/Thunder, Elk, and Beaver. Each clan has its own origin story for how the Báxoje came to be in the world. There is not a unified "Ioway" creation myth. They aren't even really called Ioway. They use the term only to distinguish themselves from the state; the official national name is Iowa Tribe of Kansas and Nebraska. The Iowa language is in the Siouan family of languages, and some believe that the word "Iowa" comes from a Dakota, Leluta, or Nakota word meaning "those who separated." It is a white settler myth that the word Iowa means "beautiful land."

In the mid-1600s, like many other western tribes, the Ioway first encountered and then rapidly domesticated the feral horses descended from those brought to the Western Hemisphere by the Spanish. The period from then until 1810 is called "Middle Ground," when Native people and Europeans interacted with increasing frequency but without actively trying to exert control over each other. The European nations, France, England, and Spain, that sought to colonize the continent sent three kinds of men to the frontiers of North America: fur trappers, traders, and priests. Priests were sent from the Arctic Ocean to South America, to convert the Native people to either Catholicism or Protestantism, hoping that planting their religion along with their flags would ensure Native participation in whatever wars might arise for the land. This worked (to some extent), back East, during the French and Indian War. But it was the trappers and fur traders who made the first real colonial impact on the Ioway. Trade for animal fur, and particularly beaver pelts, was so active and so profitable that the Ioway began to fall behind on their farming duties, making them dependent upon the fur trade to keep their families alive through winter and spring. Beaver fur was an excellent source material for felt, and European markets bought as much as they could get.

By the start of the eighteenth century, France, Spain, and Great Britain were well underway in their centuries-long, sometimes semantic, nearly always lethal conflict over which of them would hold dominion over the continent of North America. That the continent was already full of people was irrelevant to Europe. And by the end of that century, when the American colonies became the American states, we picked up that flag and ran with it; by 1805 we'd run all the way to the Pacific Ocean.

By the 1820s the Ioway had moved south into what is now northern Missouri. Conflict had expanded between the Dakota tribe to their west and the Sac and Fox to their east, trapping the Ioway in the middle. In addition, the increased contact with European Americans exposed the Ioway, like all Native people, to diseases like smallpox, which killed them in enormous numbers. The Ioway settled in the southern reaches of their ancestral territory and tried to resume their lives there.

During his tenure, President Thomas Jefferson wrote that he considered Native people both noble and equal to white men. However, after he bought most of what is now the United States from the French in the Louisiana Purchase, he wanted Native lands for American farmers. As he knew while preparing Lewis and Clark for the Corps of Discovery expedition, the only way to get American settlers west of the Mississippi was to ensure a means of getting their crops to market, and sending settlers west was the only way to maintain America's hold on the western half of the continent. As his presidency progressed, he encouraged traders to let Native hunters run up debts for essential goods, which would force them to cede their lands to the government for payment. At best, he wanted them to settle down in one place, on individual land plots, and become farmers.

In 1824 No Heart's older brother White Cloud was appointed chief of the Ioway by the U.S. government. "Chief" is a white word and, at least for the Ioway, a white governmental construct. Before the arrival of Europeans, the dominant clans of each Ioway branch, Sky and Earth, passed leadership responsibilities between each other according to the season. Buffalo Clan, of the Sky Clans, was the leader during spring and summer, the season of agriculture. Bear Clan, of the Earth Clans, policed the tribe in fall and winter. Disagreements were handled by discussion.

White Cloud also had a "kin brother" named Great Walker. Great Walker was a celebrated warrior in a culture where bravery, honor, and military service were and remain prized values. White Cloud and Great Walker were invited to Washington to negotiate a treaty with outgoing President James Monroe, and they went. Once there, the two Ioway men were shown a display of all the power and might of the new capitol. They were wined and dined. Their portraits were painted by George Catlin, who made a career out of painting Native people. Only after this did the government bring them in to "discuss" the tribe's land. For most of those discussions, the Ioway had no interpreters.

William Clark, by then superintendent of Indian Affairs, urged them to sign a treaty ceding the northern half of what is now Missouri, from the Missouri River to what is now the Iowa border, for $5,500. White Cloud felt that working with the Americans—even assimilating—was important, and signed it. Great Walker disagreed. When they got home, Great Walker took forty warrior families and left the rest of the tribe.

And all the while, white settlers and squatters were moving into Native lands. This tension increased conflicts between different tribes, and the U.S. government tried to settle things down by creating boundaries and buying land. Often, they placed outside tribes between warring tribal factions, adding to the stress. Finally, in 1830, Andrew Jackson signed the Indian Removal Act, making it legal to seize all Native land east of the Mississippi River, laying the foundation to seize any and all land west of the river, and forcibly marching eastern Native people across most of the continent to "Indian Territory," which is now Oklahoma. And the Ioway braced themselves.

The U.S. Army built its western forts on rivers, including the Missouri. There were strategic purposes for this; rivers enable supplies to be moved easily, and the line of sight is, at least on the waterfront, unimpaired. Fort Leavenworth was originally planned to be on the banks of the Missouri until flood patterns convinced the military to shift the fort twenty miles inland. The difficulty with riverfront forts is that they also cut trade and supply routes for anyone who isn't the military, or under military protection. And they establish a leadership presence, for good or bad, on land that other people had been living on and managing for millennia.

Tensions continued to rise among the Ioway, and at the same time, the U.S. government became increasingly involved in Native issues. Great Walker and his band fought with settlers; they also fought with other tribes. In 1831 he and a Nakota warrior fought hand-to-hand, and killed each other. Later that year, a conflict began between the Ioway and the Omaha tribe. Ioway warriors killed six Omaha warriors, avenging the killing of an Ioway leader. The military demanded the Ioway soldiers be brought into custody. White Cloud turned them in, and the accused Ioway warriors were held at Fort Leavenworth. In 1834 two of them escaped. They tracked White Cloud to his hunting camp in southwest Iowa and killed him. In 1836 White Cloud's son, named Francis by the priests at the mission school White Cloud had sent him to as a boy, led what was left of the people to the Great Nemaha Agency on the Kansas–Nebraska border and settled them onto the reservation.

The land surrounding the White Cloud Casino, most but not all of which is owned by the Ioway, is farmland. It is a beautiful place, hilly, shifting between woods and fields. Below the hills, the Great Nemaha River, a tributary of the Missouri, passes the reservation. The traffic sign, when you drive from the casino to the cabins, has an English Stop sign hanging over a second sign, the same size, shape, and colors, that reads in Báxoje "Nasda ne." Turn left, and in a few seconds you see a pretty stone building with white trim. This is the Báxoje Wósgaci, the Iowa Tribe Culture Center and Museum. Built in 1940 from local stone, it holds hundreds of books, films, and artifacts from the tribe.

From a legal perspective, the land is a checkerboard of tribal, state, federal, and non-Native land. The original reservation, under the treaty of 1830, was two hundred square miles. By 1860 it was 10 percent of that. In 1887 Jefferson's notion of convincing Native people to become assimilated individual farmers on individual plots of land was codified into federal law as the Dawes Act. The Dawes Act, in an effort to save the federal government the time and money dedicated to the reservation system, dismantled the reservations and sold any land the Native people couldn't afford to purchase to settlers and the big businesses of the Gilded Age. Tribes were forced to adopt a capitalist idea of land as individual property, rather than the tribal cooperative property concepts that they had lived with for thousands of years. Unsurprisingly, this further destabilized their cultural identities. The Dawes Act was one of the most destructive policies ever enacted on Native people and their cultures.

According to Lance Foster, a former member of Ioway tribal government, archaeologist and tribal historical preservation officer who died in January 2025, the Ioway are holding on as much as possible to what is important to them. That is a struggle, for the Ioway and for all Native people. As anthropologist William Green put it, stories are part of the identity of all people, both family stories and, for lack of a better term, tribal stories. But the United States' early policy toward Native people—forced marches off their homelands, forced education in boarding schools far removed from their families, forced learning of a new language, forced abandonment of their own languages—stripped those stories from generations of the Ioway, and generations of other tribes all over the continent. As honorary Ioway tribal member and amateur archaeologist John Palmquist says, if you deny people's history, you dehumanize them. And if you dehumanize them for long enough, they lose that history, in part or in full, and are left to struggle with not only who they are but who they were. Where they came from. And what it means to exist in the world without knowing those things.

Even in the nineteenth century, however, the Ioway engaged actively with the government of the United States. Despite their appalling treatment, the Ioway, like many tribes, sent forty of their own young men to fight for the Union in the U.S. Civil War. Ioway tribal members have fought in every American war since.

Today's Ioway tribe have taken some major steps to reasserting their place in their new homeland in Kansas and Nebraska. On tribal lands, they are restoring prairies and placing historic and cultural sites under protections. They are, when possible, repurchasing lands given to them as part of the original reservation and then taken back by the U.S. government and sold to farmers. Some of their historic sites, and the historic sites of their distant ancestors, the Oneota, are now under state and federal protection. And for the first time in almost two hundred years, the tribe now holds title to some land inside the state of Iowa, land that had been their home for centuries.

In 2020, in the midst the COVID-19 pandemic and after years of careful effort, the tribe established Báxoje Mowatanani, the Ioway Tribal National Park. Báxoje Mowatanani is made up of four sites on tribal lands, beginning with the Leary Site, which had been a village between 1200 and 1400. The Leary Site had been an important trading post between the Ioway and the Pawnee, on the southern edge of the Ioway's historic lands. It includes ancient Hopewell mounds, ceremonial and burial monuments, but it has been farmed for more than a century, and it has suffered a great deal of damage. The tribal national park designation protects it from any more. The other sites are Rulo Bluffs, a parcel of restored prairie, Iron Monument, where the borders of Nebraska and Kansas divide, and finally the Ioway Sac and Fox Presbyterian Mission, which brought the Christian boarding school experiment to the Ioway.

Báxoje Mowatanani is not the first tribal national park; the Red Cliff Ojibwe had established the Frog Bay Tribal National Park on the northern tip of Wisconsin in 2017. Foster says that the advantage of the tribal national park designation is twofold. It will attract visitors, surely, but more importantly, it will give the Ioway people a connection with not only their land but their own history. It will, I hope, help to restore their stories.

And then, in 2021, they did something more. The Executive Committee of the Iowa Tribe of Kansas and Nebraska recognized the status of Nyisoje and its ecosystem as a legal entity all its own:

WHEREAS: The Tribe and its members have had a strong relationship with Nyisoje, also known as the Missouri River, since being moved to this area in 1836, after we signed the Platte Purchase Treaty that brought us by 1837 to this reservation in what was then Indian Country, and Báxoje culture, ceremonies, religion, subsistence, economics, residence, and all other lifeways are intertwined with the health of the River, its ecosystem, and the multiple species reliant on a thriving Missouri River ecosystem;

WHEREAS: The Missouri River ecosystem encompasses the surrounding areas in and around the reservation, the sacred high country, its contributing tributaries and underground aquifers, and through and past the estuary into the Mississippi River;

WHEREAS: All species connected to the Missouri River are environmentally and culturally significant and should be protected in their traditional forms, natural diversity, and original integrity;

WHEREAS: The Iowa Tribe of Kansas and Nebraska's Executive Council recognize that to protect the Missouri River, its ecosystem, species, and our people, the Tribe must secure the highest protection of the Missouri River through the recognition of legal rights.

NOW THEREFORE BE IT RESOLVED: That the Iowa Tribe of Kansas and Nebraska's Executive Committee now establishes the Rights of the Missouri River to exist, flourish, and naturally evolve; to have a clean and healthy environment free from pollutants; to have a stable climate free from human-caused climate change impacts; and to be free from contamination by genetically engineered organisms.

The Missouri River, to the Ioway, has legal personhood. It is, under tribal law, human.

Legal personhood for bodies of water is not new. In 2017 the Whanganui River in New Zealand became the first river granted personhood on the planet. There, as for the Missouri, the effort was spearheaded by Indigenous people. The Maori, like the Ioway, see their river as sacred, a part of their culture for millennia, to whom they owe care, protection, and support. In 2019 the people of Toledo, Ohio, granted personhood to Lake Erie after a toxic algae bloom cut off the city's water supply for four days. Bangladesh recognized all of its rivers as persons. And in California, the Yurok tribe gave personhood to the Klamath.

Practically speaking, the Missouri's "personhood" doesn't provide much protection, physically or even legally. The Delaware River is protected by the four-state Delaware River Basin Commission and Compact, which means that all states downstream must sign off on any riverside project upstream. The Missouri River has no such agreement. But what the Ioway's personhood designation does do is start conversations. Conversations about environmental issues impacting the river, conversations about the importance of the river, and conversations about the Ioway themselves. And this is a conversation the rest of us should be having, about the Missouri and about all rivers.

Despite smallpox, and forced relocation, and systemic oppression, despite a serious attempt by the United States to completely erase their land rights, their human rights, their history, their language, and their culture, the Ioway have survived. They farm and work and celebrate, they protect their history, and they care for their tribal land. They hold powwows every September. Since the passage of the Native American Graves Protection and Repatriation Act, they have federal protections for not only the bones of their ancestors, but for any historic objects discovered by archaeologists, amateur or professional, on all federal or tribal lands, or conducted by any organization that receives federal funding. An Ioway man, Jimm GoodTracks, has created an online digital dictionary for the Báxoje language. They have struggles, of course, just like every community. But they endure, like the Missouri River, whether the rest of us are paying attention to them or not, and they deserve our respect, and our gratitude. They certainly deserve mine.

In the second half of the nineteenth century, almost twenty years after the Ioway moved to the reservation in Kansas and Nebraska, a young man from Hoorn, Holland, got off a steamboat on the Mississippi River and entered the new state of Iowa. He made his way to Pella, a small Dutch immigrant community about forty miles southeast of Des Moines. There, he met and married another Dutch immigrant named Helena Corteweig, and as soon as they could, they moved to the western edge of the state. There, he and Helena bought as much farmland as they could afford, just as the federal government was offering land on the frontier for pennies on the dollar. His name was John Gleysteen. He was my great-great-grandfather.

John must have been a good farmer, because he managed to send all twelve of his children to college. The family farm was divided and subdivided and subdivided further as the generations went by. When my great-grandmother died, she left all eight of her grandchildren land. My mother and her three sisters all sold their shares, mostly to help send their children—me, my brother, and our cousins—to college. When my mother died in 2019, my brother and I inherited a one-eighth share in the last piece of land that my part of the family owned, a small holding midway between Alton and Orange City, Iowa.

John's farm helped pay for my education, and for my mother's education, for her father's education, for his father's education. It helped pay for the cottage, where the FloteBote began its life with my family. It ensured that John's children, and theirs and theirs and theirs, in addition to our educations, could have good nutrition and health care, and the best start he could give us. In short, I am a direct recipient of all of his efforts and his good fortune.

And what I have to grapple with, what I will always grapple with, is that all that benefit came to me as the result of a nineteenth-century land grab, achieved through appalling violence, cruelty, lies, and manipulation, by the government of my own country. Why I was born of that land as the descendant of John and Helena Gleysteen, and not the descendant of two of White Cloud's people, is unanswerable. John didn't buy the land from the Ioway, or even the Sac and Meskwaki, who, having driven the Ioway south to Missouri in the 1820s, ultimately signed over the land between the Missouri and the Mississippi to the United

FIG. 7. Bales of hay on the Ioway Tribe of Kansas and Nebraska reservation, White Cloud, Kansas. Photo by the author.

States in 1842, before John or Helena ever set foot in North America. But that doesn't undo the damage.

I don't know what I can do about this, or what the Ioway would want me to do. One of the only things I can do is tell the story of my brief time with the Iowa Tribe of Kansas and Nebraska. Of the people I met and spoke with, all of whom were unfailingly kind to me. Of Kyle, the laughing young artist, who saw leaving his tribe and his home as the best shot at the life he wanted. Of Lance, who grew up far from tribal lands but returned to serve his community as a historian, an archaeologist, and an advocate for his people, their history, and their land. Of the older woman who handed me the key to my little cabin, and the security guard much older than Kyle who held the door for me the next morning when I turned it back in. Of the whole Iowa tribe, who hold the Missouri River so close to their hearts that to them it is a person. The Báxoje are their own people with their own stories, and I am grateful and indebted to them for much more than just their kindness to me.

When I got up the next morning, I dressed and went out for a walk. The hills and trees of the Iowa Tribe, and of Kansas, were gray and misty, but it wasn't raining. I walked over the hill and looked at a long line of round hay bales, and at rolling fields of corn and beans. Then I turned to the southeast, looking at the edges of the hills that I knew overlooked the river, and went back to my cabin to pack up my things and head back to the river.

8

Invasive Species

> It is not the strongest species that survives,
> not the most intelligent that survives. It is
> the one that is the most adaptable to change.
>
> —Charles Darwin

In the morning it was misty and cool, but the birds were singing as Lee and I waited by our cabins for Rod to pick us up. As we drove back into Nebraska to the FloteBote, Dirk pointed out the changing geography.

"This must be the flood plain," he said, indicating a wide swath of flat land, bounded by a low rise. "Where they divert water. The levee must be a quarter mile from the river."

When we got back to the boat ramp in Rulo, three men in a pickup were unloading coolers and fishing tackle from a bass boat. It was about 8:30 a.m.

"How'd you do?" Rod asked them as we made our way down to the FloteBote, the tarp still draped over the outside of the deck railings.

"Not bad," one of the men said. "Got two big catfish for the church fish fry, so we're happy."

Dirk asked about the catfish, and I heard the man say one of them was about three feet long.

One of the others looked at me and smiled. He pointed to my University of Iowa sweatshirt.

"Hawkeye, huh? Got enough running backs to avoid getting crushed this year?"

The rest of them laughed, and I made a joke about Big Ten football, like I had any idea what I was talking about. I might be from the

East Coast, but I know enough not to argue with Nebraskans about the Huskers.

We got the boat squared away and set off. Lee was driving the van again; the next day was his last on the river, as he was flying home from Kansas City. The fog hung heavily in the trees along the river, and I couldn't make out the land behind it on either bank. It reminded me of a night I'd driven across Utah once, on my way to a week-long backpacking trip. It was pitch dark, and I hadn't seen the moon, but I could feel the mountains rising around me. Here, on the Missouri, I could sense the landscape beneath the fog.

The birds were out in force. We saw Great Blue heron, Turkey vultures, and masses of swallows. The swallows circled around the boat like seagulls over a boardwalk, and Dirk wondered if the boat disturbing the surface of the river was driving insects up around us. On the western bank, we passed a cache of red buoys piled on the bank. Rod said they were probably there in case a serious problem arose, which made me wonder if there was something in the river we should be worried about.

There was a high flash of silver to the Kansas side of the boat, followed by a splash.

"Asian carp," Rod said.

We were passing through a heavily wooded section of the river, with tree branches overhanging on both sides. As we spluttered along, I moved over to the most rearward of the boat boxes, staring at the trees. Nearly every one of them had at least one Bald eagle perched in it. I tried to count them and gave up at about thirty-five. They all gazed down, imperious and impervious, just past us, as if we were beneath their considerable notice. Eagles are opportunists; I wondered if they were hunting for jumping carp.

We'd had Asian carp sporadically leaping alongside the boat since the first hour of the trip, and every time they made me jump a little. Native to eastern Asia, four species of Asian carp were deliberately introduced to American wastewater treatment facilities and private fish farms in the 1970s as a "natural" solution to pond grasses and algae growth in holding ponds. However, as Michael Crichton memorably pointed out in *Jurassic Park*, "nature finds a way." During flooding in the 1990s, some of them escaped into the Mississippi River. In the ensuing years, they have spread to four other major rivers, including the Missouri, and countless tributaries, and have been reported in at least twenty states.

Asian carp are just one of what the federal government calls "injurious species," animals, insects, and plants that are either brought intentionally into the United States as pets, game, or decorative plantings, or arrive unintentionally, most often by hitching a ride into the country on ships, packages, or airplanes. In 1900 President William McKinley signed a law that offered protections against overhunting or overfishing of native animals and mandated both civil and criminal penalties against anyone caught violating it. A predecessor to the Endangered Species Act, the law is called the Lacey Act after the Iowa congressman who introduced it. Today, the Lacey Act also prohibits the importing of foreign animals, plants, and timber.

Conservationists call these animals and plants "invasive." This can sometimes be confusing; the first invasive species I remember learning about as a child was kudzu, the Japanese vine that has been overrunning the American south for decades. Kudzu was introduced as a solution for eroding or poor soil; primarily, it was planted on fallow land to serve as grazing fodder for small livestock like goats. Today, if you drive along almost any highway in the south, you'll see kudzu on the sides of the road. It climbs, wraps, contracts, covers whole trees and buildings, often pulling them to the ground. When my father pointed it out to me and explained what it was and what it was doing, he referred to it as an invasive species. I assumed that he meant that "invasive" species were plants (and animals) that moved, that invaded spaces before they destroyed them.

They often are, it turns out, but they don't have to be. Simply put, invasive species are any plant or animal that enters a foreign ecosystem and survives. The problem is that many of them don't just survive. They flourish.

The more troubling thing that invasive species do in their new environment is that they outcompete the native plants and animals in the same area. This kills native plants and robs native insects and animals of significant, sometimes vital, food sources. Nonnative species don't have natural predators; even if they are edible to native wildlife, it takes a while for the natives to figure that out. I have been battling a collection of invasive plants, some planted, some that just spread from other places, in my own yard for years: English ivy, Virginia creeper, pachysandra, porcelain berry, Japanese stiltgrass. The ivy and the porcelain berry are spreaders and climbers; they're trying to strangle my trees, rip the bricks from my walls, and tear the gutters from my roof. One year, an ambitious sprig of English ivy pushed its way between the window frame and the wall and grew across the ceiling of my guest bedroom before I noticed it. In the animal world, things work the same way. This is perhaps best known in the swamps of Florida, where people have spent decades dumping all manner of nonnative snakes, Burmese pythons and Boa constrictors in particular, after initially adopting them as pets. These feral snakes are wreaking havoc on the Florida Everglades food chain and creating big headaches for Florida's animal control.

Invasive species are problematic all over the planet, not just in the United States. In the 1970s in Japan, there was a brief, cartoon-incited fad for importing raccoons from North America as pets. Once raccoons reach sexual maturity, at about a year, they often become both large and aggressive, and they either escaped or the pet raccoon owners turned them loose, where they killed native animals for food and damaged farm crops, and, of course, reproduced. While Americans may think of raccoons as ubiquitous raiders of our trash bins, they are only native to North American and are in zoos on other continents. Fifty years on in Japan, they are still making trouble.

Such invasive tendencies are also why the Asian carp are such a problem. Some varieties feed on phytoplankton and zooplankton, the microscopic plant organisms that are the base of the aquatic food chain. Others feed on plants, and still others on mollusks and snails; all of these are needed foodstuffs for native fish species. However, carp are generally larger, stronger, and faster than native species like bass, and they beat the native fish to the food. In addition, carp are spectacularly good at reproducing. The average female carp can produce anywhere from 150,000 to more than 5 million eggs in a spawning, and they can spawn more than once a year. They also reduce the quality of the water, which jeopardizes native freshwater mollusks, one of nature's greatest water filtration systems.

But that's not what Asian carp are best known for by the people who use the waterways the carp have infested. They are best known for their ability to jump.

If you want a good idea of what these fish can do to a river, look up a video of Asian carp on the Illinois River. There are videos of fishers and wildlife researchers and regular people in boats surrounded by hundreds of leaping carp, carp flashing through the air, carp landing inside the boats, carp bouncing off the humans. They are silver, tan, or dark gray, and routinely reach twenty pounds; big ones can get up to eighty pounds. Apparently the noise and agitation of boat motors disturb them, causing them to leap out of the water, sometimes as high as nine feet above the surface. They have no natural predators in American rivers, save humans. And while we have been trying to develop our own strategies to control them, their birth rates give them a big advantage.

One of the main concerns about the spread of Asian carp is how to keep them out of the Great Lakes, where they would have a serious impact on the region's $7 billion sport and commercial fishing industry, to say nothing of recreational boating. In Chicago they've installed a set of electric "fences" along the Chicago River before it gets to Lake Michigan. Electric pulses are pushed through the water along several locations, repelling larger fish. Apparently small fish, two inches long or so, can manage to sneak through the barriers, and there is a study under way to see whether barges passing through the barriers open larger windows in the electric fields. But so far, the barriers seem to be working.

One of the obvious solutions to, if not eradicate the carp, then at least control their numbers, is for humans to start catching and eating them, preferably at industrial levels. The Missouri Department of Conservation went so far as to turn up at the Missouri State Fair with free samples. According to them, the carp don't taste very "fishy," and might be nice for people who don't like stronger-tasting fish. The U.S. Geological Survey reports that they have firm, white flesh, are low in fat, and, because they aren't bottom feeders like catfish, are less likely to have absorbed dangerous contaminants. And unlike native sport and pan fish, there are no limits on how many Asian carp a fisher can take home.

The problem is that they also have small bones within the filet muscles, which makes them hard to clean and their meat potential choking hazards. Some commercial fishers on the Mississippi and its tributaries are net-fishing for Asian carp to use as bait, but as of now, these strategies are not making much of a dent. On the Missouri, thankfully, the infestation is not—yet—severe. They're down there, obviously, but nowhere near as many of them as in some places.

Back on the river, we stopped on the eastern bank to stretch our legs and take a photo of the boat sailing by with Mary in the rocking chair. Once I'd taken it, they came as close to shore as Dirk dared. The mud was thick enough at the shoreline that he stopped some ten feet from the bank to keep the motor safe, so I waded out to hold the prow line, as if the FloteBote was a horse I was grazing on a lead line. I was almost knee deep in muddy brown water, and it was startlingly warm. The mud held me solidly, and I looked around. There is remarkably little litter floating around the river, at least here in the no-man's-land between Kansas and Missouri. It helps that we haven't seen a building in a while. It also helps that several times a year the nonprofit Missouri River Relief, based in Columbia, Missouri, organizes massive trash cleanups along the river and its tributaries.

We got back under way and Mary drove for a while. The rest of us made lunch: ham and cheese sandwiches with tomato and the last of the avocado we'd brought from the lake. It was getting a little brown anyway. Mary and Lee had stopped to see some friends of their mother's the day before, and the friends had given them a bag of Cheetos, though I passed on those. I took a handful of cherries for dessert and looked back out over the river, the mist finally gone, but the sky still overcast. As I dropped a cherry pit into the river, I wondered what how long it would take for the pit to disappear down in the mud and sand of the bottom.

Of course, nothing long-lasting grows in the boat channel. The channel is designed to be self-scouring, and when it isn't, dredges come along periodically and suck the bottom up. In addition, so little light makes it through the water that photosynthesis is a challenge. Even in the shallows near the banks, the current prevents almost anything but algae and the microscopic plankton from taking hold. In the reservoirs formed by the dams upstream, however, grasses and other water plants grow, including some that are fast becoming hazards to those artificial lakes. And like other crafty invasive plants, they are skilled at using humans to move themselves around the landscape.

The most significant of these plants is Eurasian milfoil, a grassy plant that is native to the Eurasian landmass that comprises all of Europe, Asia, and the Middle East. Scientists believe it was introduced into U.S. waters sometime in the 1940s, either hitching a ride on a foreign ship, or because someone dumped the contents of a fish tank into a pond or stream, as it was sometimes used as a decorative aquatic tank plant. By now, it's spread to thirty-three states and has been found as far west as Colorado. It's a complicated problem. Typically, Eurasian milfoil grows from three to ten feet tall, rising from the bottom of a pond or lake to the surface, but it can grow up to thirty-three feet. Like most invasive species, it takes hold in the human-disturbed places where it doesn't have to compete with established species of aquatic plants and grasses, but once it gets established, it winds itself together, forming floating mats in the water and at the surface, which keeps light from getting to other plants.

Worse, it doesn't need to seed to propagate itself, though a single plant can produce up to a hundred seeds a year. If a piece breaks off—if the plant gets hit by a propeller or an anchor, or a dredge, or a barge, for example—the piece will float around until it finds a suitable habitat and start a whole new colony. In lakes, one of the easiest ways for it to spread is when boaters clean weeds off an anchor and throw them back in the water. Eurasian milfoil is a fast-spreading, fast-growing threat to reservoirs, ponds, lakes, and rivers less managed than the Missouri. And it is already in the Missouri, at least below the dam at Fort Peck in Montana. Dam spillways pull water from below the surface, so it's probably not getting around through the dam, but it is moving downstream into the other reservoirs and, presumably, settling in the river if it can find a place to land.

Of course, there is a native species of milfoil, Northern milfoil, that belongs in our waters. The two are hard to distinguish from each other, though. Both plants look very similar; Northern milfoil has fewer leaves and branches, and the leaves stay stiff when you pull it out of the water. However, they are both hard to identify without side-by-side comparison.

Northern milfoil also belongs in our waterways. It provides underwater cover for fish and insects, and some waterfowl even feed on it. However, it will hybridize itself with its Eurasian cousin, given the opportunity. What those hybrids do to their ecosystems remains unclear. Maybe some of them are better for the system. Maybe some of them are worse. The Midwest has implemented rules about cleaning boats before moving them from one body of water to another, and particularly the cleaning and proper disposal of anchor debris, but Eurasian milfoil continues to make its way into new waterways every year. Of course you can zap it with an aquatic herbicide, but that will kill everything in the vicinity, the good native plants that purify water and feed animals and invertebrates along with the bad.

The FloteBote had been in drydock for almost a year when we put her into the Big Sioux for the trip, so we were confident we hadn't brought anything from the lake with us. Even as we moved downstream from Rulo toward the cities of Missouri, we saw no recreational boaters at all, and only one barge. The land was still hilly and heavily wooded, with no visible houses or roads until we passed a rough boat ramp.

"That's Jentell Brees," Rod called, pointing to it. "We're getting close."

Jentell Brees appears, at least from midriver, to be in the middle of nowhere, but it is more or less the point from where, on July 6, 1804, Sergeant Floyd wrote in his journal "Set out prossed on a Jentell Brees from the Southwest." I looked the name up on my phone and then dug out the journals and read the entry aloud.

We weren't allowed to anchor the boat there overnight, so we passed it by. Lee had called from the Vanagon; he'd spoken to someone named Bruce at the St. Joseph Boat and Yacht Club in St. Joseph, Missouri, and they were happy to let us tie up to their dock overnight and put our tents up on their lawn. The St. Joseph Boat and Yacht Club sounded pretty fancy for the FloteBote, but hopefully they'd let us stay if we promised to be gone early, before anybody saw us.

Of all the invasive species on the river, we were certainly the strangest looking.

The last big threat to native waterways, plants, and animals is perhaps the most expensive, at least so far. The Zebra mussel is native to Eastern Europe and Russia, and scientists think it arrived in American waterways from the discharge of ship ballast tanks into the Great

Lakes sometime in the late 1980s. Zebra mussels have been moving west ever since. The U.S. Geological Survey maps them, and as of 2024 their territory covers all the Great Lakes and the state of Michigan, with blobs spread over Wisconsin, Minnesota, and New York. They reach west into central North Dakota and south all the way to central Texas. In the east, they stretch from the top of Chesapeake Bay up the Hudson River, and as far north as the Maine–Quebec border.

Adult Zebra mussels are about two inches long, about the size of a thumb, which doesn't much until you consider that a female can produce more than a million eggs in a year, and they all can live between two and five years. They can survive out of water for up to five days.

They are shaped sort of like a pointy capital D, with light and dark brown striped shells. The juveniles, which are invisible to the naked eye, float freely in the water for several weeks before settling on whatever hard surface they come across. A submerged log. A rock. The bottom of a kayak, or a barge, or a container ship. A dam. A power plant intake. To make things worse, Zebra mussels are the only freshwater species that secrete what are called byssal fibers, strong, elastic bands that they use to create barnacle-like formations on whatever surface they encounter. Some of these colonies can be more than a foot deep.

Once they take hold, they get to work. All mussels eat by sucking water and filtering out the plankton they eat and then spitting the remainder back out. But the sheer number of Zebra mussels dominate an ecosystem and starve native freshwater mussels. Their numbers can over-filter the water, allowing plants like Eurasian milfoil to grow exponentially faster. Though they have a number of predators in their home waters, including birds and fish, only a few species of American fish, along with freshwater crayfish, will eat Zebra mussels. Humans, however, definitely cannot. There are too many toxins, including pesticides and heavy metals, absorbed in their bodies.

And their impact on power and dam structures is profound. In fifteen years, between 1989 and 2004, they cost businesses and taxpayers almost $270 million in the Great Lakes region alone. The states most affected by Zebra mussels ask boaters to clean and drain their boats and equipment thoroughly before moving them from one body of water to another. If possible, to scrub the undersides with soap.

Beginning in 2014, the Gavins Point Dam in Yankton, South Dakota, a hydroelectric dam on the Missouri, began having problems with its intake efficiency. Investigation showed the pipes were clogged, sometimes completely, by living and dead Zebra mussels. More than once a month, the mussels made it all the way into the generators and stopped power production altogether. When the plant is working properly, Gavins Point produces enough electricity to power about 68,000 homes. In the years between 2014 and 2018, Gavins Point used almost 2,500 work-hours, which is about the equivalent of one person working 62 full workweeks, clearing mussels.

The first time I went to Gavins Point to see the dam, in 2019, I waded into the water about half a mile downstream from the spillway. Even once I was knee deep in the river, I could still see my feet.

In some places, Zebra mussels have been successfully eradicated by draining small lakes or ponds and overwintering them on dry ground. However, that isn't an option for the reservoir at Gavins Point, which is not only enormous but also a chief source of drinking water for the region. So in 2019 the Corps of Engineers installed an ultraviolet light system in the dam's pipe system. The UV light kills the larvae that would otherwise attach, mature, and reproduce in the pipes. They also installed much smaller filters to keep out anything larger than one-eighth of an inch and began plans to replace the piping and cooling system with mussel-resistant materials. The price tag for all of this? Almost $1.5 million. And, if Zebra mussels are in the Gavins Point Dam, they are in the Lower Missouri all the way to the mouth in St. Louis, and all the way down the Mississippi to New Orleans.

Back on the river we came down a straight stretch, passing mile marker 445, and spotted a long, low floating dock perpendicular to a high bank on the Missouri side ahead of us. A group of people—three or four, it looked like—were standing on it, looking upstream. One immediately began waving his arms at us: Lee. We had found the St. Joseph Boat and Yacht Club.

There were a number of speedboats already moored along the dock, so we made our way close to the bank, sailed past the dock, and made a U-turn. The engine thrummed, working to move us upstream against the current. Rod stood on the prow and tossed a line to Lee, and he pulled us in. The rest of the men walked down, grinning at the sight of us, or maybe of the boat. Once we got the FloteBote secured to the dock, they helped us disembark.

"There are showers in the clubhouse, if you'd like," one of them said, and I raised my hand and nodded. They laughed, and a couple of them started talking to Rod and Dirk about the boat and the trip and how it was going and, really, why on earth we were doing it. I clambered back on the boat and got my backpack and Mary's shower kit from the boxes. We climbed up a long aluminum ramp up to the top of the bank. At the top was a big fire pit and some folding chairs, right on the edge overlooking the river. About twenty-five yards inland, perched atop stilts and a small pedestal area, stood a tan metal building. A big cottonwood stood near the edge of the bank with a sign for the Boat and Yacht Club, and the river mile marker 444. We'd come 290 miles since we got on the Missouri.

A young couple were waiting for us under the clubhouse, where they had a couple of big refrigerators and a huge gas grill. Bruce, who'd introduced himself, showed us the doors to the bathrooms, where the showers were. Apparently after talking with Lee, he'd called a bunch of members, and those who could make it had come down to meet us.

The sign on the first door said "Outboard." The woman saw me looking at it and laughed.

"Women are 'Inboard,'" she said, and pointed a little further down. I raised my eyebrows a little, and she laughed again. "There's a hair-dryer in there you can use," she added, and I thanked her.

I took a shower and changed. If you've ever done even a short adventure, a long camping trip, maybe, or a few days of backpacking, you learn to appreciate a good shower. The water pressure at the St. Joseph Boat and Yacht Club is very good, should you ever have the opportunity. The guys had invited all of us to come to dinner with them, at a restaurant in town owned by another member of the club. I didn't have anything respectable to wear to a restaurant, so I put on the cleanest shorts I had, a fresh T-shirt, and a zip-up fleece jacket.

When I came out, everyone was getting to know each other. The young couple had to go home to have dinner with their kids, but Bruce and the other two men were joining us for dinner. Helpfully, they were both named Chris.

Lee and I got in a pickup with one Chris and we headed for the restaurant. Chris told us that St. Joseph was where Jesse James had lived with his family, and where one of his own gang ultimately shot and killed him in his living room. Lee pointed to the stockyards as we passed through them. And Chris told us that one of the most enduring images of the Wild West, the Pony Express, sent its first rider on a ferry across the Missouri from St. Joseph on April 3, 1860, with bags of mail from back East bound for Sacramento.

The restaurant, Adam's Bar and Grill, turned out to be a family place, with lots of local decor and funny signs. The owner and his wife came over to the table to meet all of us, armed with a couple of baskets of deep-fried something. He placed one down on the table between me and Chris.

"What is that?" I asked, looking at them. They looked a bit like fried clams.

"Turkey fries," Chris said, and grinned.

I tried to imagine what that meant. I'd heard of chicken fries, which are thin slices of deep-fried chicken served as a side dish. I assumed these were some version of that, made of turkey.

"They're fried turkey testicles," he said.

I must have blanched, because he laughed again. Apparently turkey fries are a regional thing. Since I hail from the land of Scrapple, it didn't seem like I could be judgmental, so I tried a bite of one. The whole table laughed. Maybe if I hadn't known what it was, I wouldn't have minded, but they're not for me. Like most fried food, they mostly taste like fried breading.

While we ate, the men (including Dirk) told fishing stories. I asked Chris about Asian carp, and he told me a friend of his had gone out fishing alone once, just up the river from the club. A carp jumped up and hit him so hard across the head that it knocked him unconscious for a couple of seconds. He was lucky he hadn't fallen into the water.

He also told me that, despite fishing on the river almost every day during the season, he had never once seen a Bald eagle at the river.

"I saw so many in the trees that I couldn't count them, about twenty miles upstream from your club, just today," I told him.

We got back to the club as it was getting dark, and the guys built a fire in the fire pit. Rod and I went down to the boat and brought up our tents, which we pitched near the cottonwoods on the bank. Dirk and Lee got permission to sleep in the main part of the club.

"You should never sleep under cottonwoods," Rod said, eyeing the big tree over the tents. "They drop their limbs too easily in the wind."

An hour later, I lay in my tent, watching the river glinting through my mesh door. I thought about the branches every time they creaked, but eventually I fell asleep.

It's impossible to spend more than a day or so in nature without recognizing that humans are the most significant invasive species. For three hundred miles we'd puttered down the river, crossing paths with birds, fish, deer, insects; it's likely that foxes and coyotes watched us from the shadows or cast a glance at the strange, tented boat as they moved along the riverbank or came down to drink. Most of these animals were so unfazed as to completely ignore us.

Invasive species of all kinds—plants, fish, animals, insects—tend to get their starts in disturbed places, spots on land or under water that have been dug up or cleared or otherwise stripped of whatever native habitat had been there before. None of the species moving into the Missouri River's territory got there intentionally or maliciously; they escaped from wherever they were born, and then escaped from whatever had brought them to the river, and found some spot to settle in. And then they began the long business of adapting to their new home. Their great advantage in that adaptation is that, in evolutionary terms, fifty years isn't nearly enough time for native species to adapt to defend against them. In 1859 Charles Darwin wrote, in *On the Origin of Species*, that "as natural selection acts by competition, it adapts the inhabitants of each country on in relation to the degree of perfection of their associates."

Wildlife from Europe and Asia aren't the only sources of invasive species in the United States either. Most prominent is the Rainbow trout, a cousin of the salmon, a particularly prized food and sport fish that is native to the cold water estuaries of the Pacific Northwest. Rainbow trout are both farmed and stocked—released into public fishing areas—for sport fishing and commercial food all over the continent. They raise them at the Gavins Point Fish Hatchery in South Dakota, mainly for stocking purposes. Fishers love them. I love them, at least for dinner. But they are outcompeting native trout and other fish in the waterways in which they are placed and doing immense damage to the invertebrates that native fish need to live.

Ironically, the wild Rainbow trout is the freshwater-only cousin of the Steelhead trout. Steelheads, who migrate between cold freshwater rivers and the Pacific, are treasured by sport fishers. And despite the proliferation of farmed Rainbow trout, one subspecies of Steelhead in California is endangered, and ten more are threatened. The Steelhead's problems are mostly to do with dams, which block access to their spawning grounds. But it's ironic that while these beautiful, wild fish struggle to survive, their invasive cousins are jeopardizing the life cycles of other native fish. Just as there is no way to return the Missouri River to a pre-human-contact state, there is no real way to stop invasive species once they've settled in. What we can do is work to prevent them spreading any further.

9

Dredging

> So have I seen a river, where nothing obstructed its course, flow smoothly on with but a gentle murmur; but, where it was held in check by dams of timber and stone set in its way, foaming and boiling it went, fiercer for the obstruction.
>
> —Ovid

Waking up next to the Missouri in summer is usually an early proposition, even when you sleep on the eastern bank, with your head facing west. The noise of the river itself is faint, more a whisper than a roar on a river this flat and wide and unencumbered by boulders and other obstacles. It's the birds and the wind that wake you up on the Missouri. The sun rises at around 6:20 a.m. in late July, so a tent starts to get light well before 7:00. On the nights we moored the boat in the river, whether we slept on it or not, we tried to moor on the inward side of a bend, where the water moves more slowly and gently. This was the first time the boat had spent the night on the eastern side of the river. I'd slept pretty well for most of the night, though it had been hot, and a loud bang woke me at about 1:30. I'd thought about the cottonwood above me, shifting in the wind, but whatever it was hadn't fallen on the small tent city we'd built on the club's lawn.

Lee came down from the clubhouse at about seven to tell us breakfast was ready. I dressed quickly in my tent and rolled up my sleeping pad and bag, and when I climbed out, sun was glinting off the far side of the river. I walked out to the edge of bank and whispered good morning to the river, then jogged across the Boat and Yacht Club's lawn to the stairs. Inside, Dirk was cooking oatmeal, and there was plenty of coffee. I mixed some canned peaches with my oatmeal; the cousins varied between peaches, orange jelly, purple basil, and butter for theirs. I ate, looking out the window at the river. Rod and I washed the dishes, and then we all walked back down to pack up the tents.

Bruce and Chris turned up to see us off, and they lit the fire pit again, like a beacon to see us off. We moved up and down the ramp to the dock, repacking the boat boxes and making sure the weight was distributed as evenly as we could get it. I pulled my camera out of my pack and took a few photos of the dock and the bank, piled with large, cobble-sized gravel and chunks of cement, and brought it up the ramp with me. Bruce stood next to the fire, some ten feet above the river.

"Are you taking pictures of our trash?" he asked me.

"No. Just trying to make sure I'll remember this."

He told me that the rubble reinforces the bank, keeping it stable and trying to prevent erosion as much as possible. Guys with construction companies bring along bits and pieces when they can.

I turned and took some pictures of the lawn and the clubhouse. Chris pointed a small metal sign bolted on the corner of the building, a couple of feet above the top of the piling.

"That's the water level sign from '93. You can see the levee there"—a mound of grass-covered earth beyond the clubhouse, probably thirty or so feet high, just on the other side of the club's driveway—"the water was lapping over the top of that. It didn't give, though."

I walked back up to it to take a picture of the sign. It had a line across the top, decorated with waves, and read: MISSOURI RIVER WATER LEVEL, JULY 26, 1993. 32.07 ft.

I turned around again and stared across the long stretch of grass, and across the lip of the bank down to the river and tried to imagine what all that water must have looked like, and how far it might have reached on the other side.

Rod ran into town in the Vanagon and came back with a couple of bags of ice for the cooler. We all said goodbye and thank you; I thought I saw Bruce holding a purple felt bag with a gold tie, and I wondered how much goodwill a handful of bottles of Crown Royal had bought us thus far. Mary was going to drive the Vanagon, so she could visit with some friends of their mother's, so the rest of us got the boat untied, started the motor, and headed back into the river.

Lee started out the drive, and I perched on a boat box, looking around. I'd managed to get mosquito bites on both legs, despite the fire pit and the bug screens of my tent, so I tried to distract myself by looking around.

The Kansas side of the river had leveled out as well, as far as I could see through the tree line. The only description I could think of for this landscape, as we moved toward the point where the river turned east into the center of Missouri, was *feral*. It wasn't terribly wild, but it wasn't tame either. It wasn't raining, but it was gray and cool and a little foggy. We wound around a bend and lost sight of the dock, but there were plenty of people out fishing, many with a dog or two in the boat with them.

If you pay close attention on a long river trip, you can tell when you've moved into a new geological area. The gravel wing dikes, which we'd grown accustomed to along both sides of the river, were reddish in Missouri, not the grayish white we'd seen consistently in Iowa and Nebraska. The rock used for side roads in northwest Iowa, southwest Minnesota, and eastern South Dakota is Sioux quartzite, a pinkish stone that crushes easily into road surfacing. It's probably too porous and too fragile for wing dikes, though, and I wondered where the rocks, all of them, came from.

There are two major industries on the Lower Missouri: commercial dredging, for sand and gravel for construction use, and, to a lesser extent, shipping. The dredging achieves two purposes: First, it keeps the navigation channel clear for large-ish boat traffic. While Major Suter of the Corps of Engineers hoped restructuring the river would create a nineteenth-century grain highway from the northern plains to the great port cities of the Mississippi, the Missouri has never really taken hold as a shipping lane. In 1929, at perhaps the height of its shipping power, the Missouri River Navigation Commission estimated that fifteen million tons of goods were moved up and down the still largely unmanaged and undammed Missouri, upstream as far as Montana. Expectations across the twentieth century were that below the dams, those numbers would rise steadily, despite freight trains and the rise of long-haul trucking. However, by 2000, the shipping tonnage was just over one million a year, and the vast majority of that was dredge materials and other large loads, like wind turbine blades. Granted, I wasn't on the river during harvest season, but I didn't see much of the infrastructure—particularly grain elevators—that farmers would need to support loading and shipping on the river in any significant way. A barge grain elevator was constructed in Blencoe, Iowa, in 2019, and in 2023 a record load, almost thirteen tons, of pipe was towed into Nebraska City from Louisiana. But in contrast, the National Park Service reports that about 175 million tons of goods are moved on the Upper Mississippi every year.

The other main industry on the Missouri is, of course, sand and gravel dredging. Dredging boats are difficult to describe. They're massive barges topped with platforms three levels high; essentially, they are small floating factories. The methods of getting sand on board include sucking, excavating, or scraping the sediment from the river bottom. The sand is carried up by large tubes and then deposited, most often onto barges, which are then transported to processing stations. There are two kinds of dredging happening on the Missouri: navigation maintenance, done by the Corps of Engineers, and private, commercial dredgers extracting sediment for construction purposes. Dredge companies are issued permits once their companies have been reviewed and approved by the Corps of Engineers, the Environmental Protection Agency, and state departments of natural resources.

As we moved away from St. Joseph, the fishing boats dropped off, and we were alone on the river once again. I looked at the cousins, thinking about the intersection of the river's landscape, the juxtaposition of human controls and nature's refusal to submit to those controls, and the genetic landscape of the humans on the boat. I didn't know the cousins that much more than I had before we set off; we weren't sitting on the boat talking about our secrets or our hidden pain. But, as is probably inevitable if you spend more than a week with the same small group around the clock, I understood things about each of them more clearly. And I could recognize certain traits. Dirk's dry humor, Lee's quiet determination, Rod's ability to quote anything, Mary's excitement at adventure. I recognized them in myself, and in others in our family. All I could think, when I looked at the group of them, was how lucky they were to all live in the same city (my brother lives 1,500 miles away, my half sister, 90), and how much I hoped I was still hatching wildly unusual plans for adventures when I was their age.

The sun came out, and I scratched the mosquito bites on my legs. Time becomes vaguely irrelevant on a trip like this; we needed to make a certain number of miles, but most days it didn't matter that much if we arrived at any particular hour. Tonight, Rod's college roommate and his wife were meeting us at the marina where we were docking for the night and taking us for dinner, so we had a rough timeline for the day, but barring the boat sinking, there wasn't any real need to focus on the passage of time.

The Osage tribe had called the Missouri Smoky River, apparently a reference to sand blowing from the many sandbars that still stretch along the un-engineered river above Sioux City, in the section designated as the national recreational river. However, we encountered very few sandbars as we moved further downstream, and this is likely the result of dredging. It must have been incredibly challenging for steamboat pilots to travel the Missouri in the old days, when sandbars and shoals would have shifted through the river's channel.

Maintenance dredging in the Missouri is managed by the Corps of Engineers, and is mainly undertaken in emergencies, like the aftermath of flooding. The navigation channel of the river is designed to be self-cleaning, as it were, and it works very efficiently. The river management structures—wing dikes—push faster water in from the outside of the river toward the channel, and all that fast water largely prevents silt or big debris, like fallen trees, from building up in the channel. When silt does begin to accumulate, however, the corps sends in dredgers to manage it.

In 2021, after flooding weakened the ability of the wing dikes to catch and hold sediment buildup, there was enough silt in the channel to make it too shallow for barge traffic to move through the river safely in some places. In response, the corps' biggest weapon, the Dredge *William L. Goetz* made its way to the Missouri from its home in St. Paul, Minnesota. The *Goetz*, named for a former Corps of Engineers employee, is a massive floating machine, 225 feet long and 39 feet wide. The structures on its deck look about as high as a two- or three-story building. Despite this, its draft—the depth of the boat in the water—is only five feet. It is considerably larger than the normal dredges on the Missouri; it is normally at work on the Upper Mississippi, keeping the shipping channel clear for the larger size and traffic of commercial ships that travel that river. The *Goetz*'s twenty-five-person crew worked twenty-four hours a day (a quarter boat, essentially a floating dormitory for crew to sleep and eat on, just like those used in the early days of river engineering, trailed behind them up the river), and cleared the sediment in a few weeks.

When there is damage to the river structures like the wing dikes, the corps will often need to dredge around the sides of the channel to clear whatever debris has begun to amass there. They work with local and federal Fish and Wildlife staff to make sure they don't jeopardize habitats, and strive to prevent degrading the river's channel, along with its navigation channel, any more than is necessary. Degradation is the term for damage, natural and manmade, that happens to the channel. It has a wide variety of causes: construction on or alongside the river, major flooding events, and heavy dam flow releases (the reservoir water let through sluices to reduce the pressure on the dams). But one of the easiest to control is commercial dredging.

Commercial dredging is the removal of sand and gravel for construction and maintenance use by and for private companies. An estimate from 2019 puts the total amount of sand dredged from both the Missouri and the Mississippi at between five and seven million tons a year. Rivers are one of the best places to get sand in those amounts; as far from an ocean as the Lower Missouri is, the only alternate option would be to mine it, which would be both expensive and damaging to land ecosystems.

Commercial dredgers, like the Corps of Engineers' maintenance dredgers, also work along the edge of the navigation channel, where the silt load is ostensibly highest. The trouble is that the more silt they remove from the river, the closer they get to all manner of problems, and the more damage they cause. For one, the methodical removal of silt interferes with the way sediment is naturally dispersed, which makes wildlife and plant habitats vulnerable. For another, it is impossible to know the impact dredging has on small wildlife: small or larval fish, invertebrates, and animals like mollusks that can't move out of the path of the dredges. However, the most serious concern is that lowering the bed of the river can expose or interfere with pipelines that run under the river, or the intake valves of power stations along the banks. Even if they aren't damaged by the dredging process, exposing them, even below the water line, makes other river traffic vulnerable to striking them, which will damage both pipelines and boats. As we sailed down the river, we periodically passed signs telling us where gas lines crossed under the river. Pipelines are dangerous enough, buried in the bed of a river that sends its water downstream for another thousand miles through densely populated areas, without the threat of their being struck accidentally. Additionally, the river is the primary source of drinking water for many of the cities downstream from us, including Kansas City; between the Kansas and Missouri metropolitan areas, a pipeline rupture in the Missouri would impact more than half a million people.

Between St. Joseph and Waverly, Missouri, the 128-mile stretch we were floating through, the Corps of Engineers has determined that there is serious degradation happening to the riverbed. This isn't just habitat loss. In 2017 the Army Corps of Engineers and the Mid-America Regional Council presented a report detailing the existing threats to infrastructure from the state of the river's bed at the time. In this stretch of the river, degradation was making a significant impact on levees and floodwalls, and rail and automotive bridge pilings. Called the "Missouri River Bed Degradation Feasibility Study Technical Report," the report suggested a total repair cost of more than $250 million to ensure that these essential structures be protected. While it didn't include a recommendation for implementing these repairs, it did suggest that one preventive measure would be to limit or ban entirely commercial dredging, at least in this stretch of the river.

After the 2019 floods, the levee failures in particular brought the Lower Missouri back to the government's attention. The 2021 Bipartisan Infrastructure Law, which included bridge and flood control repair, included $248 million for the Lower Missouri River, from Rulo, Nebraska, to St. Louis. Which is excellent news, of course, but broadly speaking, anything to do with infrastructure will require concrete, and that brings us back to more dredging.

The nonprofit organization Environment Missouri issued a statement in 2021 that supported the dredge limit-or-ban recommendations from the report. In it, former State Director Bridget Sanderson wrote:

> Among the report findings of the risk and uncertainty analysis was that degradation in Kansas City would not have occurred if "the commercial sand and gravel mining was absent from the channel. This was determined by running the calibrated model from 1994 to 2014 with and without the commercial sand and gravel mining. In the absence of commercial sand and gravel mining, the Missouri River in the Kansas City area would have been in a recovery phase following the 1993 Missouri River Flood."

Like everything on the Missouri, the dredging industry is a complex issue. Broadly speaking, American infrastructure around the country needs attention. Highways, bridges, tunnels, all of these systems—all of which I used to drive out to the boat—are in need of maintenance and repair. And all of these systems require sand. However, there must be a way to balance the need for these materials with the need to keep the people and animals who live and work in, on, or near the Missouri, and as important, the river itself, safe.

One of the most complicated and long-range issues regarding dredging, beyond the risks it presents to the river's ecosystem and the manmade structures that surround the river, is what that silt—in a natural river—is meant to be doing. Silt is meant to be moving downstream, building up land masses on bends and shallow sections, and particularly around the river's mouth. The mouth of the Missouri, of course, is its confluence with the Mississippi, so the Missouri's sediment should combine with the Mississippi's and make its way to Louisiana, and then out into the gulf. That it doesn't, because much of it is trapped upstream by dams, along with the tonnage removed by both maintenance and commercial dredging, has made a very real impact on the state of Louisiana. In "Louisiana's Vanishing Coastline," a 2009 article in the *New Yorker*, Elizabeth Kolbert described the amount of coastal land Louisiana had lost by then as the equivalent of the entire landmass of the state of Delaware. Without that upstream silt washing into the wetlands and barrier islands that protect mainland Louisiana from the Gulf of Mexico and the powerful storms that form there, Louisiana must purchase sand to restore these marshy islands, or risk more serious repercussions, even from weaker storm systems.

All of us need to remember that everything we do to the river has consequence, not only on the place where we are standing, but on the whole of the system. A dam release in the mountains of Montana will have repercussions in New Orleans, for good or bad. And we must be willing to embrace the complexity of each of these situations, and each of our choices in addressing them. Even the small backyard creek by my house is complex, and part of a vast and complicated system much larger than itself. The choices we make about the Missouri are exponentially larger, and while we need to act swiftly, we also need to act thoughtfully, considering all of the potential impacts we can imagine.

I took over steering for a few miles just south of Leavenworth, Kansas. Steering, even in decent weather, is more tiring than you might expect. The FloteBote didn't want to go in a straight line; I don't know if it was an issue with the distribution of weight on the deck, or simply whatever the currents on the river are doing, or something else altogether. As we moved through this area, the daybeacons in Kansas seemed further apart than upstream. There are also fewer river mile signs, though I don't know why. It's possible that there is simply so much less river traffic on the stretch between St. Joseph and our destination, Parkville—we saw no fishers at all—that if daybeacons and mile signs fell over, no one bothered to report it.

Lee was looking at the charts, and as we came around a slight bend, he pointed downstream to a red daybeacon on the Missouri side.

"Look, Lisa," he said. "It's the Delaware Bend. And the Delaware daybeacon."

As we got closer, I wondered aloud why they'd named it that. Maybe an early cartographer with the Corps of Engineers also came from Delaware, or perhaps the first person who handled the old lamp daybeacons in this area had. As we got closer, I saw that mile marker 389 was bolted to the same stakes. I obediently crossed to the left channel, and refocused on keeping the boat pointed straight downstream.

As we moved past the Delaware Bend, I could see a big sandbar reaching downstream ahead of us on my left. Below that, a tugboat, the first we'd seen on the Missouri, moved toward us, pushing two huge barges full of gravel ahead of it. I turned the boat a little toward the center, needing to be sure we would stay clear of the sandbar and any shoal that might spill into the channel. I tried to give the tug and its barges as much of the river as possible. As soon as the tug was past, I cut the wheel hard to cross his wake and get back to where we belonged.

"And not a drop of water on the deck," Rod said, smiling at me.

Nine days and 335 miles, and I was finally getting the hang of this.

One thing I was beginning to realize about myself was that I had no ability whatsoever to judge distance on the boat. I couldn't see spatially enough to even guess whether we were one hundred yards from shore, or one thousand. I would learn, a few years later, when I finally started using a GPS in the car, that I couldn't measure distance accurately there either. I wrote in my journal that day that I needed "different ideas" about measuring distance by sight.

Still haven't figured that one out.

A mile or so later, Dirk stepped in to drive, and I sat down, flexing my fingers a little to work the vibration of the steering wheel out of my system. Behind us, another tugboat was pushing three barges downstream in front of it, also loaded with gravel. Either they were going at the exact same speed as we were, or they'd slowed down to stay as far away from whatever they imagined the FloteBote was, because they stayed about the same distance from us for the rest of the day.

We didn't see the *Goetz* on our trip. We were passed, though, by dredgers and barges hauling gravel and sand moving upstream daily, sometimes multiple times daily. Their captains usually waved to us from the steering cabin, high atop the machinery on the deck, too far away to see if they had any reaction to our sudden, strange appearance on their route.

Once again, this process, the dredging of the river channel, the maintenance of the flood controls, all of these actions that interfere with the river's natural systems, are what allowed us to go on the river safely in the first place. I have no idea what the draft on the FloteBote was. Empty, it was probably around two feet; packed with all of us and all of our stuff, it's impossible to know. But because of all the work done on the channel, we could safely assume we had at least ten feet of water beneath us. The charts said fourteen, but then again, the charts also admitted that things could have changed.

Eventually we came around another bend and spotted, on the very steep Missouri bank, the Missouri River Boating Association of Parkville, Missouri. Like the St. Joseph Boat and Yacht Club, the

FIG. 8. Towboat pushing empty dredge barges upstream. To get a sense of size, the canopy of the FloteBote, about eighteen feet long and five feet high, is in the lower left corner. Photo by the author.

Missouri River Boating Association had a clubhouse, which they had kindly offered us for the night, and a handful of them came down to meet us. We pulled up to their floating dock and tied up as Rod's old roommate, Walt, and his wife Ruthie hugged the cousins. The boat club members took us up to the clubhouse, which was high on a bluff over the river, with a lovely plank deck holding a grill and a picnic table. We cleaned ourselves up a little and headed off to dinner in Kansas City at Arthur Bryant's Barbeque, a classic Missouri barbecue place. I had a hot turkey sandwich with french fries and a beer, and I looked at the photos of celebrities that covered the walls and listened as Walt and Ruthie and the cousins caught up.

On the way back to the boat club, we stopped at English Landing Park and walked around. Walt was a doctor, but they owned a farm, and Ruthie told me about the plants and trees and her dog, and I enjoyed having a long walk. The sun went down, and it seemed like it had been a pretty perfect day.

Until we got back to the club. The members, understandably needing to get back to their own lives, had given up on us and locked up their lovely, air-conditioned building. We tried all the doors we could find, but to no avail. Ultimately Mary and I pitched our tents in the small lawn between the building and the boat ramp, and Dirk elected to sleep on the deck. Rod and Lee went home with Walt and Ruthie for the night.

It was our fault, not the boat club's, and it would have been fine, despite the lack of air conditioning, except for two things: Between our campsite and the road, which turned out to be a major route into the network of highways around Kansas City, lay a freight train line. I've looked at a map, so I can tell you with some certainty that the train tracks are about two hundred yards from the clubhouse, and the road another two hundred yards beyond that. I can't tell you how many trains and semis went by, but clearly there was a road crossing somewhere not far up the tracks, because every time a train came through, it blew its horn. For our purposes, anyway, this was redundant; when you are lying on the ground that close to a moving freight train, you don't need a horn. It feels mildly like a sustained, low-level earthquake. Up the road just a bit was a twenty-four-hour gas station, which explained a lot of the truck traffic. Finally, we weren't that far from the Kansas City airport, evidently, because they offered their low, rumbling counterpoint to all the other vehicles moving past us in the dark. I think I woke up at least once an hour, each time fuzzily remembering how much I'd enjoyed that walk in the park that had kept us out too late.

When I dragged myself out of the tent the next morning, Mary and Dirk were already packing up, albeit a little blearily. It had dropped from well above eighty-five degrees the day before to sixty-five overnight, and fog hung low over the river and in the trees on the opposite bank. We pulled out my little backpacking camp stove and made some inadequate coffee, and I got my tent disassembled and went to sit at the picnic table on the deck. We had a pretty short day planned; Lee had to get to the airport in Kansas City, so we were planning to dock the boat in their riverfront park and look around a little until he had to leave. I watched a Nuthatch trot, facing downhill, down the trunk of one of the big maples that overhung the deck. More tugs were pushing barges full of gravel upstream; likely they were bound for either bank erosion projects or wing dike repairs, but we had no way to know.

Pretty soon Rod and Lee turned up, and Walt and Ruthie decided to join us for the day. I was eager to get on the river, mostly because I knew my days on the trip were running short. Apparently barges had been moving overnight as well, or had gotten an early start in the morning. There were puddles on the dock and the boat boxes, but the boat deck was dry.

Dirk suddenly said "Look!" and pointed at the bank. A young raccoon was making a brazen play for the bird feeders the boat club had along the bank. I looked around the boat deck, but it didn't look like it had gotten on the boat overnight.

The river was moving fast and the temperature was rising already, burning off the fog. We got moving downstream a little after 8 a.m., looking forward to the day.

10

Steamboats of the Missouri

> And the boat IS rather a handsome sight, too. She is long and sharp and trim and pretty; she has two tall, fancy-topped chimneys, with a gilded device of some kind swung between them; a fanciful pilot-house, a glass and 'gingerbread,' perched on top of the 'texas' deck behind them; the paddle-boxes are gorgeous with a picture or with gilded rays above the boat's name; the boiler deck, the hurricane deck, and the texas deck are fenced and ornamented with clean white railings; there is a flag gallantly flying from the jack-staff; the furnace doors are open and the fires glaring bravely; the upper decks are black with passengers; the captain stands by the big bell, calm, mposing, the envy of all.
>
> —Mark Twain, *Life on the Mississippi*

It's impossible to think about big, Midwestern rivers without picturing steamboats. Huge, white, dripping with Victorian trim, a paddlewheel splashing cheerfully on the stern, a bunch of men with long mustaches and striped pants, and perhaps top hats, playing banjos on the prow. They must have been astonishing to see in the nineteenth century, so long and tall, and moving at such speed through an undeveloped frontier.

People started developing the idea of a steam engine as early as the first century, but it was the late 1700s before people began experimenting with using them to propel boats. The first successful American steamboat was built by Philadelphian John Fitch, who launched the *Perseverance* on the Delaware River in 1787 before delegates from the

Constitutional Convention. By 1790 he was ferrying people on round-trip voyages between Philadelphia and Burlington, New Jersey. In 1807 another inventor, Robert Fulton, steamed a steamboat up the Hudson from New York City to Albany, covering 145 river miles in about eight hours.

Steamboats took off, becoming the most effective and efficient means of river transportation available throughout the nineteenth century. Most of us picture the large passenger paddleboat "show-boats" when we think of steamboats. To this day, just behind Jackson Square in New Orleans, on the northern bank of the Mississippi is the SS *Natchez*, a sternwheel paddleboat with a century-old steam engine and an oak-and-steel hull. According to its website, the *Natchez*, built in 1975, is the oldest steamboat operating on the Mississippi. You can ride it down the river, standing on the prow and watching the city go past, or sitting in a velvet Victorian armchair in the parlor, enjoying a drink.

In their heyday, however, steamboats in a number of designs operated on the country's rivers. Along with the sternwheel model, in which the paddle is at the back of the boat, there were sidewheelers, which had the paddles amidships on both sides of the boat. Steam towboats moved barges up- and downstream; snagboats cleared trees and other debris from the rivers; packets carried people, mail, and materials; and fuelers transported wood and coal to boats already in transit. In the early years, steamboats were so popular that they created their own environmental hazards. Crews and fuelers clear-cut many riverbanks for wood to keep the steam engines moving, which resulted in bank erosion and more significant flooding.

On the Missouri, steamboats, mostly sidewheelers, sailed as far upstream as Montana. The first one on the Missouri, the *Independence*, set out from St. Louis in 1819 and traveled about 250 miles, to the mouth of the Chariton River on what is now the Iowa—Missouri border. Despite the Missouri's pre-engineering challenges, by the second half of the nineteenth century, steamboats were making routine trips from St. Louis to the Rocky Mountains. Still more boats ferried people across the river between established states and territories while settlers built homesteads and towns, trappers sent furs to market, and the U.S. Army moved into the northern plains.

This didn't mean that steamboat travel was safe. Steam engines exploded or started fires, which quickly spread through the wooden boats. Snags, submerged logs and trees, or sandbars and shoals caught them midstream, punched holes in them, broke them apart, and pulled them down. The first steamboat wreck on the Missouri was in 1819, when the *Thomas Jefferson* hit a snag near the mouth of the Osage River. By the end of the century, almost three hundred steamboats had been destroyed by the river, including some that were damaged in the river, repaired, and then wrecked again. Most Missouri River steamboats had a life expectancy of about four years.

Historians have spent ample time charting the estimated or known locations of wrecked steamers on the Missouri, beginning in the late 1890s and continuing today. There are wreck maps indicating where, or near where, most of the boats went down. Modern technology means that the scientists working on the river have stumbled across several lost wreck sites; the U.S. Geological Survey, using sonar to track Pallid sturgeon habitat, spotted an unidentified wreck buried in the river's bottom in their scans in 2022. During drought years, parts of wrecks sometimes become visible, or are easily detected by the scientists and engineers working on the river. But of all the steamboats that were lost in those years, only seventeen have ever been excavated.

We moved downstream in the hot sun, coming quickly to the confluence of the Kansas River and the hard bend to the east, where soon we would have Missouri on both sides of the river. A line of bridges crossed the river in front of us, and we could see the skyscrapers of Kansas City in the distance. Kansas City is the largest city on the Lower Missouri, with over two and a half a million residents. We passed under the string of bridges over the river and made our way to a marina near the city's River Market. Lee and Ruthie were waiting for us, and we walked into the River Market, looking quite a bit less urbane than those around us, even on a Thursday morning in August. And at the end of the Market, in a grand, glass-fronted building about the size of an airplane hangar, we walked in to the *Arabia* Steamboat Museum.

The *Arabia* was built just outside of Pittsburgh in 1853. A sidewheeler, she was sent to the Missouri River, where she moved passengers and tons of supplies, equipment, and mail up the river into the frontier. In early September 1856, the ship, headed for Sioux City with 150 passengers and crew, 200 tons of supplies, and a mule, hit a snag, a submerged tree hidden in the river's depths, and sank in less than half an hour, about six miles west of Kansas City. Fortunately, the boat stuck in a fairly shallow place in the riverbed, and the upper decks remained above water for several hours. All the passengers and crew made it off the ship safely. The mule's owner told reporters he'd cut the mule loose, but she was "too stubborn" to leave the sinking ship, the sole fatality. The *Arabia*, and everything on board, sank into the thick sandy silt at the bottom of the river, and disappeared.

In 1988, 132 years later, a Kansas City businessman, David Hawley, identified exactly where the *Arabia* went down. Along with his father, brother, and two other local businessmen, Hawley set out to excavate the wreck, now forty-five feet under a Kansas cornfield, a half mile west of the bank of the river. Eventually they found the steamboat, and a great deal more. Because the boat was completely encased in zero-oxygen mud, where no air or light could get to it, because when it sank, the Missouri River was able to change its channel and move around the landscape, and would do so for another seventy years, because so much silt and soil built on top of the wreck before it was located that it stayed safe from plows and other farm equipment, because of all of these factors, the cargo in the ship, along with the huge trunk of the walnut tree that had brought the ship down, were almost perfectly preserved.

As was, sadly enough, the skeleton of the mule, still saddled and tied to the deck of the ship, belying her owner's statement to the press.

Once the team realized what they'd found—a few hundred tons of mainly intact furniture, dishes, food, clothing, and supplies—they began carefully removing it all, and looking for a museum space to hold the *Arabia*'s contents. To this day, there are still artifacts from the excavation waiting to be restored and put on display. Restoration is done by employees of the museum, and you can watch some of them working on the artifacts during the tour. They've been cleaning and restoring relics for more than thirty years, and they estimate that there is still close to fifteen years' worth of restoration to complete.

It's a fascinating museum, with whole sections of the boat, a big hunk of the tree, the skeleton of the poor mule, and room after room of perfectly preserved nineteenth-century china, glassware, fabric, gowns, boots, and more. There is a whole cabinet filled with intact jars of pickles, ketchup, and preserves. They've replicated one of the paddlewheels, but the paddlewheel motor survived intact and is on display below the wheel. The *Arabia* Steamboat Museum gives us a peek into what people moving west in the early days of the American West felt was important enough to take with them. We poked around the museum, and Mary and I listened to a talk one of the restorers gave about the methods they used to save all the delicate fabrics and buttons and shoes.

Snags were one of the foremost ways that ships on the Missouri were damaged or sunk. Explosions and fires were the other. Steamboats were either entirely made of wood or of a wood and iron hybrid; not until the Civil War did metal ships come into regular use. But wooden boats have always been susceptible to fire, and early boilers were particularly prone to exploding. At the end of the Civil War, a steamboat carrying former Union prisoners of war up the Mississippi exploded, causing more than a thousand deaths.

Probably the most famous American steamboat pilot, Samuel Clemens, suffered a loss from a boiler explosion when, in 1858, his younger brother Henry died on board the steamboat *Pennsylvania*. Samuel, already working as a pilot, had gotten Henry the job, and would carry the guilt with him for the rest of his life.

Samuel Clemens wanted to be a steamboat pilot from young childhood. His family moved to Hannibal, Missouri, on the banks of the Mississippi, in 1835, when he was four. Clemens dropped out of school in the fifth grade to become a printer's apprentice and by age twenty-two had moved around the East, working as a printer and educating himself in public libraries. In 1857 he gave up printing and became a cub pilot to a captain who worked steamboats on the Ohio, Mississippi, and Missouri Rivers. There is some debate among Twain scholars as to when he first sailed on the Missouri, but he was definitely on the Missouri in 1861, because he included a scathing description of it in his 1872 book *Roughing It*: "the boat might almost as well have gone to St. Joe by land, for she was walking most of the time, anyhow—climbing over reefs and clambering over snags patiently and laboriously all-day long."

Clemens returned to his beloved Mississippi River for most of his brief piloting career, but in one important regard, he carried his steamboat years into the future with him to international renown. "Mark Twain," the pen name he had settled on by 1863, was a riverboat call. A boatman, checking that the river's depth was enough for a boat to pass, would drop overboard what is called a sounding line, marked in fathoms, to check the water's depth. If the line goes into the two fathoms (twelve feet) mark, the water is deep enough for the boat to proceed, and the boatman would call out "Mark! Twain!"

The author Twain is, of course, best known for his novels *Tom Sawyer* and *Huckleberry Finn*. However, in his lifetime he was better known for his travel writing, and he wrote quite a bit about rivers. He complained, in *Life on the Mississippi*, that the trouble with becoming a professional steamboat pilot was that in order to know a river well enough to command a boat through it night and day, you learned it so thoroughly that you lost sight of its personality. He wrote of having to identify specific trees along the banks, and learning how to read the river's surface to identify new shoals and snags and shallow water. In short, by getting to know the river too well, he lost sight of his love for it.

Lee and Mary went off to the airport, with Mary intending to drive to spend the night with some friends outside Kansas City. Walt decided to come along with us for the day, and perhaps the night as well. Ruthie drove back to the farm; she would meet us in Orrick that night for dinner. We walked back to the city marina, where the FloteBote bobbed in her mooring, sitting a little higher on the pontoons with all of us on shore. I cast a look around at the sleek city speedboats and shining fishing boats, and then back at the FloteBote. Even the *Kon-Tiki* looked more sophisticated than we did, but affection overlooks a multitude of flaws. Rod, Dirk, and I settled in on the boxes, and Walt drove us out of the city. As soon as the landscape returned to trees, I smiled. I was in no danger of learning the Missouri by heart, but I was beginning to realize that it was working its way into my heart. Even with all its power and threats, even after only a week and a half, the Missouri, and particularly the feral parts, was beginning to feel like home to me.

Broadly speaking, the term "steamboat" refers to boats used on rivers, lakes, and canals. While the first oceangoing steamboat sailed successfully down the coast of England from Leeds to Yarmouth in 1813, the fuel these boats needed to keep the boilers running made ocean crossing by steam nearly impossible for decades. The weight and bulk of the wood needed to keep the fires stoked meant the space for freight was limited, and that made long trips in open water economically inefficient or impossible. On inland journeys, steamboats could run close enough to shore to keep fuel within sight if they needed it.

In the early years of the steamboat boom, large boat trips would often wait to depart until spring, when the snowmelt from the Rockies ensured that the river was as deep as possible. This must have meant moving upstream against an even stronger current, which in turn would likely both require more fuel and strain on the engine. Boat builders began designing steamboats with much lower drafts than the boats they built for deeper rivers like the Mississippi and the Ohio. The earliest regular run began in 1829, between St. Louis and Fort Leavenworth, in Kansas. By 1857 twenty-three steamboats were offering regular trips between St. Louis and Sioux City, some three hundred miles further upstream. Steamboats regularly traveled from St. Louis, not just to Omaha and Sioux City, but all the way into what is now central Montana. The first steamboat to arrive in Fort Benton, about fifty miles south of the Canadian border, arrived in 1859, set a new long-distance record for steamboats, and established Fort Benton as "the world's most innermost port." Fort Benton, 3,300 miles from St. Louis, was the furthest port in regular use from an ocean on the planet. The trip from St. Louis had taken three months.

The early Montana expeditions mainly served the fur trapping industry, but by the 1870s, gold had been discovered in the Rockies. Army forts and prospectors began settling along the river all the way to Fort Benton and established a new overland route to the Pacific to compete with the Oregon Trail, ending in Walla Walla in what is now southeast Washington.

Passenger steamboats were staffed by between seventy and ninety people. According to Phil Chappell, a steamboat clerk on the Missouri from 1857 to 1860, in addition to the captain, there were pilots, engineers, mates, a watchman, a lamplighter, cooks, a steward, chambermaids, a barber, a bartender, cabin crews, and deck crews. Decks were crewed by three categories of workers: steamboat mates, roustabouts, and firemen. Firemen were, of course, on constant watch for fire from the boilers. Roustabouts did the hardest labor; they were the ones physically pushing the boats off sandbars and snags. Reverend John Todd, a minister in Fremont County, Iowa, across from Nebraska City, reported in 1848 that it routinely took crews weeks at a time to get the boats unstuck. The mates ensured that the roustabouts got their jobs done.

It was the captains, however, who brought the most business to the steamboat industry. A good pilot, one who could read and perhaps even understand the Missouri, developed a reputation for safety and reliability with both potential passengers and traders. The best captains not only remembered where sandbars lay in the river; they could estimate, by the river's behavior, where new ones would form. According to Chappell, a mid-nineteenth-century Missouri River steamboat captain could make two hundred dollars a month.

Both passenger and freight travel in the 1850s was expensive and dangerous; the *Arabia*'s insurance payout after the wreck was $10,000 for the boat, and $8,200 for the cargo. Passengers came from all walks of life: settlers heading for the west, including Mormon settlers headed for Utah, prospectors hoping for gold in the Colorado or California territories, all manner of people hoping for a new life or boundless riches or both. The steamboat designers rose to meet this challenge. Some of the passenger boats were as stylish as their larger Mississippi River counterparts, and cost some $30,000, the equivalent of more than $1 million in the twenty-first century. The larger boats had as many as forty-six staterooms, nurseries for infants and small children, parlors, and even, in some cases, orchestras, which meant there was often dancing in the evenings. They weren't fast; the upstream journey from St. Louis to Sioux City took more than a month, and sometimes closer to two, but they were as comfortable as they could be.

Back on the boat, a tug went by us, pushing a barge piled high with sand. A bird flew over us, and I asked Walt what it was.

"Eastern kingbird," he said, and I wondered if our turn into the state of Missouri had brought us far enough east for the bird habitats to change. Dirk said we were in a Bald eagle breeding area; certainly we were seeing more birds than we had the day before, upstream from Kansas City. Then we came through a bend, and Rod called out, and pointed over the starboard side. A lone American White pelican paddled slowly downstream, its big orange beak pointed straight down at the water. I'd never seen one this far north before. I thought of pelicans as southern, oceanic birds, but their migration passes through much of the country west of Indiana, heading for breeding grounds as far north as Alberta. A few years later, I would see a whole colony of them on the downstream side of the Gavins Point Dam in Yankton, South Dakota.

According to a display sign in the *Arabia* museum, the river had been a mile wide here in the 1850s. In 2013, as far as I could estimate from the Corps of Engineers chart, it was about a thousand feet wide, a good bit less than a quarter mile. Engineering and dams had made the Missouri almost six times narrower in less than a century.

By 1860 the steamboats were dropping supplies and passengers at upstream ports and returning to St. Louis with crops of corn and potatoes, and Thomas Jefferson's plans half a century earlier had come to fruition. However, things were already changing.

The Civil War brought the steamboat industry to a standstill. The federal government commandeered many of the boats for use as troop and supply transports in the East; others were stolen or burned by both armies. In addition, because Missouri was a "border state" and therefore its citizens were divided, with some supporting the Union and some the Confederacy, the harbor in St. Louis was blockaded by Confederate sympathizers. Towns upstream that had been flourishing in the 1850s were in economic freefall by 1861, with supplies and crops only able to travel overland for the duration of the war. Steamboats returned to the river once peace was declared, and in larger numbers than before the war, but that was not to last.

In 1862 three railroad companies began work on what was in those days called the Pacific Railroad and is now referred to as the Transcontinental Railroad. Union Pacific began building track westward from Council Bluffs, Iowa, across the river from Omaha, while Central Pacific Railroad Company picked up from Sacramento and built east from there. The lines came together at Promontory Point in Utah Territory in 1869. By 1870 the line from Sacramento to San Francisco was completed, and the future of transportation would change forever.

Steamboats continued to work on the river until the 1930s, but in greatly diminished numbers. By the start of World War II, diesel engines had supplanted steam. We'd already met one of the last steam-powered sidewheelers built for the Missouri, though; the 1932 *Captain Meriwether Lewis*, dry docked on the riverbank near Brownsville, Nebraska, where we'd eaten lunch in the easing rain.

We've been trying to control the Missouri River since Lewis and Clark got back in 1806. For safety, for productivity, for transportation, with shovels and levers and human bodies, with dredgers and wing dikes. Before we could physically change it, we built boats custom-designed for shallow water and heavy obstructions to get up and down it more quickly. A lot of people we'd met along the way down the river had asked us why we were doing this on a pontoon boat. Our answer was always some version of "It's the boat we have, and it won't be much of a loss if it goes down," compounded with the details about how we were going to give it away in St. Louis, to anyone with a boat trailer. And it was a risky proposition, beyond the obvious threats that the Missouri can present. A forty-year-old boat, even one that had been well cared for, is probably not what veteran adventurers would recommend.

We did see some pontoon boats on the Missouri, but they are more suitable (and much more common) on lakes and reservoirs. Barring a significant snag in the boat channel, what I would call a speedboat—one used for cruising or water skiing—would do well on the Missouri. If it was fancy enough, it might even have a cabin, with an actual roof. And a bathroom. With a shower.

But the thing I liked about the physics of the FloteBote was that it reminded me a little of what life might have been like on a paddleboat. Low in the water, without much of a draft, moving slowly enough to observe birds and trees and whatever else there was to look at. Noisy, breezy, and a little unsafe.

A velvet armchair, a bartender, and an orchestra would have been a nice touch, though.

We tend to romanticize the past, focusing instead on a stylized, curated, carefully presented Hollywood version of what things might have looked like at their very best. I tried to picture a steamboat as it would really have run, rumbling along day and night for more than a month, crammed with strangers, presumably with limited chances to bathe, unless you were willing to take your chances in the river. The boat grinding to a halt on sand bars or snagged trees. If you moved up the river in summer, which was when the bulk of the steamboats ran, the mosquitoes must have been oppressive. Add to that, because I am a woman, the corset, the petticoats, the floor-length dresses, the heat.

Even with all of that, though, I imagine some of the passengers sat as I do, watching the land roll past them, land that perhaps they'd never seen before. Some of them must have wondered what the crew was watching for in the water, and how they would know it if they saw it. Some of them, even weeks into the journey, must have woken every morning with a little tingle of excitement, wondering what they would see that day.

We came around a long bend and saw someone standing on a boat ramp on the north side of the river. As we got closer, we could see that it was Ruthie. She waved to us, and we pulled the boat up to the bank and anchored it in at both ends. The banks were cleared of trees near the ramp, but we walked up the ramp to a wide stretch of marsh and grassland. We were spending the night in the most isolated spot of the trip thus far: Cooley Lake Conservation Area. Cooley Lake is an oxbow lake: A former bend in the Missouri's channel, the ends had silted up during some flood or drought event and formed a long, narrow lake. Even though we were fewer than ten miles from downtown Kansas City, Cooley Lake is mainly used for hunting and fishing and, from the river's edge, anyway, looks like the middle of nowhere.

Ruthie drove us south of Orrick, a small town a little to the southeast of Cooley Lake, to Fort Osage. A national historic landmark, Fort Osage was a log military fort constructed by the U.S. Army on the south side of the river in 1808,and commanded by George Sibley, for whom the small town that arose around the fort site is named. The fort, built on the edge of the frontier, supported trade and became a launch site for new settlers on their journeys west. As western expansion spread, however, the fort fell off the main travel routes, and in 1827 the army abandoned it. In 1941 local residents located the original site of the fort and built a historical replica in its place. The site has a factory and officers' and soldiers' quarters, and is surrounded by a log stockade with tall square guard towers looking out over the stockade in each direction. There is also a cemetery, dating back to 1810, and a stretch of restored prairie outside the stockade.

I walked back out of the fort and stared down at the river, a railroad bridge visible in the distance, and wondered what the steamboat passengers might have seen, fifty years after the fort was abandoned. The prairie had probably taken back much of it by then, and it must have looked a little eerie, as ruins tend to.

We got back in the car, crossed over the river again, and went to dinner at a little restaurant called Fubbler's Cove. Walt decided to spend the night with us, so there were three of us sleeping on the boat deck. As we got the boat ready for the night, heavy, dark clouds moved in from the west, and I wondered what tomorrow would be.

11

Recreation

> Even when one reaches the Missouri, there is little in that ugliest of all rivers to divert one's attention. . . . Deserted, monotonous, hideous, treacherous, with its forever shifting sands and snags, it almost seems to repel settlement, even as it repels poetry and art.
>
> —Bayard Taylor, letter to the *New-York Tribune*, 1866

In 1968 the U.S. Congress enacted the Wild and Scenic Rivers Act, granting certain rivers protection from damming or channel engineering, so that rivers around the nation would remain in a natural state. The act specifies three categories: wild rivers, which have never been dammed or managed and are not easily reached by road; scenic rivers, which have never been dammed or managed but are able to be reached by road; and recreational rivers, which have been either dammed or managed or both, but some portion of them has been preserved in as natural a state as possible.

Ten years later, the Missouri National Recreational River was created, encompassing fifty-nine miles of the Missouri, from just below the Gavins Point Dam in South Dakota to Ponca State Park in Nebraska, just upstream from the top of the engineered channel. In 1991 Congress added thirty-nine more miles to the designation, upstream from Gavins Point, from the Fort Randall Dam near Pickstown, South Dakota, downstream to Niobrara, Nebraska. These two sections, the dams notwithstanding, have been left to their own devices ever since. Apart from the headwaters of the river in Montana, these sections are as much like what the river would have looked like before 1880 as we can imagine.

The Missouri National Recreational River is very different from the river we were traveling on. Below Gavins Point, it is wide; the Vermillion–Newcastle Bridge, which crosses the Missouri about twenty miles downstream from the dam, is nearly half a mile long. Up there, the river is full of huge sandbars, some so big they look more like islands, often several of them spread across the river in a single stretch. The current moves in complex ways, as the water runs through natural channels that are spread across the riverbed, faster in some places, slower in others. Up there, the river truly is feral, not quite wild, but certainly not tamed. There are places to park and get to the river's edge, though unless it's at a boat ramp, this usually involves hiking quite a way through often dense undergrowth. The water is every bit as muddy as it is in Missouri, and every bit as strong; according to the National Park Service, currents normally run between three and five miles per hour. I've swum in the river up there; you can swim freestyle upstream as hard as you can and never move forward, like you're using some kind of muddy swimming treadmill. It is for this reason that the park service discourages swimming in the Missouri and recommends a personal flotation device anytime you are in or on the river. Despite this, from Montana to Missouri, the river is beloved by swimmers, boaters, fishers, birdwatchers, and the occasional strange, long-haul tourists.

It was my day to drive the van, so once the FloteBote was on its way downstream, I got in the car and headed for Lexington, Missouri, a twenty-mile drive. It was surprising how strange it was to have a clearly defined route, a steering wheel that didn't vibrate so hard that the bones in my wrists rubbed together, and a vehicle that actually turned the second I asked it to. I headed out of the Cooley Lake reserve and turned down the county highway, surrounded on both sides by corn and soybeans.

Most of the recreational boating we had seen were fishers, though the couple at St. Joseph Boat and Yacht Club told us they did some water skiing. In the reservoir behind the Gavins Point Dam, however, speedboats, pontoon boats, and sailboats are moored in marinas or out on the water during summer. In the managed section of the river, we never saw an anchored fishing boat; presumably, if you threw an anchor, the current would spin you in circles around the anchor line until you either got sick or found yourself and your boat snarled into a spiderweb of fishing line.

Up in the recreational area, there are boaters as well, including kayaks and canoes. Apparently kayaks and canoes are very popular around the urban areas of the river, and a number of people have kayaked the length of the Missouri, from the headwaters to St. Louis. We didn't see any in the engineered section of the river, though. But once a year, in late July, the nonprofit Missouri River Relief, which holds volunteer river cleanups, hosts lectures, and teaches schoolchildren in Missouri about the river and its history, also sponsors the World's Longest Nonstop Paddle Race.

The MR340 was created by Scott Mansker of Kansas City, Kansas, to raise awareness about the river and its importance to the community. It began in 2006 with a total of 15 paddlers and 11 boats from as far away as North Carolina. By 2012, they had 526 boats. In 2023, the number of entrants was up to 701, from all over the world. Paddlers compete solo, in pairs, or in teams of up to ten called dragon boats. And "boats" here is a broad category. Competitors come with rafts, canoes, kayaks, stand-up paddleboards, and anything else that can float and be propelled by a person. The race runs the 340 miles (thus the name) from Kansas City to St. Charles. Paddlers have a total of eighty-five hours to complete the race, and the current record, from a five-person canoe team, is thirty-three hours and one minute. Competitors start a little above the confluence of the Kansas River, just west of Kansas City, and paddle as hard and as long as they can. The river towns are spread out almost perfectly through Missouri, about twenty miles apart, so they arrange check-in sites all the way down the route, and safety boats accompany the racers throughout the whole route.

When he was twenty, Mansker and a few of his friends built a raft and managed to sail it down the Missouri for five days, and he began imagining a long-distance paddle race on the river. In 2005 he decided to give it a try. He built a website, expecting maybe two or three paddlers to sign up. He figured that would make for a good proof of concept. He was surprised, therefore, when he got fifteen, many of them veteran paddle racers.

The first race launched in early August of 2006. It was a very hot summer; the Missouri was so low that barge traffic had been severely restricted. Scott and another experienced paddler manned two safety boats, with Scott at the back of the pack. As night fell, a big storm blew in from the southwest, and he urged the paddlers around him to make it to the shore in Waverly, Missouri. As they pulled their boats on shore, he could hear branches breaking across the river.

For about fifteen minutes, the storm pummeled the river. Waves crashed along the shore, swamping his boat, tied some four feet up on the bank. Once the wind had passed, Mansker checked in with the other safety boat, by then almost thirty miles upstream of Waverly, and while his friend and the race leader were fine, Mansker began to wonder how the rest of the racers were.

"My goal for that first race was simple," Mansker remembers. "I needed for somebody to finish, and for nobody to die."

A few minutes later, his cell phone rang. It was a friend of a racer from North Carolina. The racer, not having Mansker's cell phone number, called home for help. She'd been washed up onto the banks by the powerful waves during the storm and was, the friend believed, injured. She had told the friend that she was on a hill under some trees, and that she'd passed under a bridge about an hour before the crash.

Mansker did some quick calculations and thought he knew where she was, so he set off again, in the pitch dark, whitecaps still roiling across the surface of the river. A half hour later, he spotted some debris on the riverbank, just about where he thought she might be. Sure enough, he found the racer curled up under a tree, battered but not badly injured. He managed to get her equipment together and got her back in her boat, and they made their way downstream a bit to an island. He put up a tent, and as the racer slept, he started to receive text messages from competitors all along the route. All of them were fine.

When he woke in the morning, the racer had already packed up her boat and gotten back on the river. She ended up winning the women's solo division.

A surprising amount of river analysis goes into racers' planning. They look for the places where the channel is deepest, and therefore fastest, to give themselves a break and their boats a boost. And in addition to headwinds and floating debris, the weather, cold and raining or dry and hot, adds to the challenge. Competitors all have ground crews, and volunteers sail with the racers to assist in case anyone has a medical problem. And the paddlers routinely fight dehydration, because it's hard to drink while paddling in a river that will spin a boat around in a circle if you pull a paddle out for more than a few seconds. But every year, more boats enter, and more volunteers turn out to help with the race.

The MR340 has become a staple of the summer, and paddle sport businesses have sprung up all along the route. It's changed the way the people in the region look at the river.

All up and down the river, groups of people will motor to large sandbars, throw down anchor, and have a beach party in the middle of the river. We sailed past a smallish sandbar adorned with a rough driftwood tent frame draped with an old bedsheet, empty, but clearly someone's impromptu summer getaway. It looked like something Huck Finn might have built. Some families camp overnight on them. This trend is popular enough that, during breeding season, Fish and Wildlife will post "no trespassing" signs on sandbars where plovers and terns are nesting. There isn't much of what could be described as "beach" up there, at least in the spots where I've been, on the banks of the river.

There are, of course, the various boat clubs and public marinas all along the river between Sioux City and St. Louis. And in many places, the states have preserved areas along the banks as state or county parks, some with campgrounds and picnic areas and what look like good spots from which to fish. But the Missouri is not a suitable place for many of the less expensive activities that lakes and smaller rivers provide.

It is, when it's behaving itself, an advantage to the small communities along its banks, though. Even using the meandering, county road route that I'd chosen, I made it to Lexington in less than an hour. I parked on Main Street and went for a walk, looking in shop windows and enjoying being able to move around more than I had been for the last eleven days. Lexington's history is tied to the river; though today it only has about five thousand residents, it was the largest town west of St. Louis until the 1850s and offered ferry service across the river starting in 1819. Once steamboats came along, Lexington established the first coal mine industry along the river. It was also the scene of one of the worst steamboat wrecks in the river's history. In 1852 the steamboat *Saluda*, transporting some 250 Mormon settlers toward the Mormon trail, suffered a boiler explosion. More than 60 percent of the passengers were killed.

I walked into River Reader Books on Main Street and poked around, purchasing an excellent cup of coffee and a couple of notebooks. But once I got out, I drove off in search of the river, more than an hour ahead of when I expected the FloteBote to come in. Nice as it was to be in town, I kept thinking about the river. I was happy to take my turn in the van, and the cousins had generously seen to it that I spent only one day off the boat. But I decided to head to the park where we would leave the boat early.

Without GPS, I tried to find a map that included the surface streets of Lexington, but all I had was a map of Missouri, so I stopped in a gas station to ask directions. I walked into the little convenience store and the bell jingled over my head. Two teenagers stood behind a counter piled with different kinds of jerky and scratch-off lottery tickets. I picked up a bottle of water.

"Can you tell me how to get to Riverside Park?" I asked as I fished money out of my wallet.

They looked at each other blankly.

"Never heard of it," one of them said.

"It's a park, by the river . . . ?" I said.

"Well, there's the marina," the other one said.

"That'll do," I said. They looked at each other again.

"Oh!" the boy said. "That's Riverside Park!"

With their instructions, I got to the park and sat on the Lexington boat ramp, watching the river. Bitterns, apparently deciding that I wasn't a threat, began poking around in the shallows. I couldn't remember what day of the week it was, but I was the only person out there.

After a few hours, the boat appeared upstream, and I stood and waved as it came in. We moored it downstream from the boat ramp. Walt had stayed on board for the day, and Ruthie was going to drive down and meet us for dinner and then take him back home with her.

We piled in the van, and Walt told me they'd seen snakes in the river, probably cottonmouths. I told him I had a snakebite kit in my pack but that I'd never seen a water snake in the wild, much less a venomous one.

"If you're ever bitten, be as still and quiet as possible," Walt said, which reminded me that he was a doctor. "Immobilize the limb if you can and go to a hospital as fast as possible. Don't worry about trying to identify the snake," he added. "You'll probably just get bitten again."

I tried to commit that to memory.

"Ruthie was bitten by a rattlesnake living under our porch once," he went on. "She was at home alone with the baby, and had to drive herself, with the baby because we had no sitter, to the hospital."

I hoped, then and now, that if it ever happened to me, I could be that cool about it.

We went to dinner, and checked into an old, slightly seedy motel on the edge of town closest to the marina. Once again, we weren't allowed to sleep on the river. In the morning, as we carried our things back to the Vanagon, I noticed a good-sized, very tidy vegetable garden along the edge of the parking lot: corn, squash, chilis, beans, okra, tomatoes, and peas. Over in a corner, a lovely weeping mulberry tree drooped artfully over a small car. Rod pulled into a small parking lot, and we loaded up and went to breakfast at Maria's Family Cafe. It was one of the best meals I had on the whole trip, but the waitress told us that the restaurant was closing at the end of the week.

"The prices are too expensive, apparently," the waitress said, and walked away.

I had prosciutto, pesto, and a soft-boiled egg on an English muffin, and thought what a shame it was that Lexington wouldn't have this as an option by the end of the week. Whenever that was.

On the way back to the boat, we stopped at the Anderson House, part of the Battle of Lexington State Historic Park, on the other side of town. The patriarch, Oliver Anderson, had a successful hemp and cotton business, and in 1853 he built his family a large brick home, said to be the biggest and finest house west of St. Louis. By the late 1850s the hemp market had collapsed, and only by shuffling the house between family members did the Andersons manage to hang onto the house until the start of the Civil War.

The Missouri River served as a sort of north–south delineation for Missouri in the Civil War, though, of course, delineation was not actually that simple. A border state, Missouri had both Union and Confederate governments, and citizens on both sides of the river fought for both sides of the war. The Union army arrived in Lexington soon after war was declared. When Anderson, a slave owner, wouldn't swear the Oath of Allegiance to the Union, the army seized the house and used it as a field hospital. Over a week in mid-September 1861, the Missouri State

Guard, essentially a Confederate militia, fought the Union throughout the town. The Anderson House changed hands three times in the first day. By the end of the week, the state guard had soaked hemp bales in water and begun using them as a kind of movable barricades, and ultimately the Union surrendered. The house itself survived the battle, but all around the building remains visible damage from bullets and cannonballs.

We got back to the boat and set off again, a bit later than usual after our tour. It was weirdly disorienting to be back on the river after the day in the car, and it took me a little bit to get readjusted. It was still cloudy and cool, and plenty of fishers were out. Down here, fishing boats were pretty much all we saw. In fairness, we were in a pretty remote part of the state. For the last two days, we had been floating through sections of the Big Muddy National Fish and Wildlife Refuge. The Big Muddy is an experiment in both animal and river management. It is a collection of (as of 2018) seventeen separate tracts, some twenty thousand acres mainly in the floodplain, that the U.S. Fish and Wildlife Service has been purchasing from private owners since the fall of 1994. These tracts are strung along the river from Kansas City to St. Louis, and Fish and Wildlife is working to restore a more natural floodplain area, which in turn is improving wildlife habitat, in the river and on land, along the whole river.

The timing of the start date is not a coincidence. The flooding of 1993 was catastrophic in Missouri, and most of this land, the bulk of which had been row crop fields, was so badly damaged by floodwaters that for many farm owners, selling was the best option. Today, the land is a mixture of floodplain wetlands and cottonwood and willow forest, all of which creates a much more effective protection barrier between future floods and private land.

Most wildlife refuges exist to protect either a specific species or a specific habitat. Big Muddy exists to protect the river, and the animals who live on or near it; by existing, it protects the humans along the river as well. The tracts are open to the public, offering fishing, hunting, hiking, berry picking, and wildlife watching, but the most popular thing humans do in there is hunt for morels, the prized, gourmet cousins of cap mushrooms that are nearly impossible to cultivate. The wildlife includes plenty of deer and small mammals, along with Bald eagles, turkeys, waterfowl, birds, snakes, turtles, and reptiles. It is a unique collection of sites, acquired to serve a unique purpose, and an enormous benefit to the ecosystem of the river.

From the FloteBote, the Big Muddy looks like wilderness. I wrote in my journal, "this looks like the setting for the *Last of the Mohicans*, just without the mountains."

I drove the FloteBote almost eighteen miles, reveling in being on the river after my day on land. We saw Canada geese in large numbers for the first time; there had been a few families of them, clustered together, in Iowa and Nebraska, but here they were beginning to flock. Canada geese overwinter in Missouri, and their numbers expand as birds from farther north migrate down to join them.

The boat traffic had dwindled as well; at one point we went more than an hour without seeing anyone. Mary asked if we could pull over to the southern shore for a few moments, and I turned the wheel over to Rod. We dropped anchor and all got off. I walked down the first real sandy beach we'd stopped on, maybe ten feet wide. There were big deer tracks in the sand leading down to the water's edge. It had become a beautiful day on the river, blue sky and lofty, puffy clouds, and I rolled my shoulders a little and stared out over the river, watching the swarms of bugs rise in small, silvery clouds from the surface, like balloons. The water was much cooler than it had been, presumably because of the weather the day before.

I carefully put aquatic cottonmouths out of my mind, sloshed back out, and hoisted myself carefully back onto the boat. The land along the river was significantly hillier than anywhere we had been so far, and Dirk said we must be in the vicinity of the Katy Trail.

The Katy Trail is the longest continuous rail trail in the United States. Running 240 miles from Clinton, a little south of Fort Osage, to Machens, near the Missouri–Mississippi confluence, the trail follows the former railroad right-of-way of the Missouri–Kansas–Texas, or MKT, Railroad. In 1968 the National Trails System Act was created to encourage people to return to the outdoors, and in 1982, the first section of the Katy Trail—named by dropping the "M" from the railroad's nickname—was opened. It is a wildly popular outdoor destination in the region for walking, running, bicycling, and horseback riding. Most of the trail runs along the northern bank of the river, winding between a fully natural setting and the small towns that rose up along the railroad's route. There are plans to add to the trail; in 2016 a forty-four-mile section called the Rock Island Spur branched northwest, nearly to Kansas City, and there is talk of connecting the Katy Trail to an interstate system of recreational trails in Kansas, Nebraska, and Iowa.

We were shooting for the Miami Access campground for the night, an undeveloped campsite above a boat ramp on the northern bank, pretty far from anything. There hadn't been a riverside boat fueling station since Kansas City, more than two days earlier, so part of our day involved loading the gas cans into the van. Our plan for the next day would have us spend the night at the only place offering riverside fuel between Kansas City and St. Louis: Cooper's Landing Campgrounds and Marina, outside Columbia.

We'd been hearing about Cooper's Landing since our first day on the river. Almost daily, whether we were speaking to boaters and fishers or people in restaurants and gas stations, someone would tell us that we had to stop in Cooper's Landing. And inevitably they would add, almost whispering with reverence, that they'd heard that Cooper's Landing had a Thai food truck that we had to try.

They weren't wrong.

Cooper's Landing is a year-round campsite, marina, and store right on the bank of the river. The store has food, bait, ice, and camping gear, plus beer, wine, and drinks. The river frontage of the store has an open porch that runs the length of the building, with a big painted sign across the back wall that reads BROADWAY. On Thursday, Friday, and Saturday nights, bands come in and perform on the porch or the adjacent stage, in front of an assemblage of picnic tables. Other nights, there are open mic shows. There are tent campsites and RV hookups, and the store arrays a handful of rental tents. There's what appears to be a bike repair shop, or maybe a bike rental, or perhaps both. And, of course, there is the food truck.

The marina offers a boat ramp, a floating dock, and plenty of space to tie up a boat. It's nowhere near as big as N. P. Dodge in Omaha, or as protected from the river as Pop-n-Doc's in Decatur, but people can launch canoes and kayaks from there, and any other private boat on the river can come in and enjoy dinner and a show.

But we wouldn't get there for another day. In the late afternoon, we passed under a tall highway bridge and spotted the boat ramp at Miami Access. People were hustling fishing boats onto boat trailers backed into the river, and above the river on the bluff we could see campfire smoke and a number of tents. We anchored the boat fore and aft and walked up to meet Rod. He'd already gotten us a campsite, so we climbed into the van and drove about ten miles to the town of Marshall, to have dinner in a nice Mexican place.

When we got back to the river, we brought the tents from the Flote-Bote and put them up. It was too hot to bother with a campfire, so we doused ourselves with bug spray. We'd brought folding camp chairs and a boat box up as well, so we sat down and decided to play cards. Mary had brought a cribbage board. Their grandmother, my great-grandmother, had taught me to play cribbage when I was about nine, on the porch at the lake, but I hadn't played since she died. Dirk gave me a quick refresher course and the three of them proceeded to thrash me in several quick games in succession.

There were seven pickup trucks in the parking lot. Plenty of other people were camping in big family-size tents around us, including one setup that involved a generator and what appeared to be a whole pig roasting on a spit. Music and laughter drifted past us and over the river. I'd said hello to a few people when I'd gone to the privy, and they were polite and friendly, though inevitably curious. I'm pretty sure we were the only campers who'd arrived by boat.

The people of the Missouri River Valley, from Montana to the Mississippi, make the most of the river, beyond drinking water and irrigation. It can be a dangerous proposition; a number of people drown every year. Some try to swim and get caught in the current and are dragged downstream until they are too tired to keep themselves above water. Some only wade in, but if they step in a hole they couldn't see and go down, they may not be able to get out in time. Officials up and down the river caution against swimming at all and encourage people to always wear flotation devices. But to me, engaging with the river is important, as long as it's done safely. Once you spend some time on a river, it becomes more real, somehow. More of an individual than a body of water. More a part of you. I'd spent one day off the river in the last twelve, and I'd missed it.

We couldn't survive without rivers, any of us. Without them we wouldn't have been able to spread around the planet, develop technologies, begin the Industrial Revolution. But they are more than simply a vehicle for our transportation or a tool for our resources. Around the world, people hold religious festivals to celebrate rivers. Any serious fly fisher will tell you that there is something meditative, maybe even holy, in the process of casting and reeling. Boats, especially canoes and kayaks, blend together the rhythm of paddling with a pace that permits, maybe even encourages, slowing down to watch the dance of the natural world. And it's a dance worth watching. These days, to quote Ferris Bueller, life moves pretty fast. But if you can get to a river, even if all you can do is sit on a rock on the bank and look at it, you'll find that things start to slow down. And once you find the rhythm of the river, it might help balance the rest.

After I'd lost my third game of cribbage, I pulled my camera out of my backpack and walked over to an oak on the edge of the bluff. Technically, we were facing north, but we had traveled out of the hills and were back to level ground on both banks. I stood, leaning against the tree, feeling the corners of the bark nudge into my T-shirt. The river smelled clean, and a little like fish, though maybe it's that fish all smell a little like rivers. The sun had sunk behind a thick bank of low clouds, and the surface of the river was rippling and golden. I leaned against the tree for a while, looking west. My time on the river was starting to run low, and I wanted to remember as much as I could.

12

Governing a River

Away, we're bound away, 'cross the wide Missouri.

—"Oh Shenandoah," American folk song

We set off early the next morning, the early sun vanishing behind increasing clouds. It wasn't raining—the National Weather Service gave us a 40 percent chance of thunderstorms for the day—but it was overcast and chilly, and there was a solid headwind blowing up the river. It was slowing us down, of course, but it was also hard to keep up a cheerful attitude in the wind and cold. There was a surprising amount of debris in the river, mostly tree limbs, much more than we had seen before. I wondered if it was from the rainstorm a few days earlier, or if there was something in the geometry of the river channel here that made it easy for debris to accumulate. The banks were covered in riprap, which suggested that this part of the river had chronic erosion problems. The channel itself was decidedly narrower than it had been at the campground.

Despite it being a cool, cloudy Sunday morning (I'd finally remembered to look at my phone and figure out what day it was), we saw only a couple of fishing boats that morning, and no other traffic. One of the boats had sped up to pull next to us. The woman on board told us she liked our "tepee." The man, understandably, asked what we were doing. After a brief conversation, they pulled away, turned their boat around, and disappeared back upstream.

As we passed through the town of Glasgow, we saw several rusty old barges high on the south bank. One of them had grass growing on it, and I wondered if they'd been placed there to further stabilize the banks, or if they'd just been abandoned there. As we rounded another bend, a hiker emerged from the woods on the right bank and waved to us. But by and large, we were alone on the river. And despite the sound of our motor, I could almost imagine what it would be like to make this trip in a canoe.

What was surprising was how much maintenance the area still needed. Despite the effort on shoring up the banks, mile markers and daybeacons were either overgrown or tipped over. More worrying, in several places the "No anchor—gas line" signs were hidden in bushes, and hard to notice if you weren't focusing on the banks.

Perhaps the most complicated thing about the Missouri River is how it is, and how it isn't, governed. Fifty years before our trip, President John F. Kennedy signed into existence the Delaware River Basin Compact, the governing body for the Delaware River. The Delaware River Basin Commission, made up of the governors of the four states that the Delaware moves through, plus one presidential appointee, was the first organization of its kind. When Congress voted to approve the compact, they stated that "there is one river, one basin, all water resources are functionally interrelated, and each one is dependent on the other." Essentially, Congress acknowledged that the Delaware, and by proxy, all rivers, are unified systems, regardless of the politics on their banks.

Among other things, the compact means that if one state wants to do anything that will utilize or impact the river—build a plant on the banks or increase the share of water they pull from the river—the governors of all the states downstream get to vote on the project before it begins. The Delaware River and Bay Authority, which oversees the ports of Wilmington, Philadelphia, and Trenton, the largest freshwater port system in the world, has its own law enforcement division, handling anything criminal that happens on the Delaware, regardless of which states are involved. This, in addition to the various state and federal environmental agencies, means that all aspects of river management are handled by a single entity.

Unfortunately, the Missouri River, like most of the rivers in this country, doesn't have anything like this in place. There was a Missouri River Commission in the late nineteenth century, but it collapsed. Today, though the Missouri is bounded by only seven states, governance is incredibly complicated. Technically the Corps of Engineers is responsible for overseeing and supporting the six quadrants of Missouri River management: flood control, water supply, hydropower, commercial navigation, fish and wildlife. However, the day-to-day management of each of these involves a collection of agencies, from the Environmental Protection Agency, the U.S. Geological Survey, Fish and Wildlife, the National Park Service, to tribal and state departments of natural resources and fish and wildlife, and tribal, state, and local governments. And that's before interstate and interparty politics comes into the equation. There is no formal agreement between all the states regarding development along the river, though any such project has to go through state and local environmental regulatory checks. Once I asked someone who worked at the EPA why there wasn't some sort of pact between all these entities to deal with the overarching issues on the Missouri, like how to manage flooding, or how to work together on bank erosion and pollution.

He laughed.

"It's the West," he said. "We don't like being told what to do out here."

We had seen the Geological Survey launching a boat when we were in Nebraska, and we'd passed a Missouri State Police boat at a boat ramp a little below Kansas City. But apart from those two, and the tribal and park officials we met on land, we had seen no officials overseeing the river. And it was surprising to me that those we had seen hadn't had more questions, given that we looked like the awkward offspring of the *African Queen* and the escape raft from *Lost*.

We began moving between limestone hills, and the river narrowed considerably. A strange warm breeze kicked up, and I looked at the sky, but it still didn't look like rain. A Great Blue heron stood perfectly still on a rock in the shallows, its head stretched out in front of its body, perpendicular to the river, its long neck straight. It seemed unfazed by the cold.

I, on the other hand, was very cold. I had packed for a few weeks in late July and early August. All I had was a lightweight long-sleeved button-down shirt to put on over my tank top, which wasn't enough, or my raincoat, which was too much. I hunched a little and tried to focus on the huge limestone outcrops, wondering about the geology of Missouri and what all that soft rock meant in terms of bank erosion here.

It wasn't as long a day as the day of rain, but it felt much longer than it was. And just as I gave in and pulled my jacket out of the boat box,

Dirk said, "That must be it," and pointed. On the left bank we could see the tops of two good-sized boats tucked in behind a large jetty piled with large rocks. We turned toward it and saw that one of them was a small sternwheel paddleboat. The other was a low green houseboat with a dinghy hanging behind the stern, and a huge plastic swan on the overhang over the prow. It had what I thought of as a diving platform moored next to it, complete with a camp chair, looking like a permanent fixture. We'd arrived in Cooper's Landing.

There was a second jetty piled with rocks on the downstream side of the paddleboat, and the bank between the jetties was piled with broken slabs of concrete. Above the bank, the end of an RV trailer peeked out of the trees. Behind the lower jetty, a floating dock with a trio of moored fishing boats reached downstream. We got the FloteBote tied up to the dock, and Mary headed up to the store and stage area in search of a bathroom. Dirk and I got everything sorted out and followed her. Near the top, a man was sitting in a beach chair, apparently unsnarling some fishing line.

"Where are you headed?" he asked, looking at us and then at the FloteBote.

"St. Louis," Dirk said.

"Hell in a handbasket," I followed. They both laughed. The man started asking about logistics and details, and I excused myself to also find the bathroom. When I came out, Rod had found Mary and Dirk. The campsites were all full and we couldn't sleep on the boat, so we were going to have to find a motel for the night, which made me sad. My last night on the river would be spent inland.

We walked over to the food truck and had a look at the menu. I ran back down to the boat to get my wallet. The guy with the fishing line was gone, but down on the edge of the dock, three twenty-somethings sat on the rocks, smoking. One of them was strumming a guitar. The young man closest to the dock turned and smiled at me as I came toward him.

"You must be one of the lucky ones who owns a boat," he said, smiling again.

"That depends on your definitions of both 'luck' and 'boat,'" I said, and pointed. All three of them stared at it for a minute and then burst out laughing.

After I'd gotten my wallet, I walked over to the jetty to have a look at the paddleboat. It was enormous compared to the FloteBote. It had a long front cabin with a wheelhouse on top, and a smaller two-story rear cabin with a patio deck on half the roof. A small sign on the port wall of the wheelhouse read *Joseph M. LaBarge*.

The human Joseph LaBarge was one of the most famous steamboat captains of the Missouri and Mississippi Rivers. He was one of the first to successfully pilot a steamboat to Montana and had once sailed with Abraham Lincoln aboard. The steamboat *Joseph LaBarge*, it turns out, is a houseboat that is permanently docked at Cooper's Landing, owned and lived on by a retired college professor and his wife. *The Swan*, the smaller, more traditional houseboat, travels around, but was in Cooper's Landing for the time being.

I got back up to the picnic area and went into the store, where I grabbed a bottle of water and a Boulevard beer. The beer was $3; the sign explained that if you didn't have cash, they would ring up your items, add $21 to the total for your credit card, and give you $20 back. At the food truck, a poster on the wall read "Chim's Thai Kitchen: Authentic Thai Food on the bank of the Missouri River." Entrées were $8, appetizers $2. I was dying to find out the backstory on Chim and the Thai kitchen, but there was an open mic happening and the chef was very busy. I ordered green curry with chicken, and while it was very spicy, it was delicious.

The four of us sat at the picnic table for an hour or so, listening to the music. As I suspected, the trio from down by the dock took the stage at one point. Another man followed and sang a song about falling in love with a girl from Delaware. Finally, Dirk and I went back to the FloteBote to make sure the boat was secure and collect our bags, and we got in the Vanagon once more. We checked into the Stoney Creek Hotel in Columbia, which for unknown reasons had a two-thirds-size plastic moose statue in their front yard. I took a shower to get myself warm and went to bed.

The next morning, I went down to the hotel's continental breakfast on my own, deeply conflicted. It was my last day. I had to get off the boat in Jefferson City and make my way to the friend of a friend's to spend the night; my friend was driving down from South Dakota to spend the night with me and then drive me back to my car in Iowa City.

FIG. 9. Store and main stage at Cooper's Landing. Photo by the author.

All these pieces were already in motion. I also needed to get home. I'd already been gone almost three weeks, and it would take me two days to drive back to Delaware.

But now I badly wanted to cancel those plans, to finish the trip all the way to St. Louis and figure out how to get to Iowa City from there. Call the house sitter caring for the dog and cat at home and see if she could stand another three or four days. I didn't want to say goodbye to the FloteBote. To the cousins. To the river.

I got a cup of coffee and walked outside to get a better look at the moose and think. After a while, still unsure, I went back in, got another coffee and one for Mary, and went up to our room to pack my bag.

Cooper's Landing is quiet on a Monday morning, even in August. We passed a couple riding out on bicycles, probably headed for the Katy Trail, and Rod dropped us by the store. He was going to work a little and then meet us at a park in Jefferson City. Mary gave me a half hug once we got on the boat.

"I'm sorry you're going," she whispered, and I smiled at her.

"Me too," I said.

We got off the dock and steered back into the river. Once again, there was quite a bit of small flotsam in the river, which made it hard to imagine what the river must have looked like before all the engineering was put into place.

After catastrophic floods in 1942 and 1943, Congress asked the Corps of Engineers to come up with a proposal to control the Missouri River. In response, two men, Lieutenant General Lewis Pick of the Corps of Engineers and Regional Director William Sloan of the Bureau of Reclamation in Billings, Montana, developed what would become known as the Pick–Sloan Plan. Pick–Sloan, authorized by the 1944 Flood Control Act, called for 107 separate dam and levee projects in the Missouri and Yellowstone River Basins, which included on tributaries of the two rivers. The Corps of Engineers was put in charge of flood control, navigation, and five major dams. The Bureau of Reclamation was authorized to build twenty-seven dams in the Yellowstone basin, and both organizations would share responsibility of hydroelectric power generation. President Franklin Roosevelt approved it, then named the Missouri River Basin Development Program, in 1944, and approved $200 million in funding, a startling amount given that World War II was simultaneously reaching its peak.

Some members of Congress instead proposed the creation of a Missouri Valley Authority, based on the success of the Tennessee Valley Authority, which provides hydroelectric power to all of Tennessee and parts of six other states. However, the proposal met with resistance in Congress, and Pick–Sloan went into action. Pick–Sloan built five of the six hydroelectric dams from Montana to South Dakota; the Fort Peck dam was part of the WPA program in the 1930s.

The most immediate victims of the Pick–Sloan Plan were, almost inevitably, Native people. More than 680,000 acres—550 square miles—of tribal lands were seized for the reservoirs, affecting twenty-three reservations, this despite treaty language that promised that no further land would be taken from the tribes. Nine hundred Native families were "relocated" to higher ground, ground both less hospitable and less fertile than the land along the river's banks. The reservoirs destroyed 90 percent of the tribe's timber and 75 percent of their game and plants. The "new" land couldn't support livestock. And the tribes had to dig up their own dead and relocate their cemeteries. Vine

Deloria Jr., a historian and member of the Standing Rock Sioux Tribe, wrote that the "Pick-Sloan Plan was, without doubt, the single most destructive act ever perpetrated on any tribe by the United States."

The most significant native land loss during the Pick–Sloan era happened in North Dakota, at the Fort Berthold Reservation. The Three Affiliated Tribes, Mandan, Hidatsa, and Arikara—the same people who had hosted Lewis and Clark and the Corps of Discovery over their first winter, and who introduced them to Sakakawea—had survived smallpox, cholera, and the Sioux Wars, and were thriving on the banks of the Upper Missouri, in a place called the Missouri River Breaks. The floodplain on Fort Berthold was rich farmland, and while the people of the Three Affiliated Tribes weren't making much income, they were amply providing for themselves, and maintaining the land that had been "their inherent property since time immemorial," according to a 1945 tribal resolution and the conditions of their treaty with the U.S. government.

Enter plans for the Garrison Dam. The Garrison Dam and its reservoir, Lake Sakakawea, would submerge 95 percent of the Three Affiliated Tribes' land. When tribal members refused to sell, the government threatened to condemn the properties and then pay even less than they had offered. In 1949 the tribes sent ten carefully chosen representatives to Washington to explain the ramifications of the dam to Congress and the impact the land loss would have on their people. The tribes had treaties, sovereignty, the Dawes Act, and basic human rights on their side.

The government ignored all of these. The final settlement, about $12.5 million, was still $9 million less than the tribes expected, and came to about $33 an acre. By 1954 the tribes had been relocated to New Town, North Dakota. The village life they had established on the Missouri Breaks was not supported during the move, and families were scattered across the reservation on isolated properties. Many left the reservation for good. It would take nearly fifty years for the federal government to admit fault and compensate the Three Affiliated Tribes fully for their land.

Of course, the dams generate electricity and, apart from extreme weather events, do help control flooding. However, the channel work done to make the river navigable for barge traffic and the subsequent erosion and habitat damage have resulted in the Corps of Engineers and Fish and Wildlife reworking as much of the river as possible. And that program, the Missouri River Recovery Program, is subject to the constant push and pull of the many political forces that operate around the river.

The Corps of Engineers, a division of the U.S. Army, takes orders from Congress. They are directed to manage complex environmental systems and, most of the time, receive only fractions of the funding they request to meet those orders. Likewise, the Fish and Wildlife Service is required by the Endangered Species Act to protect and preserve all threatened or endangered species, but their funding is not sufficient, and certainly not enough to adapt their restoration plans as they learn what works and what doesn't. And both organizations are also subject to the heavy crosswinds of local, state, and federal political will. In the meantime, all the agencies tied to the river do what they can with whatever they have.

As we made our way downstream, the sun came out. Another carp jumped next to the boat, just into my eyeline. It had to have been two feet long and jumped at least three feet in the air.

There was a loud noise, sort of a combination of a crunch and a bang. Dirk swore and immediately pulled the boat out of gear.

"It has to be a big branch," he said, as Mary and I hung over the rails, trying to see. We drifted for a few seconds, and then Dirk put the motor in reverse and backed us off of what turned out to be about a seven-foot tree limb.

"Well," Dirk said, smiling, "if we hadn't gotten that done quickly, that thing would have jammed our rudder and we'd have been in real trouble."

Dirk has been boating on Puget Sound for decades and has had a lot of experience with all manner of boating situations, thank heavens. Apparently if you do spot a large, floating piece of debris too late to steer around it, you can shut off the motor and drift into it, then throw a fixed stern anchor in. Once it takes hold, the anchor, theoretically, will whip the boat around in the current and pull the boat off the object.

This is not a maneuver I would feel comfortable attempting, even in the fourteen feet of water in the Missouri.

We checked the pontoons as best we could as Dirk carefully steered us around the branch.

The river widened, and I took over steering, now fixated on the muddy surface of the water, searching for any indicators of logs or branches.

I was steering us down the channel on the left side of the river when a small pilot boat began crossing toward us from across the river. As they got closer, Mary said, "It's the police."

I had the exact same feeling that I get in the car when a police car appears in the rearview mirror with its lights on. Even if I'm driving the speed limit, even if I know that there is no reason why a police officer would pull me over, I get a jolt of nervous adrenaline, wondering if regardless of all this, I am about to be pulled over, followed by a sense of relief when they speed past me. But in this instance, there was no one else for the police to be speeding toward.

One of them announced over a PA system for me to kill the motor, and the adrenaline pump in my brain went into high gear. Dirk whispered to me: "Be charming."

I shut off the motor and the police boat pulled alongside the FloteBote. There were two men on board, and one of them moved to the side of their boat and grabbed hold of our deck rail. They shut off their motor as well and we all began, slowly, to revolve in the current. The cop holding the boats together asked for my driver's license and the boat registration. Mary passed me my wallet, and Dirk pulled out the big Ziploc bag of important papers and began shuffling through them.

I pulled out my license and passed it to them, smiling as charmingly as I could. They didn't smile back. The cop in the boat took it and pulled out a laptop. He peered at my license in the bright sun and started typing. Dirk handed over the FloteBote's registration, and the one holding us together started asking Dirk and Mary about flotation devices. I was still watching the one on the laptop, hoping my unattributed guilt wasn't showing. My friends tell me that I have no poker face abilities whatsoever. And still we spun slowly downstream in the current, like two sumo wrestlers slowly trying to grapple each other to the mat.

The standing cop asked Dirk what we were doing out here, and he and Mary began explaining about the boat and the trip and who we all were to each other. I couldn't see the cop's eyes behind his sunglasses, but he did manage to keep his mouth from falling open. After what seemed like half an hour, I tried to smile charmingly at the cop on the laptop.

"So, am I wanted for anything?" I asked him.

He didn't look up.

"Not yet," he said, and tapped the keyboard again.

Maybe the Wi-Fi booster on the boat wasn't as strong as it could have been, out in the middle of the river. Maybe time moves more slowly when you're on one of a pair of boats, held together by a human body, making lazy, counterclockwise loops in the middle of the longest river in America. Maybe being pulled over in somebody else's state, whether in a car or a boat, is more worrying simply because you aren't sure what the rules are. Maybe it's a combination. Whatever it is, the more I peeked at the cop on the computer, the more nervous I became.

He finally shut the laptop, put it back in the wheelhouse, and stood up. He passed me back my license.

"All good, then?" I asked.

"You're not wanted today," he said, stone-faced, and then smiled.

Dirk asked why they'd pulled us over. The one holding the railing pointed toward pontoon at the prow.

"We've never seen a registration number that short before," he said.

Apparently there really aren't a lot of forty-year-old boats sailing down the Missouri River.

They told us that they could have ticketed us for failing to have a throwable device on board, but since Mary had promised that she would call Rod and have him buy one, they would let us go. The one holding the railing told me to wait to turn on my motor until they'd moved off. He dropped our railing and moved back into the boat, and the one with the laptop started their motor once they'd drifted ten or so feet away from us. I turned the wheel to at least straighten us out, and once they'd started heading upstream, started our motor again.

I looked at Dirk and grinned.

"Very charming," he said. "But Mary gets the credit for this one."

I looked around at the banks, trying to figure whether we'd missed a daybeacon while pirouetting down the river, decided we hadn't, and got us back in the boat channel and back under way.

I'm sure that every state police department in the country has a water patrol; we all have lakes and rivers and some of us have oceans, and I'm sure that the police use them for emergencies and water search and rescue and so forth. The Missouri State Police Water Patrol has responsibilities on the Missouri, the Mississippi, the Osage River, the Lake of the Ozarks, and undoubtedly a host of other bodies of water. I didn't ask them why they were out on the water that day, or what a patrol day on the river looked like, and I doubt they would have told me if I had.

According to their website, the Missouri Water Patrol oversees boater education, handles navigation markers, issues permits to marine events like the MR340, and offers water search and rescue. But I'm not sure how jurisdiction is handled on the river, because technically, the river isn't within Missouri's jurisdiction. Technically, the Missouri River belongs to the United States government.

In 1824 the U.S. Supreme Court heard a case arguing that one state on a multistate river could not enable shipping monopolies by granting exclusive shipping permits to one company for a whole state. *Gibbons v. Ogden* had to do with steamboats on the Hudson River, and specifically with the section of the Hudson that is bounded by New Jersey on the east. The court determined that the commerce clause of the Constitution gave the federal government, and not the states, jurisdiction over interstate commerce, which included "navigable waters." Justice John Marshall wrote in the opinion that "power over commerce, including navigation, was one of the primary objects for which the people of America adopted their government."

Technically, then, the U.S. Coast Guard is responsible for the navigational aids along the Missouri, distant as it is from any U.S. coastline. The Corps of Engineers oversees dams and maintenance, the EPA administers the air and water, and Fish and Wildlife manages the fauna. Everything else is a patchwork of state and local agencies. Arguably this is the easiest to manage once the river turns inland into Missouri, which may explain why we didn't see any marine law enforcement for almost six hundred miles.

I don't know if an interstate compact between the seven states that abut the Missouri would make things better or worse along the 2,300 miles of the river. But I wish they would consider it. Despite the combative politics of the twenty-first century, the thing Americans have always been good at is compromise. The Missouri is a big, complex system, and the issues it's facing will only get more challenging as the planet grows warmer. From drinking water, irrigation, and pollution

FIG. 10. Bridges over the Missouri. Photo by the author.

to navigation, both commercial and recreational, the people—and the river—would benefit.

About an hour after our midriver run-in with the police, just upstream from a big bridge, the gold dome of the old state capitol gleaming in the sun on the southern bank, we pulled up to the bank at the Ellis–Porter Riverside Park in Jefferson City. A man was sitting on a bench, watching us place the anchor. Rod was heading down the path from the parking lot, and Mary passed him going up to the public bathrooms. I sifted through the contents of my boat box, stuffing everything loose back into my backpack. In a corner of the deck, behind my box, I spotted a washer that looked brand new, like it had ended up on the boat in case we needed to do some minor repair. I looked around the boat and then picked it up and stuffed it in my pocket.

The man walked up and asked us what the story was just as Mary got back to the boat. She told him the same story we'd told everyone down the river, and he laughed just like they had. But he stopped when she got to "And then we're going to give the boat away."

"Really?" he asked. "Who are you giving it to?"

"Anyone who wants it," she said.

I jumped off the boat and walked up to the restrooms. When I came out, he was putting his cell phone back in his pocket. It turned out that his ex-brother-in-law had a house on the Osage River, and he was on his way to the park now, to see about taking the boat once the cousins made it to St. Louis.

The ex-brother-in-law showed up, and I watched him eye up the boat. He talked to Dirk and Mary for a while, and I climbed back on board. I sat down one last time on my empty box and looked around. Both Rod and Mary came up to hug me and say goodbye. They promised to let me know how the rest of the trip went, and I promised to check in every night until I got home. And, as the future owner of the FloteBote walked back up to the parking lot, I pulled my backpack onto my shoulders and jumped down into the Missouri for the final time. I bent down and filled my hand with brownish river water. I raised it to my face and sniffed it, and then opened my fingers and watched it drain back into the river.

"I'll see you again," I whispered.

Dirk had decided to drive me to the friend's house, so I dropped my pack in the sand and he and I waded in to push the boat back out into the river. Mary turned and waved, and I waved back. And she and Rod started the motor, turned the boat downstream, and headed down to cross under the bridge.

Earlier, after we'd gotten free of the police and I'd turned the driving duties over to Mary, I'd sat in the sun and watched the river ahead of me and decided that it didn't matter where I got off. There wasn't much difference between finishing Jefferson City or St. Louis. Or Memphis. Or New Orleans. Wherever I got off was going to be hard, because leaving the river was going to be hard. And that was a good thing. Somewhere in the six hundred miles between Sioux City and Jefferson City, somewhere in the mud and the thrum and the current, somewhere, the river had made its way inside me and taken up residence. I would never completely leave it behind.

Epilogue

> The river has great wisdom, and whispers
> its secrets to the hearts of men.
>
> —Mark Twain

What, then, is a river?

Rivers have always been significant to humans, far beyond drinking water and transportation. Since at least the middle of the first millennium, Hindus have celebrated Maha Kumbh Mela, a rite held every twelve years. During the auspicious days of the celebration, pilgrims travel to one of four holy rivers in India where, according to Hindu tradition, the gods dripped nectar from a pitcher—a *kumbh*—to calm the waters. The pilgrims immerse themselves in the water, and the rivers carry their sins away. The 2013 Maha Kumbh Mela was the largest peaceful gathering of humans in the history of the world; on Valentine's Day, more than eighty million people washed themselves clean of sin in the Ganges.

The Hindus are not the only ones to ascribe religious meaning to rivers. Ancient Jews and early Christians alike revered the River Jordan. According to the Quran, the Nile and the Euphrates originate in Paradise. The Havasupai Indians of the American Southwest were building kivas—rooms built to hold, among other things, religious and ceremonial events—into their houses on the banks of the Colorado, at the bottom of the Grand Canyon, five hundred years before Columbus landed. And of all religious groups, Buddhists perhaps pay tribute to rivers the most beautifully; during the festival of Loy Krathong, small bowls filled with leaves, incense, and candles are floated onto the water, carrying bad luck away as the rivers carry the bowls off to the sea.

And so rivers are more than just water and rock and gravity and topography. They hold sacred spaces in our religions, philosophies, and art. Most of the landscape painters of antiquity and of the Renaissance—artists from Greece, Italy, France, the Netherlands, and the other great seagoing nations of history—painted the oceans, but in the late fifteenth century, the Flemish painter Simon Bening began painting rivers. By the nineteenth century, the American painters of the Hudson Valley School had brought river paintings into the forefront of the art world. And in my own corner of the country, the three generations of the Wyeth family began what is now called the Brandywine River School.

Likewise, much of our literature centers on rivers and their symbolic and metaphoric possibilities—of birth, baptism, and the cleansing of sin, of journeys, and of threats. From Joseph Conrad to Annie Dillard to Norman Maclean, rivers run through our literary consciousness and canon.

And then there's Twain.

Perhaps no one in literature—and certainly no one in American literature—has done as much for rivers as Mark Twain. He etched the Mississippi into the framework of the country's psyche, making it a sacred presence, a metaphor, and a warped version of an American Eden all at once. Huckleberry Finn arrived in U.S. bookstores in February of 1885, and ever since, everyone carrying a latent childhood fantasy—or even an adult one—of running away from home has had a model.

Twain's river is wide and dignified and slow-moving. It rolls majestically southward past his hometown of Hannibal, Missouri, extolled in song, verse, and print. Abraham Lincoln, upon hearing that General Grant had finally won the months-long siege of Vicksburg, Mississippi, in 1863, wrote in a campaign letter that "the Father of Waters again goes unvexed to the sea."

U.S. presidents have not waxed lyrical about the Missouri.

But, lyrical or not, rivers are essential to us. They generate our electricity, transport our goods, and provide our drinking water. From inner-city parks to quiet mountain passes, they provide us with scenery and recreation. The Missouri cuts through one of the richest swathes of farmland on the planet. At the head, it is home to Brown and Rainbow trout, and some of the premiere fly-fishing on the continent. Near its mouth, I met a fisherman who told me he'd shot a 125-pound catfish with a handgun when the catfish began winning the battle to get it on the boat. The long tradition of fishers lying through their teeth notwithstanding, apparently catfish that large aren't even unusual as the Missouri runs close to the Mississippi.

But rivers bring us something more as well. They serve us metaphorically, reminding us of forward motion, of baptism, and of rebirth. They offer the Zen lesson of flow, a concept both evocative of and a step further than Heraclitus's metaphysics. Zen Buddhists see rivers as lessons in acceptance and impermanence, showing us a willing adaptation to a changing world. A tree falls in a river, and the river moves through it, around it, or over it. Or perhaps all three at the same time. Whatever is the smoothest path. And so rivers teach us that the only way out is through.

Almost as soon as I got off the river, people began to ask me how the trip had changed me. Initially, my answer was that it hadn't. I hadn't had some kind of revelation that solved all my problems or changed my life or transformed me into the person I wanted to be. Now, in the decade that's gone by while I've worked on this book, my answer is different. It did change me. I hope that it made me more patient, somehow. More tolerant of change. More accepting of the things that are beyond my control, and more aware of just how many things are. Of the value of taking a risk. And of the remarkable capacity of people, relatives and strangers, to be kind. But maybe the most important thing it did was remind me how important it is to pay attention. To look and really see.

Moving downstream on a boat at a speed that a reasonably fit bicyclist could keep up with means that you have very little else to do but pay attention. Initially, the riverscape looks unendingly the same: water, trees, muddy banks, some birds, some insects. A monoculture. But as with most things, the longer you watch a river, the more you begin to see.

When I was about eleven years old, my father handed me a copy of *Pilgrim at Tinker Creek* by Annie Dillard. I didn't understand all of it, but what I took away from it even at that young age was the importance of bearing witness. It's not something we do very often, and apart from brief moments of great joy or great tragedy, it's not something we often do well. I don't know that I was actively bearing witness every second that I was on the river. Certainly, there were hours where I was cold and tired, or hot and tired, or just tired. Those moments tend to make you self-absorbed, and self-absorption doesn't lend itself to bearing witness. But there were moments when I managed it. Catching sight of a Bald eagle on a dead tree limb, her white head nearly invisible against the cloudy sky, her body blending with the bark of the tree, and wondering what she was thinking. Listening, on still mornings, to the sound of the river moving over its bed. Hearing stories about the cousins' lives, stories of my own family that I would never have learned otherwise. Watching the river change as the sun moved across the sky, or as the wind rose in the west. Looking up from the boat at night, watching the same constellations that Heraclitus and Sakakawea and Twain had watched.

Whenever I need a little peace, I pick up my key ring. There, between my house key and the old leather fob, is the washer I'd picked up out of the corner in my last moment on the boat. It reminds me that out there, 800 miles to the west of me, and then for 2,300 miles west of that, the Missouri is moving through the landscape. My time on the river was a single tick, one heartbeat in its history, which reaches back for millennia. I made no impact on the river. But it has made an enormous impact on me.

The day I drove the van from Orrick to Lexington, I took small, two-lane county roads instead of looking for highways. I wasn't ready for traffic or speed; I wanted to stay at the slow, rolling pace of the river. The county roads in Missouri use letters instead of numbers, and somewhere in the middle of the cornfields, alone on the road for as far as I could see, ahead or behind, I saw a county road sign. I braked, pulled the Vanagon onto the gravel shoulder, and got out. A little way ahead of me was a crossroads. I walked to the sign and looked up at it. At the top was a small horizontal sign that read JCT. Below it, two larger vertical rectangles next to each other: OZ. I laughed out loud, still alone, and went back to the van and got my camera. The Junction of Oz pretty much sums up the time I spent with the Missouri River.

I go back to the river every year, usually up above the engineered section, near Vermillion, South Dakota. Even in the midst of the engineered section, the Missouri is both immeasurably wild and incalculably sacred. It is a river of both destruction and creation, of contradiction and extremes, of failure and of possibility. No one can really see any river, apart from satellite images, or maybe from the International Space Station. The Missouri is too big, too long, too hyperbolic. But it's worth sitting on a river's bank, any river's bank, for an hour, or an afternoon, and letting it find its way into you. Like all rivers, the Missouri changes every day. The river I'll see this year won't be the same as the one I saw last year. But I know that however many times I go back—and I will, again and again—I'll never really see it.

Dirk said once that if we ever did this again, he'd slow down even more, run the motor only as much as we'd need it to steer, so we could really see the country as it went by. Maybe in fifteen or twenty years, I can do something like this again with my nephews, who will be adults by then, though if so I should probably go ahead and buy us an old pontoon boat now. Maybe we can go finish the 130 miles that I missed.

Three days after I got off the boat, Mary and Dirk pulled up to a dock in St. Louis and picked up Rod. The three of them motored the FloteBote through the confluence of the Mississippi and crossed it to Illinois, then turned the boat around and headed back to St. Louis. There, in a marina, the man we'd met in Jefferson City was waiting with a truck and a boat trailer. And Mary gave the FloteBote away, just as she'd planned.

I went to the Missouri with no real idea what I'd see, or what might happen. A lot happened, and I saw even more. I will always be pulled to the Missouri, and I'll always pay attention to what is happening with it. It is a big, muddy, nondescript river, but it is also stunningly beautiful, and it has its own personality. Even with everything we've done to it, when you're on it, you know that you are no longer entirely in charge.

The Missouri River is facing challenges on many fronts in the future, and it can't defend itself alone. From invasive species to climate change, what is happening on the Missouri will affect all of us, not just the people who live along it. And the same can be said for rivers all over the country, and all over the world. There are organizations and government divisions and scientists working on these issues, but they need our support. And so do the rivers. We need to stop thinking of them as things we drive over and start thinking of them, if not as persons, then at least as powerful, sensitive systems. Systems that we need if we're going to survive.

These days, when I see a river, I can see a lot more than I used to. I can recognize the places that have been structured, and the places where it's most likely to flood. I watch the wind across the surface, and watch the far bank, wondering what it would look like from the deck of a boat. I'm not a scientist or a hydrologist or a civil engineer. But I got to spend a couple of weeks living on the Missouri, and unlike Twain, the more time I spend with it, the more I admire it.

On the second day on the boat, I was sitting on my boat box, scribbling down something in my journal about wing dikes or birds or tow barges, when Rod came over and sat down near me. I looked up at him, and he nodded at my journal.

"What are your expectations for this trip?" he asked.

"Oh, nothing," I answered, and he looked a little surprised. "The river is going to give me whatever it gives me, and my job is to figure out what to do with whatever that turns out to be."

I'm still figuring that out. But for what it has given me, I will be forever grateful.

Bibliography

"About the Initiative." Sturgeonfest. Accessed September 25, 2024. https://sturgeonfest.org/about-the-initiative/.

"About Us." Iowa Tribe of Kansas and Nebraska. Accessed September 26, 2024. https://iowatribeofkansasandnebraska.com/about-us/.

Albeck-Ripka, Livia. "How to Scare an Invasive Fish? A Menacing Robot Predator." *New York Times*, December 16, 2021. https://www.nytimes.com/2021/12/16/science/mosquitofish-robot.html.

Almukhtar, Sarah, Blacki Migliozzi, John Schwartz, and Josh Williams. "The Great Flood of 2019: A Complete Picture of a Slow-Motion Disaster." *New York Times*, September 11, 2019. https://www.nytimes.com/interactive/2019/09/11/us/midwest-flooding.html.

American Philosophical Society. https://www.amphilsoc.org/.

Anderson, Aaron. "In Fight Against Invasive Carp, Missouri Scientists Explore New Frontier: Track the Babies." *Frederick News Post*, January 15, 2022. https://www.fredericknewspost.com/news/lifestyle/travel_and_outdoors/in-fight-against-invasive-carp-missouri-scientists-explore-new-frontier-track-the-babies/article_567dc006-43ff-5c1f-b8e8-e76fc5704938.html.

Anderson, Bryce. "Drought Maintains Grip on Western Corn Belt." DTN Progressive Farmer, November 17, 2022. https://www.dtnpf.com/agriculture/web/ag/news/article/2022/11/17/drought-maintains-grip-western-corn-2.

Anderson, Julie. "Nebraska, Iowa and Missouri Governors Meet in Omaha About Missouri River." *Omaha World-Herald*, December 14, 2023. https://omaha.com/news/state-regional/government-politics

/nebraska-iowa-and-missouri-governors-meet-in-omaha-about-missouri-river/article_b0aa2de2-9a0a-11ee-b65a-d7e5520c4f23.html.

Andreoni, Manuela. "Invasive Species Are Costing the Global Economy Billions, Study Finds." *New York Times*, September 4, 2023. https://www.nytimes.com/2023/09/04/climate/invasive-species-cost-ipbes.html.

Anthes, Emily, and Chang W. Lee. "Should We Change Species to Save Them?" *New York Times*, April 14, 2024. https://www.nytimes.com/2024/04/14/science/australia-wildlife-assisted-evolution.html.

"*Arabia*'s Story." *Arabia* Steamboat Museum. Accessed September 26, 2024. https://www.1856.com/arabia-story.

Arens, Curt. "Districts Protect Nebraska's Land Resources for 50 Years." *Nebraska Farmer*, September 15, 2021. https://www.farmprogress.com/husker-harvest-days/districts-protect-nebraska-s-land-resources-for-50-years.

"Asteraceae *Artemisia frigida Willd.*: Fringed Sagewort." Native American Ethnobotany Database. Accessed September 26, 2024. http://naeb.brit.org/uses/5242/.

"Basics." Applied River Engineering Center. Accessed September 25, 2024. https://www.mvs-wc.usace.army.mil/arec/Basics.html.

"Battle of Lexington State Historic Site." Missouri State Parks. Accessed August 13, 2025. https://mostateparks.com/park/battle-lexington-state-historic-site.

Baumel, C. Phillip, and Jerry Van Der Kamp. "Past and Future Grain Traffic on the Missouri River." Institute for Agriculture and Trade Policy, July 2003. https://www.iatp.org/sites/default/files/Past_and_Future_Grain_Traffic_on_the_Missouri_.pdf.

Baumhoff, Richard G. *The Dammed Missouri Valley: One Sixth of Our Nation*. Knopf, 1951.

"Báxoǰe: Maps, Material Culture, and Memory: On the Trail of the Ioway." Iowa Archaeology Month 2007. https://digital.lib.uiowa.edu/islandora/object/ui%3a29668/datastream/obj/view.

"Baxoje Wosgaci: Iowa Tribe Culture Center/Museum." PocketSights Tour Builder. Accessed September 25, 2024. https://pocketsights.com/tours/place/Baxoje-Wosgaci%3a-Iowa-Tribe-Culture-Center-Museum-1646:242.

Beck, Robert E. "The Wandering Missouri River: A Study in Accretion Law." *North Dakota Law Review* 43, no. 3 (1967): 429–66. https://commons.und.edu/ndlr/vol43/iss3/2/.

Berman, Mark, and Reis Thebault. "Two Dead, Two Missing amid 'Historic' Flooding Across the Midwest." *Washington Post*, March 18, 2019. https://www.washingtonpost.com/nation/2019/03/16/emergencies-declared-across-midwest-amid-historic-flooding/.

Bernhard, Blythe. "Mississippi River Is Second-Most Polluted U.S. Waterway." *St. Louis Post-Dispatch*, March 22, 2012. http://www.stltoday.com/lifestyles/health-med-fit/health/mississippi-river-is-second-most-polluted-u-s-waterway/article_bce8579e-7449-11e1-9b27-001a4bcf6878.html.

"Big Muddy National Fish and Wildlife Refuge." FWS.gov. Accessed September 26, 2024. https://www.fws.gov/refuge/big-muddy/map.

Blaine, Martha Royce. *The Ioway Indians*. University of Oklahoma Press, 1995.

Boggs, Kelsey. "'A Hero': Wolf Point Teen Drowns After Saving a Life in the Water." KTVQ, September 8, 2023. https://www.ktvq.com/news/local-news/a-hero-wolf-point-teen-drowns-after-saving-a-life-in-the-water.

Brown, Matthew. "Bridger Pipeline Break Spills 45,000 Gallons of Diesel in Wyoming." PBS, August 12, 2022. https://www.pbs.org/newshour/nation/bridger-pipeline-break-spills-45000-gallons-of-diesel-in-wyoming.

Brunkhorst, Marissa. "Missouri River Sandbars Closed to Protect Endangered Birds." SDPB, July 28, 2022. https://listen.sdpb.org/environment/2022-07-21/missouri-river-sandbars-closed-to-protect-endangered-birds.

Buck, Rinker. "How America's River Wanderers Built a Life on the Water." Literary Hub, August 8, 2022. https://lithub.com/how-americas-river-wanderers-built-a-life-on-the-water/.

"Buddhist Festivals and Special Days." Buddhanet. Accessed September 25, 2024. https://www.buddhanet.net/festival/.

Butler, James Davie. "The New Found Journal of Charles Floyd, a Sergeant Under Captains Lewis and Clark." *Proceedings of the American Antiquarian Society* 9, no. 1 (April 1894): 225–52. http://www.americanantiquarian.org/proceedings/44769410.pdf.

"Canoeing and Kayaking." National Park Service. Accessed September 25, 2024. https://www.nps.gov/mnrr/planyourvisit/canoeing-and-kayaking.htm.

"Chicago District." U.S. Army Corps of Engineers, Great Lakes and Ohio River Division. Accessed September 26, 2024. https://www.lrd.usace.army.mil/chicago/.

Chittenden, H. M. *History of Early Steamboat Navigation on the Missouri River*. Ross and Haines, 1962.

"Class of 1863: Charles W. Howell." *George W. Cullum's Biographical Register of the Officers and Graduates of the United States Military Academy at West Point, New York, since its establishment in 1802*. Accessed September 25, 2024. http://penelope.uchicago.edu/Thayer/E/Gazetteer/Places/America/United_States/Army/usma/Cullums_Register/2001*.html.

Coalition to Protect the Missouri River. "About the River." January 7, 2021. https://morivercoalition.org/about-the-river/.

Cohen, Jonathan B. *Management and Protection Protocols for the Threatened Piping Plover (Charadrius melodus) on Cape Hatteras National Seashore, North Carolina*. U.S. Geological Survey, Patuxent Wildlife Research Center, 2006. https://parkplanning.nps.gov/showFile.cfm?projectid=13331&mimetype=application/pdf&filename=102805+usgs+Protocols+-+Piping+Plover.pdf&sfid=17974.

Cohn, Amy L. *From Sea to Shining Sea: A Treasury of American Folklore and Folk Songs*. Illustrated by Molly Bang. Scholastic, 1993.

Columbia Environmental Research Center. Missouri River Natural Resource Bibliography. Accessed September 25, 2024. https://www.cerc.usgs.gov/pubs/moriver/morivbib.htm.

"Contractors Assemble a Dike in the Missouri River East of Jefferson City." *Columbia Missourian*, July 29, 2022. https://www.columbiamissourian.com/news/contractors-assemble-a-dike-in-the-missouri-river-east-of-jefferson-city/image_065fd260-0eb5-11ed-b4d1-3bfea93a9a2e.html.

"Cooley Lake Conservation Area: Missouri River—Excelsior Springs Junction, US." Paddling.com. Accessed September 26, 2024. https://paddling.com/paddle/locations/cooley-lake-river-access.

"Cooper Nuclear Station near Brownville Sandbagging as Missouri River Rises." *Omaha World-Herald*, March 14, 2019. https://omaha.com/news/nebraska/cooper-nuclear-station-near-brownville-sandbagging-as-missouri-river-rises/article_ab98ece2-cd55-5fd7-8b26-db197ca0e52e.html.

Cooper's Landing, MO. https://cooperslandingmo.com/.

Corbin, Annalies. *The Material Culture of Steamboat Passengers: Archaeological Evidence from the Missouri River*. Kluwer Academic, 2005.

Corbin, Annalies, and Bradley A. Rodgers. *The Steamboat Montana and the opening of the west: History, excavation, and architecture*. University Press of Florida, 2008.

Coren, Michael J. "What Happened When I Went Hunting for Iguanas in Florida's Suburbs." *Washington Post*, April 16, 2024. https://www.washingtonpost.com/climate-environment/2024/04/16/iguanas-invasive-florida-hunting/.

Cvannoy. "History: Jim Bridger Part 1, Beginnings and Tall Tales." Sheridan Media, October 8, 2022. https://sheridanmedia.com/news/117152/history-jim-bridger-part-1-beginnings-and-tall-tales/.

Dalton, David A. *The Natural World of Lewis and Clark*. University of Missouri Press, 2008.

"Dams, Climate Change Threaten Missouri River Cottonwood Forests." Yale Climate Connections, June 17, 2022. https://yaleclimateconnections.org/2022/06/dams-climate-change-threaten-missouri-river-cottonwood-forests/.

Darwin, Charles. "The Principal Works of Charles Darwin: *The Origin of Species*. *The Descent of Man*." In *Evolution and the Origin of Species*. John B. Alden, Publisher, 1886.

Davidson, Jordan. "Missouri River Drought Was Its Worst in 1,200 Years, Study Finds." EcoWatch, December 9, 2021. https://www.ecowatch.com/missouri-river-drought-climate-crisis-2645979607.html.

"The Day the President—and the World—Got a Stunning View of the Flood of 1993." *St. Louis Post-Dispatch*, July 17, 2023. https://www.stltoday.com/news/archives/the-day-the-president---and-the-world---got-a-stunning-view/article_fef70b40-c0f4-53dc-b575-4b42a17c39a5.html.

DeLonay, Aaron J., Kimberly A. Chojnacki, Robert B. Jacobson, Patrick J. Braaten, Kevin J. Buhl, Caroline M. Elliott, et al. *Ecological Requirements for Pallid Sturgeon Reproduction and Recruitment in the Missouri River—Annual Report 2014*. Open-File Report 2016-1013. U.S. Geological Survey, in cooperation with the U.S. Army Corps of Engineers, Missouri River Recovery Program—Integrated Science Program, 2016. https://pubs.usgs.gov/of/2016/1013/ofr20161013.pdf.

"Desalination Plants, Not Mississippi River Water, Are the Solution to West's Water Needs." *Desert Sun*, July 13, 2022. https://www.desertsun.com/story/opinion/readers/2022/07/13/desalination-not-mississippi-river-water-solution-west-drought/10025117002/.

De Voto, Bernard. *Across the Wide Missouri*. Houghton Mifflin, 1998.

De Waal, Louise C., Andrew R. G. Large, P. M. Wade, and P. Max Wade. *Rehabilitation of Rivers: Principles and Implementation*. Wiley, 1998.

Dickey, Michael E. *People of the River's Mouth: In Search of the Missouria Indians*. University of Missouri Press, 2014.

Dobney, Fredrick J. *River Engineers on the Middle Mississippi: A History of the St. Louis District, U.S. Army Corps of Engineers*. U.S. Army Corps of Engineers, 1978.

"Dock and Swim Area Products: Weed and Muck Control." Lake Restoration. Accessed September 6, 2024. https://www.lakerestoration.com/product/dock-swim-area-products/.

Donnella, Leah. "The Standing Rock Resistance Is Unprecedented (It's Also Centuries Old)." NPR, November 22, 2016. https://www.npr.org/sections/codeswitch/2016/11/22/502068751/the-standing-rock-resistance-is-unprecedented-it-s-also-centuries-old.

Doppelt, Bob. *Entering the Watershed: A New Approach to Save America's River Ecosystems*. Island Press, 1993.

Douglas, Walter B., and Abraham Phineas Nasatir. *Manuel Lisa*. Argosy-Antiquarian, 1964.

"Down Year for Missouri River Hydropower." Radio 570 WNAX. Accessed September 25, 2024. https://wnax.com/news/180081-down-year-for-missouri-river-hydropower/.

"Dredge *Goetz* Makes Rare Visit to Missouri River." *Waterways Journal*, November 12, 2021. https://www.waterwaysjournal.net/2021/11/12/dredge-goetz-makes-rare-visit-to-missouri-river/.

"Dredging Is Key to Missouri River Repairs." *Waterways Journal*, July 5, 2023. https://www.waterwaysjournal.net/2023/07/04/dredging-is-key-to-missouri-river-repairs/.

Dulle, Brian. "Atchison Asking People to Limit Water Use due to Ice Jam in the Missouri River." KSN, December 21, 2022. https://www.ksn.com/weather/weather-stories/atchison-asking-people-to-limit-water-use-due-to-ice-jam-in-the-missouri-river/.

Duncan, Dayton. *Scenes of Visionary Enchantment: Reflections on Lewis and Clark*. University of Nebraska Press, 2013.

Dura, Jack. "North Dakota Missouri River Acreage Adjustment Releases $120M." *Bismarck Tribune*, October 4, 2022. https://bismarcktribune.com/news/state-and-regional/north-dakota-missouri-river-acreage-adjustment-releases-120m/article_88b1502e-43fb-11ed-ba8e-cbe8eb019ca0.html.

Dyer, Robert L. "A Brief History of Steamboating on the Missouri River with an Emphasis on the Boonslick Region." *Boone's Lick Heritage* 5, no. 2 (June 1997). https://web.archive.org/web/20101128113801/http://riverboatdaves.com/docs/moboats.html.

Ebert, Joel. "The Great Flood: Recalling the Missouri River Flood and Ice Gorges of 1881." *Capital Journal*, September 24, 2019. https://www

.capjournal.com/news/the-great-flood-recalling-the-missouri-river-flood-and-ice-gorges-of-1881/article_74bb4c08-8a3e-11e3-9ea6-0019bb2963f4.html.

"Educator Guide: Earth's Fresh Water." *National Geographic*. Accessed September 26, 2024. https://education.nationalgeographic.org/resource/earths-fresh-water/.

"Effigy Mounds National Monument: Effigy Moundbuilders." National Park Service. Accessed September 26, 2024. https://www.nps.gov/efmo/learn/historyculture/effigy-moundbuilders.htm.

Eggert, Amanda. "High Temperatures Trigger Widespread Fishing Restrictions in Montana, Yellowstone." Associated Press, July 23, 2024. https://apnews.com/us-news/waterways-montana-heat-waves-general-news-6fc51ec1d032f36fee269c0bf9aa5a63.

Eggert, Timothy. "Army Corps to Implement 'Lessons Learned' from 2022 Low Water Levels." FarmWeek Now, June 11, 2024. https://www.farmweeknow.com/policy/national/army-corps-to-implement-lessons-learned-from-2022-low-water-levels/article_24408690-e9ce-11ed-b33c-f3a6f7d76da2.html.

Einhorn, Catrin. "The Most Important Global Meeting You've Probably Never Heard of Is Now." *New York Times*, October 14, 2021. https://wwpw.nytimes.com/2021/10/14/climate/un-biodiversity-conference-climate-change.html.

Eligon, John, and Richard Pérez-peña. "Record Floods Affect Millions in the Midwest." *New York Times*, December 30, 2015. https://www.nytimes.com/2015/12/31/us/missouri-flooding-st-louis-mississippi.html.

Ervin, Heather. "Missouri Port Secures $3.5 Million in Grants for River Terminal Infrastructure." Marine Log, July 13, 2022. https://www.marinelog.com/inland-coastal/inland/missouri-port-secures-3-5-million-in-grants-for-river-terminal-infrastructure/.

"Eurasian Watermilfoil (Myriophyllum Spicatum)." Minnesota Department of Natural Resources, August 1, 2024. https://www.dnr.state.mn.us/invasives/aquaticplants/milfoil/index.html.

"Eurasian Water-Milfoil (Myriophyllum spicatum)." Weeds Gone Wild: Alien Plant Invaders of Natural Areas. Accessed September 26, 2024. https://www.invasive.org/alien/pubs/midatlantic/mysp.htm.

Everett, Avery. "Army Corps of Engineers Signs Off on Flood Resiliency Study in Jefferson City." KOMU, November 28, 2022. https://www.komu.com/news/midmissourinews/army-corps-of-engineers-signs-off-on-flood-resiliency-study-in-jefferson-city/article_0b9cdf3e-6f4f-11ed-9e22-0baf03ffee35.html.

Ewers, John C. *The Blackfeet: Raiders on the Northwestern Plains*. University of Oklahoma, 2003.

Ewing, Tom. "US Inland Waterways: Looking for Rainmakers." MarineLink, November 10, 2022. https://www.marinelink.com/news/us-inland-waterways-looking-rainmakers-500857.

"Faces of Standing Rock: Stories from the Pipeline Protest." *Billings Gazette*, November 20, 2016. https://billingsgazette.com/news/state-and-regional/montana/faces-of-standing-rock-stories-from-the-pipeline-protest/collection_761b7934-910f-5dd8-a557-41b499fb0a24.html.

"Fact Sheet 30: Dredge Fleet." U.S. Army Corps of Engineers, St. Paul District, May 24, 2015. https://www.mvp.usace.army.mil/Media/Fact-Sheets/Fact-Sheet-Article-View/Article/588283/fact-sheet-30-dredge-fleet/.

Fairholme, William, and Jack B. Tykal. *Journal of an Expedition to the Grand Prairies of the Missouri, 1840*. Arthur H. Clark, 1996.

Farzan, Shahla, John Dankosky, and Charles Bergquist. "What Worsening Floods Mean for Superfund Sites." Science Friday, April 26, 2024. https://www.sciencefriday.com/segments/superfund-sites-flooding-climate-change/.

Fears, Darryl. "America's Longest River Was Recently Drier Than During the Dust Bowl. And It's Bound to Happen Again." *Washington Post*, May 11, 2020. https://www.washingtonpost.com/climate-environment/2020/05/11/missouri-river-drought-climate-change/.

———. "Drought Threatens to Halt Critical Barge Traffic on Mississippi." *Washington Post*, January 6, 2013. https://www.washingtonpost.com/national/health-science/drought-threatens-to-halt-critical-barge-traffic-on-mississippidrought-threatens-to-halt-critical-barge-traffic-on-mississippidrought-threatens-to-halt-critical-barge-traffic-on-mississippi/2013/01/06/92498b88-5694-11e2-bf3e-76c0a789346f_story.html.

Ferrell, John, and George Kishmar. *Soundings: 100 Years of the Missouri River Navigation Project*. U.S. Army Corps of Engineers, 1995. https://apps.dtic.mil/sti/tr/pdf/ADA322235.pdf.

Fettig, David. "Missouri River Is the Lifeblood of the Northern Great Plains." Federal Reserve Bank of Minneapolis, April 1, 1992. https://www.minneapolisfed.org/article/1992/missouri-river-is-the-lifeblood-of-the-northern-great-plains.

Flavelle, Christopher, Somini Sengupta, and Mira Rojanasakul. "How America's Diet Is Feeding the Groundwater Crisis." *New York Times*,

December 25, 2023. https://www.nytimes.com/interactive/2023/12/24/climate/groundwater-crisis-chicken-cheese.html.

Flavelle, Christopher, Raymond Zhong, Zach Levitt, and Mira Rojanasakul. "Weeks of Storms Test California's Approach to Taming Nature." *New York Times*, January 5, 2023. https://www.nytimes.com/2023/01/05/climate/california-floods-drought-preparedness.html.

Forté, Chanese A. "Missouri Community and Its Children Grappling with Conflicting Nuclear Waste Exposure Reports." *The Equation* (blog), December 8, 2022. https://blog.ucsusa.org/chanese-forte/missouri-community-and-its-children-grappling-with-conflicting-nuclear-waste-exposure-reports/.

"Fort Leonard Wood USACE Area Office." Defense Visual Information Distribution Service. Accessed September 25, 2024. https://www.dvidshub.net/unit/usace-nwk.

Fort Osage National Historic Landmark. https://fortosagenhs.com/.

"Fort Peck Reservoir Fisheries Management Plan (2023–2032)." Montana Fish, Wildlife and Parks, October 16, 2023. https://fwp.mt.gov/conservation/fisheries-management/fort-peck-reservoir.

Foster, Lance. Personal interview. June 25, 2023.

French, Brett. "Pallid Sturgeon Passage: New Dam Bypass on Yellowstone River Luring Fish Upstream." *Spokesman-Review*, May 20, 2022. https://www.spokesman.com/stories/2022/may/23/pallid-sturgeon-passage-new-dam-bypass-on-yellowst/.

———. "A Tour of Fort Peck Dam: Engineering Marvel Holds Back Massive Missouri River." *Billings Gazette*, July 11, 2011. https://billingsgazette.com/news/state-and-regional/montana/a-tour-of-fort-peck-dam-engineering-marvel-holds-back/article_d5271d92-8f09-536d-89bf-92b0c9321656.html.

Gaarder, Nancy. "Could a 2011-Level Missouri River Flood Happen Again? Short Answer: YES." *Omaha World Herald*, May 31, 2016. https://omaha.com/news/nebraska/could-a--level-missouri-river-flood-happen-again-short/article_7d6b3a01-3c28-5c7c-b7c0-f70a417b49c8.html.

———. "Nearly 20-Mile Ice Jam on Missouri River Poses Risks Through Winter." *Omaha World-Herald*, January 13, 2023. https://omaha.com/weather/nearly-20-mile-ice-jam-on-missouri-river-poses-risks-through-winter/article_178dd466-9136-11ed-8bdd-ebd29ab336ec.html.

Gaarder, Nancy, and Martha Stoddard. "Current Flooding in Nebraska, Iowa Rivals Most Devastating Years as Multiple Rivers Flood." *Omaha World-Herald*, March 15, 2019. https://www.omaha.com/news/

nebraska/current-flooding-in-nebraska-iowa-rivals-most-devastating-years-as/article_95dde7e0-7927-5309-ba7f-d1acdcf69488.html.

Ganic, Eldin. "Bank Stabilization Navigation Project Kicks off along Missouri River." Dredging Today, November 18, 2022. https://www.dredgingtoday.com/2022/11/18/bank-stabilization-navigation-project-kicks-off-along-missouri-river/.

———. "Florence Bedrock Removal in Full Swing." Dredging Today, May 30, 2022. https://www.dredgingtoday.com/2022/05/30/florence-bedrock-removal-in-full-swing/.

Garth, Gary. "Big Muddy Refuge: How Midwest Floods Created a Wildlife Wonderland." usa *Today*, December 21, 2018. https://www.usatoday.com/story/travel/destinations/2018/12/21/big-muddy-fish-wildlife-refuge-missouri/2390142002/.

"Goose Facts." GeesePeace St. Louis. Accessed September 26, 2024. https://www.geesepeacestlouis.org/goose-facts.

"Government." Iowa Tribe of Kansas and Nebraska. Accessed September 25, 2024. http://iowatribeofkansasandnebraska.com/government/.

Grigg, Neil S. "Missouri River Governance: Collective Action and Basin-Wide Problems." *Journal of Water Resources Planning and Management* 146, no. 5 (2020). https://ascelibrary.org/doi/full/10.1061/%28asce%29wr.1943-5452.0001196.

Hafen, LeRoy R. *Fur Traders, Trappers, and Mountain Men of the Upper Missouri*. University of Nebraska Press, 1995.

Haldiman, Jeff. "Corps Gets More Money to Repair Banks of Missouri River." *Fulton Sun*, August 22, 2022. https://www.fultonsun.com/news/2022/aug/22/corps-gets-more-money-to-repair-banks-of-missouri/.

Hanson, Joseph Mills. *The Conquest of the Missouri, Being the Story of the Life and Exploits of Captain Grant Marsh, with Map and 36 Illustrations*. Murray Hill, 1946.

Hart, Henry C. *The Dark Missouri*. University of Wisconsin Press, 1957.

Hawley, Matt. Personal interview, April 7, 2024.

Heimsoth, Josie. "How Microplastics Are Threatening Water and Land Across Missouri." *Columbia Missourian*, June 20, 2022. https://www.columbiamissourian.com/news/local/how-microplastics-are-threatening-water-and-land-across-missouri/article_bd4092fc-ec0b-11ec-a059-2b00303c349b.html.

Hicks, Nancy. "Plan Calls for City to Pull Water from Missouri River." *Lincoln Journal Star*, June 1, 2014. https://journalstar.com/news/local/govt-and-politics/plan-calls-for-city-to-pull-water-from-missouri-river/article_b900688a-c677-53d1-adaa-c61a3befaaf6.html.

"High Temperatures Exacerbated by #climatechange Made 2022 Northern Hemisphere Droughts More Likely: 'The Models Analysed Also Show That Soil Moisture #drought Will Continue to Increase with Additional #globalwarming'—World Weather Attribution #ActOnClimate." *Coyote Gulch* (blog), October 8, 2022. https://coyotegulch.blog/2022/10/08/high-temperatures-exacerbated-by-climatechange-made-2022-northern-hemisphere-droughts-more-likely-the-models-analysed-also-show-that-soil-moisture-drought-will-continue-to-increase-with-additiona/.

Hill, Christina Gish, Matthew J. Hill, and Brooke Neely. *National Parks, Native Sovereignty: Experiments in Collaboration*. University of Oklahoma Press, 2024.

"Historical Vignette: The Engineers Come to the Missouri." *Omaha District*, January 16, 2015. https://www.nwo.usace.army.mil/Media/Fact-Sheets/Fact-Sheet-Article-View/Article/560338/historical-vignette-the-engineers-come-to-the-missouri/.

"Historic Floods on the Missouri River: Fighting the Big Muddy in Nebraska." Nebraska Department of Natural Resources, 2008. https://semspub.epa.gov/work/07/30022840.pdf.

"History." MHA Nation. Accessed September 26, 2024. https://www.mhanation.com/history.

"History of the Union Pacific Railroad." Wikipedia, September 17, 2024. https://en.wikipedia.org/wiki/History_of_the_Union_Pacific_Railroad.

Hoagland, Edward, and Peter C. Mancall. *Land of Rivers: America in Word and Image*. Cornell University Press, 2019.

Holt, Edgar A. "A Voyage of the Omaha." *The Palimpsest* 6, no. 4 (April 1925). https://iagenweb.org/history/palimpsest/1925-Apr2.htm.

Hotchkiss, Rollin H. "U.S. Army Corps of Engineers." *Encyclopedia of the Great Plains*. Accessed September 25, 2024. http://plainshumanities.unl.edu/encyclopedia/doc/egp.wat.034.

Howells, Robert Earle. "Paddle 340 Miles of the Mighty Missouri—Nonstop." *National Geographic*, August 2, 2010. https://www.nationalgeographic.com/adventure/article/race-missouri-340.

Hudson, Marilyn Cross. "The Mandan, Hidatsa, and Arikara People and the Flood Control Act of 1944—Points West Online." Buffalo Bill Center of the West, June 15, 2014. https://centerofthewest.org/2014/06/15/points-west-online-mandan-hidatsa-arikara-people-flood-control-act-1944/.

"Hydroelectric Power: How It Works." U.S. Geological Survey. Accessed September 25, 2024. https://www.usgs.gov/special-topics/water-science-school/science/hydroelectric-power-how-it-works.

Hytrek, Nick. "Dry Conditions Continue as Army Corps of Engineers Cut Missouri River Releases to Winter Rate." *Sioux City Journal*, December 7, 2022. https://siouxcityjournal.com/news/local/state-and-regional/dry-conditions-continue-as-army-corps-of-engineers-cut-missouri-river-releases-to-winter-rate/article_66fda3ec-e125-5aee-864e-08de1b8646f7.html.

IllumiNative. https://illuminative.org/.

"Improving Transportation." U.S. Army Corps of Engineers Headquarters. Accessed September 25, 2024. https://www.usace.army.mil/About/History/Brief-History-of-the-Corps/Improving-Transportation/.

"Injurious Wildlife Listings—Keeping Risky Wildlife Species out of the United States." U.S. Fish and Wildlife Service. Accessed August 27, 2025. https://www.fws.gov/program/injurious-wildlife-listings-keeping-risky-wildlife-species-out-united-states.

"In 'Momentous' Act, Regulators Approve Demolition of Four #KlamathRiver Dams—The *Los Angeles Times*." *Coyote Gulch* (blog), November 18, 2022. https://coyotegulch.blog/2022/11/19/in-momentous-act-regulators-approve-demolition-of-four-klamathriver-dams-the-los-angeles-times/.

"Invasive Species: Rainbow Trout." Columbus Audubon. Accessed September 26, 2024. https://columbusaudubon.org/invasive-species-rainbow-trout/.

"Iowa's Biological Communities Series: Iowa Wetlands." Iowa Association of Naturalists. Accessed September 26, 2024. https://www.campsilos.org/wp-content/uploads/2021/09/IAN204.pdf.

Ioway, Otoe-Missouria Language. https://iowayotoelang.nativeweb.org/index.htm.

"Ioway Map of 1837." National Archives Catalog. Accessed September 26, 2024. https://catalog.archives.gov/search?q=Ioway+Map+of+1837&rows=20&typeOfMaterials=Maps+and+Charts.

Ioway Tribal National Park. https://iowaytribalnationalpark.org/.

Jackson, Donald. *Voyages of the Steamboat "Yellow Stone."* University of Oklahoma Press, 1987.

Jacobs, Dillon. "How to Invest in Water like Dr. Michael Burry from the *Big Short*." FinMasters, March 1, 2024. https://finmasters.com/michael-burry-invest-in-water/.

Jacobson, R. B., M. E. Colvin, D. Marmorek, and M. Randall. "Science to Manage a Very Rare Fish in a Very Large River—Pallid Sturgeon in the Missouri River, U.S.A." American Geophysical Union, fall meeting 2017. https://ui.adsabs.harvard.edu/abs/2017agufmpa23a0366j/abstract.

Jacobson, Robb, Aaron DeLonay, and Casey Hickcox. "Unprecedented Pallid Sturgeon Larval Drift Experiment." U.S. Geological Survey, Columbia Environmental Research Center, July 1, 2019. https://www.usgs.gov/centers/columbia-environmental-research-center/unprecedented-pallid-sturgeon-larval-drift.

Johnson, Laura. "Efforts Continue to Stop Spread of Invasive Zebra Mussels in Missouri River Dams." SDBP Radio, May 18, 2022. https://listen.sdpb.org/2022-05-18/efforts-continue-to-stop-spread-of-invasive-zebra-mussels-in-missouri-river-dams.

Jones, Sheritha. "Reminisce: Missouri River Flood of 1952." *Omaha World-Herald*, April 16, 2023. https://omaha.com/news/local/history/reminisce-missouri-river-flood-of-1952/article_534f7f60-da27-11ed-914e-db54292ad6fb.html.

Journals of the Lewis and Clark Expedition Online. http://lewisandclarkjournals.unl.edu/.

Kauffman, Gerald J., Jr. "The Delaware River Revival: Four Centuries of Historic Water Quality Change from Henry Hudson to Benjamin Franklin to JFK." *Pennsylvania History: A Journal of Mid-Atlantic Studies*, November 3, 2010. https://muse.jhu.edu/article/400911.

Kane, Jerry. "Public Urged to Clean, Drain, Dry After Zebra Mussels Found in Private Lake." Nebraska Game and Parks Commission, June 23, 2023. https://outdoornebraska.gov/about/press-events/news/public-urged-to-clean-drain-dry-after-zebra-mussels-found-in-private-lake/.

Kennedy, Mary. "Mississippi River Barge Movements Restricted Due to Critical Low Water Levels." DTN Progressive Farmer, October 3, 2022. https://www.dtnpf.com/agriculture/web/ag/news/article/2022/10/03/mississippi-river-barge-movements-2.

Kim, Stephanie. "The New Legalities of Floating Missouri Waterways." *Daily Journal*, July 27, 2022. https://dailyjournalonline.com/2022/07/27/the-new-legalities-of-floating-missouri-waterways/.

King, Teagan. "Likely Shipwreck Site Found in Missouri River near Boonville." *Columbia Missourian*, August 24, 2022. https://www.columbiamissourian.com/news/local/likely-shipwreck-site-found

-in-missouri-river-near-boonville/article_ad12ede4-23f6-11ed-9edb-7bab325e110a.html.

———. "Sturgeon Research Along Missouri River Guides Habitat Restoration Projects." *Columbia Missourian*, October 22, 2022. https://www.columbiamissourian.com/news/local/sturgeon-research-along-missouri-river-guides-habitat-restoration-projects/article_af7a7720-41d6-11ed-841a-778426728b98.html.

Kirst, Marian Lyman. "Can Pallid Sturgeon Hang On in the Overworked Missouri River?" *High Country News*, January 26, 2024. https://www.hcn.org/issues/44.16/can-pallid-sturgeon-hang-on-in-the-overworked-missouri-river.

———. "Pallid's PR Problem." *High Country News*, January 24, 2024. https://www.hcn.org/issues/44.16/can-pallid-sturgeon-hang-on-in-the-overworked-missouri-river/pallids-pr-problem.

Kite, Allison. "Lawmakers Hope to Block Missouri Water from Being Exported to Other States." *Missouri Independent*, February 1, 2024. https://missouriindependent.com/2024/02/01/lawmakers-hope-to-block-missouri-water-from-being-exported-to-other-states/.

———. "Officials Plan to Truck 6,000 Gallons of Water from Missouri River across Kansas." *Kansas Reflector*, February 27, 2023. https://kansasreflector.com/2022/10/21/officials-plan-to-truck-6000-gallons-of-water-from-missouri-river-across-kansas/.

Knott, John R. *Imagining Wild America*. University of Michigan Press, 2002.

Koch, Sophie. "Invasive Zebra Mussels." National Park Service. Accessed September 22, 2025. https://www.nps.gov/articles/zebra-mussels.htm.

Kolbert, Elizabeth. "Louisiana's Disappearing Coast." *New Yorker*, April 1, 2019.

Kondolf, G. Mathias, Matt Smeltzer, and Lisa Kimball. *Freshwater Gravel Mining and Dredging Issues*. White Paper Prepared for Washington Department of Fish and Wildlife, Washington Department of Ecology, and Washington Department of Transportation. Center for Environmental Design Research, December 10, 2001. https://wdfw.wa.gov/sites/default/files/publications/00056/wdfw00056.pdf.

Kurz, Rudolf Friedrich, Carla Kelly, and J. N. B. Hewitt. *On the Upper Missouri: The Journal of Rudolph Friederich Kurz, 1851–1852*. University of Oklahoma Press, 2005.

"Lake Oahe Could Rise Five Feet as Corps Looks to Balance Reservoir Storage." KCCR, December 9, 2022. https://www.kccrradio.com/2022/12/11/lake-oahe-could-rise-five-feet-as-corps-looks-to-balance-reservoir-storage/.

Lambrecht, Bill. *Big Muddy Blues: True Tales and Twisted Politics Along Lewis and Clark's Missouri River*. St. Martin's, 2014.

LaRose, Naomi. "Major Nebraska Rivers and Their Drainages Part 2—The Elkhorn and Missouri Rivers." Morning Ag Clips, May 4, 2023. https://www.morningagclips.com/major-nebraska-rivers-and-their-drainages-part-2-the-elkhorn-and-missouri-rivers/.

Larsen, Lawrence H., and Barbara J. Cottrell. *Steamboats West: The 1859 American Fur Company Missouri River Expedition*. Arthur H. Clark, 2010.

Larson, Lee W. "The Great USA Flood of 1993." Presented at International Association of Hydrological Sciences Conference, Destructive Water: Water-Caused Natural Disasters—Their Abatement and Control, Anaheim, California, June 24–28, 1996. https://www.nwrfc.noaa.gov/floods/papers/oh_2/great.htm.

Lass, William E. *A History of Steamboating on the Upper Missouri River*. University of Nebraska Press, 1991.

———. *Navigating the Missouri: Steamboating on Nature's Highway, 1819–1935*. University of Oklahoma Press, 2023.

Lawson, Michael L. *Dammed Indians: The Pick-Sloan Plan and the Missouri River Sioux, 1944–1980*. University of Oklahoma Press, 1994.

———. *Dammed Indians Revisited: The Continuing History of the Pick-Sloan Plan and the Missouri River Sioux*. South Dakota State Historical Society Press, 2009.

"Learn About the River." U.S. Army Corps of Engineers, Kansas City District. Accessed September 25, 2024. https://www.nwk.usace.army.mil/Locations/Missouri-River-Sites/Learn-About-the-River/.

"Least Tern." American Bird Conservancy, August 31, 2023. https://abcbirds.org/bird/least-tern/.

Leonard, Diana. "California Is Drought-Free for First Time in Years. What It Means." *Washington Post*, November 8, 2023. https://www.washingtonpost.com/weather/2023/11/08/california-is-drought-free-first-time-years-what-it-means/.

"Lewis and Clark: A Missouri River Adventure." U.S. Bureau of Reclamation. Accessed September 25, 2024. https://www.usbr.gov/gp/lewisandclark/index.html.

Liermann, Martin, and Phil Roni. "More Sites or More Years? Optimal Study Design for Monitoring Fish Response to Watershed Restoration." *North American Journal of Fisheries Management* 28, no. 3 (2011): 935–43. https://afspubs.onlinelibrary.wiley.com/doi/10.1577/m06-175.1.

Lincoln, Abraham. "Letter to James C. Conkling." Abraham Lincoln Online. https://www.abrahamlincolnonline.org/lincoln/speeches/conkling.htm.

Little, Jane Braxton. "The Ogallala Aquifer: Saving a Vital U.S. Water Source." *Scientific American*, February 20, 2024. https://www.scientificamerican.com/article/the-ogallala-aquifer/.

"A Long Time Coming." News-Press Now, November 24, 2023 (page discontinued). https://www.newspressnow.com/opinion/editorials/a-long-time-coming/article_3386e2c0-4f28-11ed-9123-b77d8d0baa4f.html.

Lowe, Peggy. "Kansas City Both Copes with Water Pollution and Creates It." KCUR, September 23, 2016. http://kcur.org/post/kansas-city-both-copes-water-pollution-and-creates-it.

"Lower Missouri River Navigation Charts: Rulo, Nebraska to St. Louis, Missouri." U.S. Army Corps of Engineers, 2010. https://usace.contentdm.oclc.org/digital/collection/p16021coll10/id/11947/.

"Low Missouri River Levels Means Less Electric Production." Radio Iowa, May 17, 2022. https://www.radioiowa.com/2022/05/17/low-missouri-river-levels-means-less-electric-production/.

Mall, Scott. "FreightWaves Classics: The Yellowstone Achieved 'Firsts' in Peace and War." barchart, May 19, 2022. https://www.barchart.com/story/news/8422026/freightwaves-classics-the-yellowstone-achieved-firsts-in-peace-and-war.

Mansker, Scott. Personal interview. March 20, 2024.

Marohn, Kirsti. "Ice Jams: Destructive, Hard to Predict, Tough to Prevent." MPR News, March 26, 2019. https://www.mprnews.org/story/2019/03/26/whats-an-ice-jam.

McDonald, David W., and Katrina Service, eds. *Key Topics in Conservation Biology*. Blackwell, 2007.

McFetridge, Scott. "Des Moines Tries Cooperation to Reduce Farm Runoff." AP, May 29, 2022. https://apnews.com/article/politics-environment-iowa-des-moines-978cc6f9edb83389af50a5c1cb05d243.

McKean, Andrew. "Unmarked Pallid Sturgeon Netted in Fort Peck Dam Tailrace." *Billings Gazette*, March 10, 2004. https://billingsgazette.com/news/features/outdoors/unmarked-pallid-sturgeon-netted-in-fort-peck-dam-tailrace/article_21f7ec30-74a8-5d48-98fc-42fa29717428.html.

"Meriwether Lewis Dredge / Museum of Missouri River History." National Maritime Historical Society. Accessed August 27, 2025. https://seahistory.org/museums-sites/meriwether-lewis-dredge-museum-of-missouri-river-history/.

"Miami Access." Missouri Department of Conservation. Accessed September 25, 2024. https://nature.mdc.mo.gov/discover-nature/places/miami-access.

Midkiff, Ken. "Just When You Thought It Was Safe to Go into the Water . . ." *Ozark Sierran*, October–December 2004. http://missouri.sierraclub.org/thb/newsletter/2004/12/mo-dnr.html.

"Millions of Hindus Plunge into Ganges River in India to Wash Away Their Sins." *The Telegraph*, January 14, 2013. http://www.telegraph.co.uk/news/worldnews/asia/india/9799882/Millions-of-Hindus-plunge-into-Ganges-River-in-India-to-wash-away-their-sins.html.

Minnesota DNR Reports. "Barrier at Lake Bella in Nobles County Stops 140 Invasive Carp." Outdoor News, August 14, 2022. https://www.outdoornews.com/2022/08/14/barrier-at-lake-bella-in-nobles-county-stops-140-invasive-carp/.

"Missouri Department of Conservation to Remove Invasive Carp from Lower Grand River September 12th through 16th." KTTN, September 5, 2022. https://www.kttn.com/missouri-department-of-conservation-to-remove-invasive-carp-from-lower-grand-river-september-12th-through-16th/.

"Missouri National Recreational River: Current Conditions." National Park Service. Accessed September 26, 2024. https://www.nps.gov/mnrr/planyourvisit/conditions.htm.

"Missouri National Recreational River: Maps." National Park Service. Accessed September 25, 2024. https://www.nps.gov/mnrr/planyourvisit/maps.htm.

"Missouri National Recreational River Tourism Creates $6,105,300 in Local Economic Benefit." National Park Service. Accessed September 25, 2024. https://www.nps.gov/mnrr/learn/news/2016economics.htm.

"Missouri River." Steamboats.org, November 10, 2020. https://www.steamboats.org/traveller/missouri-river.html.

"The Missouri River: A View from Upstream." *Prairie Fire*, December 2007. Accessed September 26, 2024. https://web.archive.org/web/20120321062645/http://www.prairiefirenewspaper.com/2007/12/missouri-river.

"Missouri River Basin." Drought.gov. Accessed September 25, 2024. https://www.drought.gov/dews/missouri-river-basin.

"Missouri River Basin." North Dakota Department of Water Resources. Accessed September 25, 2024. https://www.swc.nd.gov/basins/missouri_river/missouri_river.html.

"Missouri River Basin." Waterwebster.org. Accessed September 25, 2024. http://waterwebster.org/MissouriRiverBasin.htm.

"Missouri River Basin Water Management Division." U.S. Army Corps of Engineers, Northwestern Division. Accessed September 25, 2024. https://www.nwd-mr.usace.army.mil/rcc/.

Missouri River Bed Degradation Feasibility Study: Technical Report. U.S. Army Corps of Engineers, Kansas City District, May 2017. https://www.marc.org/sites/default/files/2022-02/mo-river-degradation-feasibility-technical-report.pdf.

Missouri River Bed Degradation Public Scoping Report. U.S. Army Corps of Engineers, 2014. https://marc2.org/assets/environment/PublicScopingmoriver20140812-sm.pdf.

"Missouri River Commercial Dredging Final Environmental Impact Statement." U.S. Army Corps of Engineers, 2011. https://usace.contentdm.oclc.org/digital/collection/p16021coll7/id/8151.

"Missouri River Commission Maps Showing Location of Steamboat Wrecks on the Missouri River (Collection)." University of Missouri Digital Library. Accessed September 26, 2024. https://digital.library.missouri.edu/node/8913.

"The Missouri River During the Lewis & Clark (Corps of Discovery) Expedition." Historical Marker Database, August 15, 2024. https://www.hmdb.org/m.asp?m=254201.

"Missouri River Flooding." U.S. Geological Survey, Earth Resources Observation and Science Center. Accessed September 26, 2024. https://www.usgs.gov/centers/eros/missouri-river-flooding.

"Missouri River Governance: Institutions, Laws, and Policies for Managing Sediment and Related Resources." In *Missouri River Planning: Recognizing and Incorporating Sediment Management*. National Academies Press, 2011. https://nap.nationalacademies.org/read/13019/chapter/5#52.

"The Missouri River. Its Habits and Eccentricities Described by a Personal Friend." *Big Muddy News* (blog), January 17, 2019. https://bigmuddynews.blogspot.com/2019/01/this-is-one-of-most-quoted-pieces-about.html.

Missouri River Mainstem Reservoir System: Master Water Control Manual, Missouri River Basin. U.S. Army Corps of Engineers, Northwestern Division, 2018. https://www.nwd-mr.usace.army.mil/rcc/reports/mmanual/MissouriMainstemMasterManual2018.pdf.

"Missouri River Navigation Charts: Sioux City, Iowa to Rulo, Nebraska." U.S. Army Corps of Engineers, 2011. https://usace.contentdm.oclc.org/digital/collection/p16021coll10/id/8418/.

Missouri River Planning: Recognizing and Incorporating Sediment Management. National Academies Press, 2011.

Missouri River Relief. https://riverrelief.org/.

"Missouri River Sand and Gravel Dredging, September 2010." U.S. Environmental Protection Agency, September 8, 2010. https://archive.epa.gov/region07/factsheets/web/html/lower_missouri_river_sand_gravel_dredging.html.

Missouri River Tourism. http://sdmissouririver.com/.

Missouri River Water Management Division. "Below Average Runoff Continues for the Upper Missouri River Basin in 2023." U.S. Army Corps of Engineers Northwestern Division, February 7, 2023. https://www.nwd.usace.army.mil/Media/News-Releases/Article/3290832/below-average-runoff-continues-for-the-upper-missouri-river-basin-in-2023/.

"Missouri Safe Drinking Water Commission." Missouri Department of Natural Resources. Accessed August 27, 2025. https://dnr.mo.gov/commissions-boards-councils/safe-drinking-water-commission.

Moreland, Janet. "The First American to Paddle the Missouri." *Canoe & Kayak Magazine*. Accessed September 25, 2024. https://www.canoekayak.com/touring-kayaks/learned/.

MR340. https://mr340.org/.

"MR340 Race Tests Missouri River Paddlers' Endurance." *Columbia Missourian*, July 25, 2013. Accessed September 26, 2024. https://www.columbiamissourian.com/sports/mr-race-tests-missouri-river-paddlers-endurance/article_0ad6dd03-f1dd-5d81-923e-58d4f342d7e9.html.

Nasatir, Abraham Phineas. *Before Lewis and Clark: Documents Illustrating the History of the Missouri, 1785–1804*. University of Oklahoma Press, 2002.

"The National Wild and Scenic Rivers System: A Brief Overview." EveryCRSReport.com, September 22, 2015. https://www.everycrsreport.com/reports/R42614.html.

"Navigation Season on Missouri River Will End Early This Fall Due to Drought." KIWA Radio, September 19, 2022 (page discontinued). https://kiwaradio.com/local-news/navigation-season-on-missouri-river-will-end-early-this-fall-due-to-drought/.

Neihardt, John Gneisenau. *The River and I*. University of Nebraska Press, 1968.

"New Hope for the Missouri." *New York Times*, July 16, 2003. https://www.nytimes.com/2003/07/16/opinion/new-hope-for-the-missouri.html.

Nicandri, David L., and Clay Jenkinson. *River of Promise: Lewis and Clark on the Columbia*. Dakota Institute Press of the Lewis and Clark Fort Mandan Foundation, 2022.

"The North Platte River—Multiuse Water Part 5—The Pick-Sloan Missouri River Basin Project—Glendo." IANR News, August 27, 2022. https://ianrnews.unl.edu/north-platte-river-multiuse-water-part-5-pick-sloan-missouri-river-basin-project-glendo.

"Northwestern Division History." U.S. Army Corps of Engineers, Northwestern Division History. Accessed September 25, 2024. http://www.nwd.usace.army.mil/About/History.aspx.

"Northwestern Division Water Management." U.S. Army Corps of Engineers, Northwestern Division. Accessed September 25, 2024. http://www.nwd.usace.army.mil/Missions/WaterManagement/MissouriRiverBasin.aspx.

Oglesby, Richard Edward. *Manuel Lisa and the Opening of the Missouri Fur Trade*. University of Oklahoma Press, 1984.

Olson, Greg. *The Ioway in Missouri*. University of Missouri Press, 2008.

———. *Ioway Life: Reservation and Reform, 1837–1860*. University of Oklahoma Press, 2016.

———. "The Ioways." Missouri Encyclopedia. Accessed September 26, 2024. https://missouriencyclopedia.org/groupsorganizations/ioways.

"Outdoor Water Use." U.S. Environmental Protection Agency. Accessed September 26, 2024. https://19january2017snapshot.epa.gov/www3/watersense/pubs/outdoor.html.

Ovid, and J. D. Reed. *Metamorphoses*. Translated by Rolfe Humphries. New annotated edition. Indiana University Press, 2018.

"Paddlefish: Regulations." Missouri Department of Conservation. Accessed September 25, 2024. https://huntfish.mdc.mo.gov/fishing/species/paddlefish/paddlefish-regulations.

Palmer, Tim. *Lifelines the Case for River Conservation*. Island Press, 2013.

Paskoff, Paul F. *Troubled Waters: Steamboat Disasters, River Improvements, and American Public Policy, 1821–1860*. Louisiana State University Press, 2007.

Peikes, Katie. "Lessons from Dakota Access Pipeline Shape Farmers' Battle over Proposed Carbon Pipelines." STLPR. May 24, 2022. https://www.stlpr.org/health-science-environment/2022-05-24/lessons

-from-dakota-access-pipeline-shape-farmers-battle-over-proposed -carbon-pipelines.

"A Pending Flood." *Omaha Daily Bee*, April 5, 1881. https://www.loc.gov/resource/sn99021999/1881-04-05/ed-1/?sp=4&st=image&r=-0.11,-0.639,1.111,1.484,0.

Petersen, William J. "Steamboating on the Missouri River." *Nebraska History* 35 (1954). https://history.nebraska.gov/wp-content/uploads/2017/12/doc_publications_NH1954Steamboating.pdf.

"The Pilings of History Along the Old Muddy." KWIT, May 16, 2022. https://www.kwit.org/podcast/small-wonders/2022-05-16/the-pilings-of-history-along-the-old-muddy.

"Piping Plover." Cornell Lab All About Birds. Accessed September 25, 2024. https://www.allaboutbirds.org/guide/Piping_Plover/.

"Piping Plover." Nebraska Game and Parks Commission, May 19, 2023. https://outdoornebraska.gov/learn/nebraska-wildlife/nebraska-animals/birds/piping-plover/.

Pivoney, Ryan. "Extreme Conditions Becoming More Common along Missouri River." *News Tribune* (Jefferson City), January 15, 2023. https://www.newstribune.com/news/2023/jan/15/extreme-conditions-becoming-more-common-along/.

"Rainbow Trout (*Oncorhynchus mykiss*)." U.S. Fish and Wildlife Service. Accessed September 26, 2024. https://www.fws.gov/species/rainbow-trout-oncorhynchus-mykiss.

Ramirez-Franco, Juanpablo, and Eva Tesfaye. "Mississippi River Basin Adapts as Climate Change Brings Extreme Rain and Flooding." NPR, October 18, 2022. https://www.npr.org/2022/10/18/1127966940/mississippi-river-basin-adapts-as-climate-change-brings-extreme-rain-and-floodin.

"Ramping Down the River." Radio 570 WNAX. Accessed September 25, 2024. https://wnax.com/news/180081-ramping-down-the-river/.

"Rare Fish Caught Out of Kansas River, KDWP confirms." KSNT. Accessed September 26, 2024. https://www.ksnt.com/news/local-news/rare-fish-caught-out-of-kansas-river-kdwp-confirms/.

"Recent Fish Kill Below Lake Bella Dam Included Largest-Ever Population of Invasive Fish Species." *Worthington Globe*, August 12, 2022. https://www.dglobe.com/news/local/recent-fish-kill-below-lake-bella-dam-included-largest-ever-population-of-invasive-fish-species.

Reitzel, Matthew T. "Down by the Old Missouri." *Capital Journal*, September 20, 2024. https://www.capjournal.com/opinions/down-by-the-old-missouri/article_6d393d76-751c-11ef-8ea3-87f16622f4c2.html.

Rekacewicz, Philippe, and Delphine Digout. "River Fragmentation and Flow Regulation." GRID-Arendal, 2005. https://www.grida.no/resources/5821.

Renkl, Margaret. "On an Endangered River, Another Toxic Disaster Is Waiting to Happen." *New York Times*, May 9, 2022. https://www.nytimes.com/2022/05/09/opinion/coal-ash-toxic-alabama-rivers.html.

"Reproduction." Pallid Sturgeon Recovery Program. Accessed September 25, 2024. http://www.pallidsturgeon.org/about/reproduction/.

"River Tools." Missouri River Water Trail. Accessed September 26, 2024. https://missouririverwatertrail.org/river-tools.

"River-Corridor Habitat Dynamics." U.S. Geological Survey, Columbia Environmental Research Center. Accessed September 25, 2024. https://www.usgs.gov/centers/columbia-environmental-research-center/science/river-corridor-habitat-dynamics.

Robbins, Jim. "A Silver Lining: Giant Floods Not Only Destroy, They Renew." *New York Times*, August 2, 2022. https://www.nytimes.com/2022/08/02/science/yellowstone-flooding.html.

Ruskin, John. *Selections from the Writings of John Ruskin*. George Allen, 1893.

Salter, Jim. "Missouri School to Close After Radioactive Waste Report." Associated Press, October 18, 2022. https://apnews.com/article/health-education-cancer-st-louis-missouri-be4a2acec5aeeae1fff94aca76f056a1.

———. "More Evacuations in Midwest as Floodwaters Head Downstream." Associated Press, March 18, 2019. https://www.apnews.com/ec2e1352a4bc4b31921e46026e078c8d.

Samuels, Sam Hooper. "Curtains for the Pallid Sturgeon." *Smithsonian Magazine*, March 2007. https://www.smithsonianmag.com/science-nature/curtains-for-the-pallid-sturgeon-148476204/.

Sanders, Scott R. Personal interview. June 7, 2015.

Sanderson, Bridget. "Testimony: Environment Missouri Opposes Further Commercial Dredging of the Missouri River." Environment Missouri, August 6, 2022. https://environmentamerica.org/missouri/articles/testimony-environment-missouri-opposes-further-commercial-dredging-of-the-missouri-river/.

Sasson, Anthony. "Freshwater Mussels in the Midwest—Part 1." Midwest Biodiversity Institute, June 1, 2020. https://midwestbiodiversityinst.org/publications/articles/freshwater-mussels-in-the-midwest.

"Saving the Whanganui: Can Personhood Rescue a River?" *The Guardian*, November 29, 2019. https://www.theguardian.com/world/2019/nov/30/saving-the-whanganui-can-personhood-rescue-a-river.

Schlesier, Karl H. *Plains Indians, A.D. 500–1500: The Archaeological Past of Historic Groups*. University of Oklahoma Press, 1995.

Schneiders, Robert Kelley. *Unruly River: Two Centuries of Change Along the Missouri*. University Press of Kansas, 1999.

Schultz, James Willard, and Eugene Lee Silliman. *Floating on the Missouri: 100 Years After Lewis and Clark*. Riverbend, 2003.

Sevigny, Melissa L. *Mythical River: Chasing the Mirage of New Water in the American Southwest*. University of Iowa Press, 2016.

Shaffer, Terry L., Mark H. Sherfy, Michael J. Anteau, Jennifer H. Stucker, Marsha A. Sovada, Erin A. Roche, Mark T. Wiltermuth, Thomas K. Buhl, and Colin M. Dovichin. "Accuracy of the Missouri River Least Tern and Piping Plover Monitoring Program: Considerations for the Future." Open-File Report 2013-1176. U.S. Geological Society, 2013. https://pubs.er.usgs.gov/publication/ofr20131176.

Shaw, Julie. "Why Is Biodiversity Important?" Conservation International, October 15, 2024. https://www.conservation.org/blog/why-is-biodiversity-important.

Sidder, Aaron. "Missouri River Floodplain Expansion, Services, and Resiliency." Eos, September 21, 2022. https://eos.org/research-spotlights/missouri-river-floodplain-expansion-services-and-resiliency.

"Silver Carp (*Hypophthalmichthys molitrix*)." U.S. Fish and Wildlife Service. Accessed September 26, 2024. https://www.fws.gov/species/silver-carp-hypophthalmichthys-molitrix.

Skipworth, William. "Interest in Steamboat Wrecks on the Missouri River up Following Discovery of Possible Steamboat Wreckage near Rocheport." *The Missourian*, September 2, 2022. https://www.emissourian.com/features_people/interest-in-steamboat-wrecks-on-the-missouri-river-up-following-discovery-of-possible-steamboat-wreckage/article_2f42faf0-2ad4-11ed-9496-37ae67c1124b.html.

Slavit, Mark. "New Report Shows Missouri River Runoff Levels Improve for Water Supply Needs." KRCG, August 4, 2022. https://krcgtv.com/news/local/new-report-shows-missouri-river-runoff-levels-improve-for-water-supply-needs.

Smith, Mitch, Jack Healy, and Timothy Williams. "'It's Probably over for Us': Record Flooding Pummels Midwest When Farmers Can Least Afford It." *New York Times*, March 18, 2019. https://www.nytimes.com/2019/03/18/us/nebraska-floods.html.

Smith, Mitch, John Schwartz, and Tim Gruber. "'Breaches Everywhere': Flooding Bursts Midwest Levees, and Tough Questions Follow." *New*

York Times, March 31, 2019. https://www.nytimes.com/2019/03/31/us/midwest-floods-levees.html.

Southard, John. "5.9: Morphology and Dynamics of Meandering Streams." LibreTexts: Geosciences, December 26, 2021. https://geo.libretexts.org/Bookshelves/Geography_(Physical)/The_Environment_of_the_Earth's_Surface_(Southard)/05%3A_Rivers/5.09%3A_Morphology_and_Dynamics_of_Meandering_Streams.

"Special Events at Katy Trail State Park and Rock Island State Park." Missouri State Parks, February 22, 2011. https://mostateparks.com/page/57941/special-events.

"Spirit of Brownville Riverboat and River Inn Resort." VisitNebraska.com. Accessed September 26, 2024. https://visitnebraska.com/brownville/spirit-brownville-riverboat-and-river-inn-resort.

"Steamboat." National Geographic Education. Accessed September 26, 2024 (page discontinued). https://education.nationalgeographic.org/resource/steamboat/.

"Steamboating on the Missouri River." MontanaKids.com. Accessed September 25, 2024. https://montanakids.com/history_and_prehistory/transportation/steamboating.htm.

"Sturgeon and Paddlefish Management." North American Sturgeon and Paddlefish Society, September 1, 2020. http://www.nasps-sturgeon.org/sturgeons/management.aspx.

"Sunken Boats on the MO River." Rivermiles, March 4, 2013. http://www.rivermiles.com/forum/YaBB.pl?num=1362427145.

"Sustainable Fishing: Empowering Fishing Communities Worldwide." Environmental Defense Fund. Accessed September 26, 2024. https://seafood.edf.org/trout.

Switzer, Ronald R. *Steamboat "Bertrand" and Missouri River Commerce*. University of Oklahoma Press, 2015.

Symington, Adam. "Mapping the World's River Basins by Continent." Visual Capitalist, January 6, 2023. https://www.visualcapitalist.com/cp/mapping-the-worlds-river-basins-by-continent/.

Tesfaye, Eva, Brittney J. Miller, and Halle Parker. "Communities Look at Nature-Based Solutions to Control Flooding." STLPR, October 13, 2022. https://news.stlpublicradio.org/health-science-environment/2022-10-13/making-room-for-the-river-communities-look-at-nature-based-solutions.

———. "When It Rains: Making Room for the River: Communities Look at Nature-Based Solutions." Investigate Midwest, October 8, 2022.

https://investigatemidwest.org/2022/10/08/when-it-rains-making-room-for-the-river-communities-look-at-nature-based-solutions/.

"Think Running Out of Water Is Just a California Problem? Talk to a Kansas Cattle Farmer." *Kansas City Star*, October 9, 2022. https://www.kansascity.com/opinion/editorials/article266967166.html.

Thorne, Tanis C. *The Many Hands of My Relations: French and Indians on the Lower Missouri*. University of Missouri Press, 1996.

Thorson, John E. *River of Promise, River of Peril: The Politics of Managing the Missouri River*. University Press of Kansas, 1994.

"Thune Secures Key South Dakota Priorities in Water Resources Bill." U.S. Senator John Thune, December 15, 2022. https://www.thune.senate.gov/public/index.cfm/press-releases?id=5cddbaba-7efe-4502-8203-a107701960d1.

Tiwari, Rosemary. "College of Engineering: The University of Iowa." Iowa Geological Survey. Accessed September 25, 2024. https://iowageologicalsurvey.org/landforms/alluvial-plains-2/.

Trafzer, Clifford E. *As Long as the Grass Shall Grow and Rivers Flow: A History of Native Americans*. Harcourt College, 2000.

Tucker, Anna M., and Michael C. Runge. "Optimal Strategies for Managing Wildlife Harvest Under System Change." *Journal of Wildlife Management* 85, no. 5 (2021): 847–54. https://wildlife.onlinelibrary.wiley.com/doi/10.1002/jwmg.22047.

Twain, Mark. *Life on the Mississippi*. Penguin, 1984.

Upper Midwest Environmental Sciences Center. "Exploring Patterns of Bird Diversity in a Floodplain River System." February 1, 2016. https://www.umesc.usgs.gov/terrestrial/migratory_birds/patterns_bird_diversity.html.

"USACE Dredge Goetz." U.S. Army Corps of Engineers, Philadelphia District and Marine Design Center, August 31, 2012. https://www.nap.usace.army.mil/Missions/Factsheets/Fact-Sheet-Article-View/Article/490717/usace-dredge-goetz/.

U.S. Army Corps of Engineers. "Upper Missouri River Basin Saw Only 75% of Normal Runoff in 2022." *Billings Gazette*, January 6, 2023. https://billingsgazette.com/news/state-and-regional/montana/upper-missouri-river-basin-saw-only-75-of-normal-runoff-in-2022/article_14ec2a66-8e14-11ed-9e6f-737d5bc820f8.html.

U.S. Department of Agriculture National Agricultural Statistics Service. "2017 Census of Agriculture Highlights: Irrigation and Water Management." https://www.nass.usda.gov/Publications/Highlights/2019/2017census_Irrigation_and_WaterManagement.pdf.

U.S. Department of Commerce. *Distances Between United States Ports*. 14th ed. U.S. Government Publishing Office, 2025. https://www.nauticalcharts.noaa.gov/publications/docs/distances.pdf.

U.S. Fish and Wildlife Service. "Endangered and Threatened Wildlife and Plants; Designation of Critical Habitat for the Northern Great Plains Breeding Population of the Piping Plover." *Federal Register*, September 11, 2002. https://www.federalregister.gov/documents/2002/09/11/02-21625/endangered-and-threatened-wildlife-and-plants-designation-of-critical-habitat-for-the-northern-great.

U.S. Geological Survey. "Culprit Identified in Decline of Endangered Missouri River Pallid Sturgeon." Phys.org, January 23, 2015. https://phys.org/news/2015-01-culprit-decline-endangered-missouri-river.html.

Vestal, Stanley. *The Missouri*. University of Nebraska Press, 1996.

Walker, B. A. "It Takes Two Sides to Debate, but Only One Side to Dictate." Missouri Coalition for the Environment, September 21, 2016. https://moenvironment.org/blog/it-takes-two-sides-to-debate-but-only-one-side-to-dictate/.

Walker, Mark, and Chris Cameron. "Plaintiffs in Long Fight over Endangered Salmon Hope a Resolution Is Near." *New York Times*, August 15, 2022. https://www.nytimes.com/2022/08/15/us/politics/salmon-dams-washington.html.

"Water." Missouri Department of Natural Resources. Accessed September 25, 2024. https://dnr.mo.gov/water.

"Water Q&A: What Does the Term 'River Stage' Mean?" U.S. Geological Survey. Accessed September 26, 2024. https://www.usgs.gov/special-topics/water-science-school/science/water-qa-what-does-term-river-stage-mean.

"Water Resources Center." Missouri Department of Natural Resources. Accessed September 25, 2024. https://dnr.mo.gov/about-us/missouri-geological-survey/water-resources-center.

"Water Resources Development Act of 2022." House Committee on Transportation and Infrastructure. Accessed September 25, 2024. https://democrats-transportation.house.gov/committee-activity/issue/water-resources-development-act-of-2022.

"Water Usage in Agriculture." Agremo, April 30, 2024. https://www.agremo.com/water-usage-in-agriculture/.

Weihe, Paul. *99wetlands* (blog). https://99wetlands.wordpress.com/.

Wells, Jeffrey V. *Birder's Conservation Handbook: 100 North American Birds at Risk*. Princeton University Press, 2007. https://www.jstor.org/stable/j.ctt7s12c.

Welte, Dean. "Sioux City Marina and Jolly's on the River Will Be Closed This Summer." KTIV, March 22, 2024. https://www.ktiv.com/2024/03/22/sioux-city-marina-jollys-river-will-be-closed-this-summer/.

"What Are Zebra Mussels and Why Should We Care about Them?" U.S. Geological Survey. Accessed September 25, 2024. https://www.usgs.gov/faqs/what-are-zebra-mussels-and-why-should-we-care-about-them.

"What Is an Ice Jam?" NOAA SciJinks. Accessed September 26, 2024. https://scijinks.gov/ice-jams/.

Williams, Chris. "Sunken Steamboat Exposed Once Again After Drought in Missouri River." FOX 4 News Dallas-Fort Worth, September 3, 2022. https://www.fox4news.com/news/sunken-steamboat-exposed-once-again-after-drought-in-missouri-river.

Williams, Jeb. "North Dakota Aquatic Nuisance Species 2021 Update." North Dakota Game and Fish Department, 2021. https://www.ndlegis.gov/files/committees/67-2021/23_5043_02000_1335presentation.pdf.

Williams, Nat. "Rising River Levels Allow More Shipments." AgUpdate, November 18, 2022. https://www.agupdate.com/illinoisfarmertoday/news/crop/rising-river-levels-allow-more-shipments/article_f0899758-65d7-11ed-9618-2b845befaac0.html.

Wischmann, Lesley, and Andrew Dawson. *This Far-Off Wild Land: The Upper Missouri Letters of Andrew Dawson*. University of Oklahoma Press, 2014.

Wood, W. Raymond. *Prologue to Lewis and Clark: The Mackay and Evans Expedition*. University of Oklahoma Press, 2003.

World Sturgeon Conservation Society. http://wscs.info/.

Zaveri, Mihir. "Record-High Floods in Nebraska Breach Levees and Isolate Towns." *New York Times*, March 17, 2019. https://www.nytimes.com/2019/03/16/us/nebraska-flooding.html.

"Zebra Mussel (*Dreissena polymorpha*)—Species Profile." USGS Nonindigenous Aquatic Species Database. Accessed September 26, 2024. https://nas.er.usgs.gov/queries/factsheet.aspx?Speciesid=5.

Zhong, Raymond, and Mira Rojanasakul. "Who Gets the Water in California? Whoever Gets There First." *New York Times*, December 14, 2023. https://www.nytimes.com/interactive/2023/12/14/climate/california-water-crisis-drought.html.

Zimny, Michael. "The Fort to Field 50 Returns, Missouri River Refuses to Cooperate." SDPB, July 20, 2022. https://www.sdpb.org/blogs/dakota-life/the-fort-to-field-50-returns-missouri-river-refuses-to-cooperate/.

Zinn, Mark. "Team Effort Continues in Fight Against Invasive Carp." News-Press Now, November 7, 2023. https://www.newspressnow.com/news/local_news/government/team-effort-continues-in-fight-against-invasive-carp/article_c41da290-3ea9-11ed-8f19-8fe23dd9b4fd.html.

———. "Why Is the Missouri River so Low?" News-Press Now, February 11, 2024. https://www.newspressnow.com/opinion/always_looking_up/why-is-the-missouri-river-so-low/article_caf3129a-8c82-11ed-8cca-33456fa4f07f.html.

www.ingramcontent.com/pod-product-compliance
Lightning Source LLC
Chambersburg PA
CBHW051229140226
39490CB00005B/15
9781496237316